International Technology Transfer

International Technology Transfer

Europe, Japan and the USA, 1700–1914

Edited by

David J. Jeremy
Manchester Polytechnic

Edward Elgar

Published by
Edward Elgar Publishing Limited
Gower House
Croft Road
Aldershot
Hants GU11 3HR
England

Edward Elgar Publishing Company
Old Post Road
Brookfield
Vermont 05036
USA

British Library Cataloguing in Publication Data
International technology transfer : Europe, Japan and the
    USA, 1700–1914
    1. Technology transfer
    I. Jeremy, David J. (David John) *1939*–
    338.926

Library of Congress Cataloguing in Publication Data
International technology transfer : Europe, Japan, and the USA,
    1700–1914/edited by David J. Jeremy.
        p.   cm.
    Includes bibliographical references and index.
    1. Technology transfer–Europe.   2. Technology transfer–United
States.   3. Technology transfer–Japan.   I. Jeremy, David J.
T174.3.I558   1991
338.9'26–dc20   90–14558
                                                                        CIP

ISBN 1 85278 317 6

Contents

Figures

Tables

Contributors

Dr James Foreman-Peck, Fellow of St Antony's College, Oxford

Professor John R. Harris, Emeritus Professor of Economic and Social History, Birmingham University

Professor Charles K. Hyde, Wayne State University, Detroit, Michigan, USA

Dr Paul B. Israel, Research Associate, The Papers of Thomas A. Edison, Rutgers University, New Brunswick, New Jersey, USA

Dr David J. Jeremy, Senior Lecturer in Economic History, Manchester Polytechnic

Professor Tetsuro Nakaoka, Faculty of Economics, Osaka City University, Osaka, Japan

Dr Keith Nier, Research Associate, The Papers of Thomas A. Edison, Rutgers University, New Brunswick, New Jersey, USA

Dr Darwin H. Stapleton, Director, Rockefeller Archive Center, Rockefeller University, New York, USA

Professor Hoshimi Uchida, Economics Faculty, Tokyo Keizai University, Tokyo, Japan

Dr Simon Ville, Senior Lecturer in Economic History, Australian National University, Canberra, Australia

Dr Kenneth Warren, Fellow of Jesus College, Oxford

Professor Takeshi Yuzawa, Faculty of Economics, Gakushuin University, Tokyo, Japan

Acknowledgements

In the mind of the editor the concept of a collection of case studies on international technology transfer allowed him to revive an interest laid aside for a number of years. Like other collections of essays, however, it was sparked by conversations at an international conference on a related topic. The topic was textile history; the conference was an Anglo-Japanese one held in Kyoto in October 1987.[1] The enthusiastic support of many Japanese scholars, a number of whom became contributors, pushed the project ahead. Professor Yuzawa was especially helpful in mobilising additional Japanese contributors. On the English side Dr Geoff Tweedale has been of great assistance in some editorial matters.

In preparing the manuscript for press I have been well supported with photocopying and postal resources by the Faculty of Management and Business, Manchester Polytechnic. Jacket illustrations have been kindly supplied by Dr B. S. Finn of the Smithsonian Institution and by Mrs Leonore Symons of the Institution of Electrical Engineers. A considerable amount of retyping has been necessary and here my younger daughter Rebecca stepped into the breach in the summer of 1990. Last, and as ever, I must thank Theresa my wife for the inspiration she has been, beyond the telling of words.

DAVID J. JEREMY
Whaley Bridge

NOTES

1.   For which see the special issue of *Textile History* published in 1988.

xiii

1. Introduction: Some of the Larger Issues posed by Technology Transfer

David J. Jeremy

Technology transfer is widely recognised as a principal means of relieving world poverty. The Brandt Commission on International Development Issues in 1980 declared that 'it can even be argued that their [developing countries'] principal weakness is the lack of access to technology, or of command of it. The acquisition of technology is crucial, not only to growth, but to the capacity to grow.[1] If only technology – which may be defined as knowledge about the ways in which processes and products are designed, made or organized – could be shared and applied, then, it is believed, developing nations might approximately follow the advanced economies of the West. As is frequently the case, however, theoretical possibilities run aground on the rocks of reality. Political, economic, sociological structures and relationships distort international flows of technological knowledge. Poverty continues to blight and prematurely extinguish the lives of 20 per cent, or 800 million, of the world's population.[2] How can technology transfer be more effectively achieved? The Brandt Commission pinpointed multinational corporations and national governments as the key actors. Certainly today's multinationals can provide technical knowledge, personnel, investment; national governments the political frameworks which may facilitate transfers. The Commission also observed that technology in the late twentieth century might be transferred in many ways: 'While some spreads through published literature, personal exchanges, imitation and copying, most is transmitted commercially. It comes with the sale of machinery and knowhow, through training and technical assistance, or through participation in the construction, operation and management of a foreign firm'.[3] Imported technology, to succeed, would also have to be appropriate to the situation and needs of receptor countries.

The importance of technology transfer, therefore, is well understood. Much less familiar are the process and the circumstances under which it effectively occurs. Indeed the Brandt Commission, in identifying needs in this area, spoke of 'a need to see case studies of where and how different systems have worked'.[4] This volume has been compiled as a contribution to this perceived need. The essays all relate to the century or more before 1914, the period when the advanced nations of today caught up with Britain, the first industrial state.

The primary lesson from these essays, as from the increasing literature on technology transfer, is that the process cannot be captured by a single formula or model. It is complex. It is the product of many ingredients. One permutation works in one situation but not in another. At one and the same time the process engages economic, cultural and technical dimensions. This introduction, rather than summarizing the contents of the essays that follow, offers pointers for a general understanding of the process.

In some respects technology transfer is governed by economic forces. Expectations of profit certainly lay behind most of the case studies presented here. Eighteenth and nineteenth-century Continental and American merchants turned to new manufacturing technology, especially textiles, in hopes of combining relatively high returns with relatively low risks. Multinationals exported telegraph and telephone technologies with the same objective. Other motives also intruded. For France and other eighteenth-century nation states, as for nineteenth-century Japan, there were strong political reasons for obtaining new foreign technology. When it came to the adoption phase (spreading the new technology in the receptor economy/society) economic factors came strongly into play. Levels of capital formation, market size and structure, relative factor (land, labour, capital) prices, the extent of entrepreneurial opportunities, the availability of financial institutions, for example, became critical: the kind of elements W. W Rostow 30 years ago controversially identified as crucial in the much broader industrialization process.[5]

Yet, as Alexander Gerschenkron noted, in some industrializing economies the state has taken the place of entrepreneurs and financial institutions.[6] As part of this strategy the state might facilitate or circumscribe the introduction of new technology. The essays below on the transatlantic transfers of iron and steel, telegraphy, the telephone and heavy chemicals, as well as the inward movement of cotton manufacturing, railway and electrical technologies to Japan, evidence varying kinds and intensities of state interventions. If the Japanese experience is indicative, however, the state has to limit its interventions, either in time or in scope.

Cultural arrangements – the values, organizational forms and material expressions of social groups – likewise influence technology transfer. Economic forces and perhaps the state may explain the timing of introductions of new technology. Cultural forces, combined with economic ones, explain the rate of diffusion within the receptor economy/society. Cultural features by themselves often shape the form of the imported technology. With economic forces they can transform and radically modify it. Sociologists have exhaustively studied the diffusion of innovations across national and cultural boundaries. While they have produced explanations that elude the tools of the economist, few of their findings are undisputed by fellow sociologists.[7] Three are generally accepted: as a process, the diffusion of innovations resembles a communication model, comprising source, message, channel, receiver and effects; adoption depends on opinion leaders; the rate of adoption over time follows an S-shaped curve.[8] The importance of culture for historians trying to understand technology, including technology transfer, has produced a number of fresh works since 1960.[9]

Then there is the technology itself. How far its manufacture or use, actual or perceived, is appropriate for a receptor economy/society will clearly influence the timing of transfer and adoption. Nathan Rosenberg has reiterated the point that diffusion is likely to be a gradual process depending on the pace at which secondary improvements perfect the original innovation; that the level of human skills, especially machine-making skills, in the receptor economy is critical; and that bottlenecks in related production activities need to be removed before an innovation can spread.[10] The nature and level of technical knowledge in both the originating and receptor economies/societies is also an aspect of the technology which is easily overlooked. Technical vocabularies, technical measuring systems, patents, technical handbooks: such manifestations of technical knowledge can present obstacles, if not always as enduring as Britain's imperial weights and measures, to technology transfer.

In the effort to learn some obvious lessons from past examples of technology transfer, all the contributors to this volume were asked to address a number of common questions insofar as their own case studies would allow. Since there are no simple answers, these questions are reproduced here to draw attention to the wide range of issues which may be involved in the effort to secure successful transfers of technology.

1   Source economy/society

(a)   What kinds of *inhibiting factors* in the originating economy slowed down (or accelerated) transfer? Were they internal to the technology: for example, were they regional and distortive (like the technical vocabularies and measuring systems the editor found in the British textile industries of the late eighteenth century[11]) or were they due to technical sophistication (like a fast pace of technical change, as signalled for example by the rate of patent registration)? Or were there other inhibiting factors internal to the technology in question?

(b)   If the *inhibiting factors* were *non-technical*, were they related to economic conditions (such as the high price of skilled labour or of capital equipment in the originating economy)? Or to the social environment of the technology (for example, attitudes of secretiveness on the part of factory owners, or policies of state protection, such as the editor found in England pre-1850)?

2   Movement

On the movement of technologies between economies and societies, what does your case study demonstrate about some or all of the following:

(a) *Vehicles of transfer*: was the technology carried by verbal descriptions, drawings and plans, patents, machine parts, or more by skilled workers, technicians and managers? The editor's study of pre-1830s textile technology transfer from Britain to the USA credited a flow of skilled workers with achieving the transatlantic diffusion of early machine spinning, weaving and printing technologies.

(b) *Networks of access to the originating economy*: how did followers get hold of the technological information in a leader economy? Did they rely on stray visitors, consular officials, students on apprenticeships or what? What problems or help did these agents encounter: foreign language barriers, culture shock, or did they share the language and social or political stances of the ruling groups in the leader economy?

(c) *Information goals of acquirers*: what kinds of target were set for agents seeking new technology: were they largely technical, or economic (such as costs of production by a given new method) or did they include social considerations (for example, an estimate of the human costs of shifting from one production method to another)?

(d) *Methods of information collection*: were these open or surreptitious? Literary or mathematical or pictorial or scientific? Did they involve single agents or groups of agents acting together?

(e) *Speed of transfer of a given technology*: can this be measured in length of time? Can it be explained?

3   The adoption of imported technology in a receptor economy/society

What does your case study reveal about some or all of the following:

(a) *Rate of adoption*: is it possible to plot the rate of adoption? Does it conform to the classic S-curve? Can local variations in the rate of adoption be explained?

(b) *Networks of distribution into the receptor/follower economy*: what part did government (national or local) play in promoting imported technology? Or did private enterprise predominate?

(c) *What hindrances faced carriers of new technology*? For example, is there evidence of technical confusion as a result of the mingling of different technical traditions if the technology came from different countries or regions (such as the editor noted in the USA's woollen industry *c.* 1810)? Or did science clash with intuitive technical tradition?

4   Modifications of the imported technology

What does your case study disclose about the conditions which reshaped the incoming technology:

(a) Were *economic conditions* such as the differentials between factor costs, or the nature of available markets of prime importance?

(b) Were *social factors*, on the other hand, more important: for example, the dictates of fashion or the taboos of religion or the rigidities of a class system (which might prohibit the employment of women and so induce their replacement by more automatic machinery)?

(c) Were *conditions in the physical environment* important in modifying an imported technology?

5 Reverse flows

Regarding modifications to the imported technology which might be appropriate for use in the originating economy/society: is there any evidence of these and how successful were they?

NOTES

1. Willy Brandt (introduction), *North–South: A Programme for Survival. The Report of the Independent Commission on International Development Issues* (London, 1980) p. 194.
2. Ibid., p. 50; the statistic is for the late 1970s.
3. Ibid., p. 194.
4. Ibid., p. 196.
5. W. W. Rostow, *The Stages of Economic Growth: A Non-Communist Manifesto* (Cambridge, 1960).
6. A. Gerschenkron, *Economic Backwardness in Historical Perspective*. (Cambridge, Mass., 1962).
7. See, for example, the large number of hypotheses with supporting and opposing empirical findings in Everett M. Rogers and F. Floyd Shoemaker, *Communication of Innovations: A Cross-Cultural Approach* (2nd edn, New York, 1971) pp. 347–85.
8. *Ibid.*
9. For a survey of the work of historians of technology, mostly in the USA, see John M. Staudenmaier, *Technology's Storytellers: Reweaving the Human Fabric* (Cambridge, Mass., 1985).
10. Nathan Rosenberg, 'Factors Affecting the Diffusion of Technology', *Explorations in Economic History* 10 (1972–3) 6.
11. David J. Jeremy, *Transatlantic Industrial Revolution: The Diffusion of Textile Technologies between Britain and America. 1790–1830s* (Cambridge, Mass. and Oxford, 1981).

PART 1

The First Industrial Nation:
Britain before the 1840s

2. Movements of Technology between Britain and Europe in the Eighteenth Century

John R. Harris*

A flow to continental Europe of technologies initiated in Britain took place from the early decades of the eighteenth century and was wholly commonplace and virtually unimpeded by 1840. In many cases movement took place sooner and more extensively than conventional thinking would indicate, frequently before the general internal or national diffusion of the British textile inventions of the 1760s and 1770s, let alone the statistical indications of increased industrial production once thought to indicate a take-off in the 1780s. We are now in a situation where the classic account of technological diffusion by W. O. Henderson has been much extended by other writers, but this extension has not been even, either in the coverage of the various branches of transferred technology or in the coverage of the different receiving countries. This unevenness demands further research if the lacunae are to be filled. The present chapter cannot fill all the gaps, but hopes to give some indicators of the dating and type of technology transferred and some impression of the geographical spread. Its emphasis will be on the period before 1800, reflecting the balance of the writer's studies, and it takes as its main example and case study, France, for the same reason. It will not attempt to describe the important, but weaker, flow of European technology to England in the same period, though France, for instance, gave Britain cast plate glass, chlorine bleaching, and Le Blanc soda; nor will it examine the long list of European technologies that had reached Britain before 1700.[1]

It would be out of the question to discuss here the many debates about the general causes of British industrialization and the extent to which a more industrialized economy had been achieved in Britain by the last decades of the eighteenth century than had been achieved elsewhere in Europe – or indeed whether that can be assumed to be the fact. However it can be shown without difficulty that in critical areas of technology a British lead had been established by then. Long before the French Revolution a deep European interest had been shown in these technological areas, and this interest had been translated into

technological transfer to other European countries, whether with the agreement and support of those who possessed the British technologies or without
it, and whether legally or illegally. Whatever the overall British industrial lead
may have been, and whatever the effect of the progress of British industry in
terms of national wealth, contemporary Europeans believed that certain British
technologies had produced advantages to Britain which they desired for their
own countries. The remarkable lengths to which they were often prepared to
go to get the technologies, by hook or by crook, show the strength of that
belief.

If there was then a technology which was available in Britain alone, and
which other nations wanted for themselves, why could not such a technology
have been created in other European countries with fairly comparable markets,
capital availability, literacy and the other social or economic assets associated
with what is sometimes called 'modernization'? Equally, wherever it was
generated, could it not have derived from a small cluster of inventions made
over a few years of the eighteenth century which had a great spin-off potential?
While such a scenario of random incidence has been suggested,[2] it may have
a value in provoking discussion, but has little factual accuracy or explanatory
use. Over the last decades of the seventeenth century and the first of the
eighteenth England had moved from being a country which had been tradition-
ally an importer of new technology, a technological debtor, to being a country
to which, on balance, others came to borrow, even steal; in other words, a
technological creditor. Nor are some contemporaries to be taken seriously
(though they have sometimes found favour with historians) when they say that
the English were mainly good improvers on the basic innovations of others.[3]
The remarkable thing about English technological advances was the creation
of new machines and processes not previously used elsewhere, and which
proved capable of forming the basis of leading technologies for long periods,
often for a century or more, while the fundamental principles behind the key
inventions proved susceptible to almost indefinite development and enhance-
ment.

While the long-term trends in technological history have been less looked
at than the histories of major inventions, it is possible to show that over a
lengthy period a shift in the basis of British technology had been taking place.
It can reasonably be argued that most technological development can be shown
to be part of an evolutionary chain, that virtually all inventions and innovations
incorporate knowledge already available, and that they largely re-employ
artefactual features already used in production for a new purpose, or with
significant modifications.[4] But this does not invalidate the observation that at
times there are strong trends in particular technological directions, and that
sometimes these trends continue to be dominant over long periods and to be of

international as well as national significance. It is these major shifts of direction which inspire the most intense efforts to transfer technology.

In the case of Britain a particular technological trend has been shown to have been of great importance, to have begun well before the eighteenth century, and to have become remarkably pervasive during it. It was emphasized in that part of the late John Nef's work which marks his permanent historical contribution, as compared with those ideas which produced much fertile discussion among historians before being generally abandoned.[5] The work of A. E. Wrigley, recently summarized and further advanced in *Continuity, Chance and Change*, with its emphasis on the shift from a society which had its economic base firmly in vegetable and animal raw materials to a 'mineral based energy economy' is of great relevance.[6] One way to describe these developments is to use the framework of the rise of a coal-fuel technology. The interest in coal use in Britain was stimulated by regional shortages of wood fuels at certain periods and by some periods of more general rising prices, but the geological endowment meant that over remarkably wide areas of Britain coal could be reached at progressively greater depths by gradual improvements in mining technology. This meant that a cheaper fuel was available, and not only in pit-head terms, for, as Wrigley rightly emphasizes, the greater quantity of heat delivered per ton by coal meant that its transport costs compared with wood as fuel were superior, while in some important cases the useful propinquity of coalfields to coastal transport was a further reason for its wide distribution. The one technological hurdle which could have impeded the expansion of coal production, and which led to an increase in price in many areas, was removed by the very timely invention of the Newcomen steam engine. The obvious motivation for a shift to coal was to obtain an expanding fuel supply at low prices over an indefinite period. The increasing success of coal production at prices lower than those ruling for wood fuel meant that there was a strong inducement to change to mineral fuel without waiting till wood shortages became acute; the problem was simply obviated.[7]

The shift in fuel use was not however a matter of simply substituting mineral for vegetable fuel. As has been emphasized elsewhere the introduction of coal almost always involved some technical innovation because it had different burning qualities, and the impurities or pollutants which it contained would seriously damage the product unless processes were modified. British industrialists were forced into a very long process of change, involving increasing technological innovation. The use of coal by smiths and nailworkers can be traced to the late middle ages, and brewing, dyeing, salt boiling, brick making and other trades used it before the end of the sixteenth century. The production of glass with coal goes back to the beginning of the seventeenth century, and this quickly became compulsory; by the 1670s the attractive new flint glass had been invented, which could only be made with coal as the fuel. Melting with coke was possible from the 1620s, cementation steel production with coal was mastered and became significant after the Restoration. Of enormous importance was the conversion of non-ferrous metal production to coal, copper being so converted from the 1680s. Gradually a range of good cheap earthenware was developed, based on cheap coal. The smelting of iron with coal was first achieved in 1709, and while its effects were mainly confined to cast iron for some decades, this limitation ceased about 1750. By 1712 the Newcomen engine was triumphantly at work; a new power source had been created, whose expansion was very great throughout the century, and would have been so without Watt's brilliant inventions of the 1760s and 1780s. Coal fuel, already applied to the production of simple chemicals in the seventeenth century, was applied to the production of sulphuric acid by the lead-chamber process from 1745; cheap sulphuric acid was the basis of the subsequent development of much of the heavy chemical industry. About the same time Huntsman created cast steel, with coke as the fuel, thus giving tool and spring steel a new quality. In the production of wrought iron the effective stamping and potting process of the 1760s was superseded in the late 1790s by Cort's classic puddling and rolling process, slowly perfected over the previous decade. In the collieries themselves, not only was steam pumping of great importance, but steamwinding came in at the end of the century, while the development of the railed way continued with the introduction of the iron rail.

The above does not cover every part of the creation of a coal-fuel technology, but it is sufficient to show that, by the middle of the eighteenth century, British industry had taken a fundamentally different direction from that of the rest of Europe over a wide front. Of course this particular technological movement does not embrace all technological advance. The classic textile inventions are in many ways a separate stream of technological development, though not wholly so. Before their arrival British textile methods were already sought abroad because of the finishes achieved through heat-using methods. Once machines began to be introduced into textile production they were soon being provided with metal parts and mechanical drives which were derived from the iron and steel industry, and from the tool-making and engineering trades which the metal industries supplied; the gradual spread of steam power in textiles and the introduction of iron-framed factory buildings helped to integrate this other important stream of technological change with the wider coal fuel technology.

Two features of technological change in Britain have to be emphasized. One is that the new techniques were evolved empirically, and that, once evolved, they became part of a craft practice. This was imparted to other people by on-the-job training, principally through formal or informal apprenticeship. Not only were there developments or refinements of existing crafts, but new crafts were created: furnace builder, crucible maker, puddler, engine erector and so on. In some industries there was a concatenation of separate crafts, members of each being unable to do effectively the work of the others. This meant that, for fully successful transfer of the techniques of a coal-using industry, a team of key workers had to be identified by the intending acquirers and successfully recruited. The empirical nature of the technology made it especially hard to transfer by written description. While there were areas where contemporary science did make some impact on industry these were very much in the minority. Consequently the writings of the savants and the literati played a very small part in the transfer of technology, apart from occasional instances, more valuable for creating awareness than procuring techniques.

The second factor is that, together with the new crafts, a collection of new equipment and processes had been formed in Britain, particularly in the new coal-fuel technology, for instance high-quality firebrick and crucibles, the coal-fired reverberatory furnace, coke making, the large casting, the furnace cone, all familiar on one side of the Channel and not on the other, and this increased the learning problem. Another factor which even Wrigley, with his emphasis on raw materials, does not fully establish, is the extent of Britain's endowment with those 'non-organic' materials needed – and in the quantities sufficient – for the early stages of industrialization. Here we may instance the range of coal types (such as coking coal), the non-ferrous ores (copper, tin, lead, calamine), fireclay, china clay, mordants (like alum and copperas), brine and rock salt. Was any other European country so variously endowed with the materials which its technologists' ingenuity could work upon?

A new and thorough survey of all the British technological transfer to Europe between the beginning of the eighteenth century and the middle of the nineteenth is now overdue, particularly because Henderson's celebrated account naturally shows its age. For Europe there is no single work to equal the comprehensive coverage of the instances, combined with analysis of the process, which has been given by Jeremy to British textile industry transference to America.[8] Language of course is a problem, and the lack of languages of so many British scholars a particular hindrance. Henderson, and all subsequent researchers, were given a flying start for France by Ballot's immensely detailed and scholarly posthumous volume on the introduction of machinery into French industry; its comprehensiveness and its accuracy perhaps have had the effect of dissuading new researchers with a wider economic and social outlook from going over that ground again.[9] Perhaps, too, recent sentiment among some French historians has inclined them to try to reverse the excessive tendency of earlier generations of Anglo-Saxon historians to mark down the vitality of French industry as compared with British in the eighteenth and early nineteenth centuries. They find the account of an age when there was 'a superiority of Great Britain over France' not a congenial tale, even when told by a great compatriot.[10] France will be returned to.

The interest of Sweden in British technological advance was as close and tenacious as that of the French. The Swedes, with an economy heavily influenced by the fortunes of iron and copper, noted the cloud no bigger than a man's hand, namely the new vogue for innovation in British ferrous and non-ferrous metals, discernible from the late seventeenth century. They began to worry about the loss of export markets. From their national mine administration, and in the late eighteenth century from their ironmasters' association, they sent knowledgeable observers with a technical, even a scientific training – including a couple of professors. Sometimes ready to engage in deliberate espionage, at other times they were ready to pay money for secrets or were able to pursue their enquiries very openly, dining with and being taken about by prominent industrialists. Since they came from an economy without coal or a colonial supply of raw cotton, it was often impossible to follow up their good information with technological transfer. Triewald, who so early understood the international importance of the steam engine, and involved himself in the erection of an early Newcomen engine in England, was in the end quite unsuccessful in transferring it to Sweden. One of the first cast steel factories outside England, however, was set up in Stockholm by Broling. Perhaps the excellent information the Swedes had from Cletscher and Odhelius in the late seventeenth century, from Triewald, Alstromer, and Kahlmeter (and even Swedenborg) in the early eighteenth century, from Schröderstierna and Angerstein in mid-century, from Andersson and Robsahm in the late eighteenth century, and from Svedenstierna at its very end, really establishes a negative: if you do not possess the right material endowment the best information cannot win you foreign technology.[11]

In Peter the Great the Russians had perhaps the most distinguished of the technologically interested visitors to Britain. The usually good relations between the two countries led to a succession of Russians in English royal dockyards in the eighteenth century and Russian officers in training with the Royal Navy. But in one period of poor relations the Birmingham metal trades raised an outcry against the apprenticeship of a large number of Russians in their region, who were feared to be taking its skills to 'his Czarish Majesty's dominions'.[12] This was an element in the protests which led to the first significant British legislation against industrial espionage in 1719. Later in the century Watt himself was twice officially approached to go to Russia but, failing him, they secured a Newcomen engine erector at the prime rate of £1 000 a year. Cannon founders were recruited in 1771 at the more modest rate of £100 a year. The manager of the Carron Iron Co., Charles Gascoigne, was persuaded to emigrate to Russia, and the Company was prepared to export cannon-founding and cannon-boring equipment, despite representations to the British government against it. They exported a steam engine and sent erectors for it, and a group of Carron men were in Russia in the 1780s. Garbett, a former

Carron proprietor, and a strong opponent of such emigration, claimed in 1786 that 170 workmen and families had gone to Russia within the last two years, and believed that the Birmingham trades would be established there. A total of 139 Scottish workers arrived at St Petersburg on a single vessel. Shipwrights, building workers, mechanics, millwrights, tanners, instrument makers were all successfully recruited at various times. The Baird brothers, associates of Charles Gascoigne, became major industrialists in the Russian iron, mechanical engineering and armaments industries. Charles Baird had built 141 steam engines by 1825. One notable and above-board export of sophisticated machinery was that of Boulton's steam-powered mint for St Petersburg, and a number of Russian officials and artisans arrived in Birmingham to have the appropriate training. In some instances they carefully acquired other skills during their stay.

Russian borrowings from English hydraulic engineering go back to Peter the Great's visit in 1698, when John Perry was recruited, but there was a particularly valuable visit between 1775 and 1777 by Korsakov, who paid much attention to the work of Smeaton and Mackell, and also to that of Brindley and his assistants, while Boulton and Watt arranged a tour of Birmingham manufactures and Wedgwood gave him introductions – the value of Russian business connections in this case outweighing their usual worries about industrial espionage. English instrument makers were brought over to Russia under Peter, Elizabeth and Catherine, while some men sent to England in 1719 for observation and training were (like the French at the same period) anxious to get the technology of the steam bending of timber for shipbuilding. This process of technological acquisition was continuous. Before the rebuilding of the great Tula metal works two celebrated technologists, Surnin and Leont'ev, were sent over to England in 1785, interested in steam engines and in the trades of Birmingham and Sheffield. They were placed for a time with leading English gun makers, including Henry Nock, who apparently assisted Surnin in industrial espionage in a wide range of industry. This he used to advantage in 15 years at the Tula works on his return, greatly improving the Russian musket and rifle manufacture. Six Russians arrived at Soho in 1796 for prolonged stays, partly in connection with Boulton's export of steam mint machinery, but some with wider remits. Deriabin in particular was concerned with mining, with copper-smelting, and with plate glass and ironworks and he had a most distinguished career as a technologist and manager of state factories when he went back to Russia.[13]

Compared with the Swedes or the French, the Austrians were fairly late in their drive to acquire British industrial methods, if we except the early entry of the Newcomen engine into some of the imperial mining regions. But from the 1760s there was a wave of government-sponsored immigrants. Interest seems first to have been concentrated on metals, on steel production and on metal-forming for buttons and other goods. Mathias Rosthorn and George Collins went to Vienna in 1766, enticed by the Austrian embassy in London, to make ordinary and gilt buttons, with the proviso that they must teach Austrian workmen; Rosthorn later tried to get more assistance from England for making pressed goods. This eventually attracted Robert Hickman, from a family of skilled metal workers prominent in Birmingham and Wolverhampton, again through the intermediacy of the London ambassador. Hickman then brought over two brothers. One, William, went back fairly openly and with bravado to Birmingham to recruit other workers, so as to help him to set up a water-powered rolling mill, to produce alloyed goods, and to establish a brass-foundry. Another immigrant was Thomas Lightowler, arriving in 1768, also a Birmingham trades expert, possibly connected with the Lightoler who had patented a file-cutting machine. Though his residence in Vienna may not have been continuous he was important enough to have been ennobled before his death there in 1796. A man of the same name, possibly a son, produced a scheme to send two men to England on an ambitious industrial espionage trip. In the 1760s a different initiative had brought over a group of English steelworkers who took new methods to Graz, where they were persisted with until their deaths. All this precedes another wave of English textile workers who went to Vienna about the turn of the century.[14]

What is now Belgium is of considerable interest. It had coal in quantity and a long tradition of using it: why it was strikingly less innovative than Britain deserves more attention than it has been given. A less complete raw material endowment may have been one factor, while the ability to produce charcoal iron without fuel supply restraints may have delayed coke iron production to the 1820s. However it provided an early site for the Newcomen engine on the Continent, from 1720, and it eventually had the densest population of steam engines outside Britain. Moreover, while the engines were not of very high quality, the Belgians produced their own before other European countries made theirs, and Belgium was not dependent on Britain for cylinders. The Belgian textile and engineering industries received a great boost from the arrival of William Cockerill and his sons about 1799. He at once started providing wool-spinning and carding machines at Verviers, and soon brought over the Nottingham mechanic, Hodson. Another important input was Bauwens' quite extensive industrial espionage operation which introduced many English cotton workers and mechanics about 1800. Belgium became an important focus of British-type industry, and a means by which British engineering, steam power and textile methods were passed to adjacent Continental countries, and even to Prussia, in the early nineteenth century.[15]

Space forbids any attempt to show the total diffusion of British technology to Europe, even if we stop our listing at 1800. It can only be pointed out that new facets continue to catch the light. For instance, Norway and Denmark turn out to have an interesting development which began in 1741 with a company originally under joint German and Danish ownership, but which was soon Norwegian controlled, and from 1776 placed under State ownership. Eventually seven glassworks were built. In the 1750s a young industrialist, Waern, came to England to get the technique of making crown glass – interesting in that England was now thought to be the leading practitioner of a process originally French, and to have 'highly perfected factories'. Waern was arrested under the English law, but jumped bail. Nevertheless he had secured five workers; the contract for one, a Bristol worker, fortunately survives. The Norwegian industry made its way with difficulty, but by 1800 it was successful with several types of glass, though two attempts to convert the industry to coal had failed. In Portugal there had also been an attempt to establish the manufacture of several sorts of glass at Coina near Lisbon in a royal manufacture (now being excavated) which had English and other foreign workers. In 1748 the works was moved to Marinha Grande under the Englishman John Beare, and in 1769 it passed into the management of William Stephens, whose name it retains. It still produces high quality flint tableglass and possesses an elegant and impressive eighteenth-century courtyard whose buildings give the dignified impression which all contemporary royal manufactures throughout Europe sought to convey. These may together serve as an example of the way evidence of the export of technology from eighteenth-century Britain is continually being found, and in an industry in which such transfer is not commonly cited by historians.[16]

Now let us take the example of France as a destination for British transferred technology.[17] As already pointed out, research is not yet at a point where it is possible to draw up with certainty a list of European countries to show their differing absorption of eighteenth-century British technology. One problem is that the range and accessibility of French records could also give some bias to such a comparison. Nevertheless it is likely that France attempted to acquire more British technology than any other country. Without going into more speculative explanations of this, two stand out. Firstly France was a country with a wide range of industry. British technological advance was at least as wide in the industrial range which it covered, and thus France was a natural borrower and, as she had much less to impart to Britain, she was potentially a considerable technological debtor. However, many of the industrial methods she sought were only slowly or imperfectly absorbed in the eighteenth century, and sometimes not secured by its end. No list compiled here could be exhaustive, but textile-related inventions (fly shuttle, jenny, water-frame, mule, improved stocking frames, hot calendering, watered silk, and copper-plate and powered roller textile printing) form an extensive group.[18] In metals and engineering there were a number of attempts to transfer cementation and crucible steel production (largely unsuccessful in the first case, wholly so in the second). Coke smelting was carried out, but badly; iron founding and cannon-boring methods, copper-sheathing of ships and cylinder-boring were all copied. So was the whole gamut of the Birmingham trades, from alloys to stamping, pressing and piercing machinery and mechanical polishing. The steam engine inventions, the Savery and Newcomen engines and the Watt engine (with its main improvements) were absorbed, though this was not a resounding success story. The glass-retort and then the lead-chamber processes of sulphuric acid production were adopted. In glass, coal-fired bottle production was quickly taken up, but the flint glass process was only transferred much later, with grotesque clumsiness and low qualitative results. In ceramics coal-fired earthenware was developed, but not competitively with the English product. Briefly vivified by a short infusion of British skills and tools at the beginning of the century, French horological technique stagnated when the transfer ended.[19]

The second element inducing a French interest in British industrial advances was of course the highly competitive position of the two countries, politically and militarily, as well as commercially, over nearly the whole of the century. While anglomania was at times prevalent among some French intellectuals, anglophobia was as common, and among the administrative, commercial and military population England was more usually seen as a perpetual rival and natural enemy. This meant that it was frequently regarded as an excellent stroke to deprive England of some technological superiority she enjoyed, and the Frenchmen acquiring the technology did not have to be particular about the means. The bribing away or suborning of foreign workers had long been a practice internationally, but a particularly flagrant case perpetuated on behalf of France had long-term consequences.

Briefly, in 1718 the British Parliament became aware of the Russian attempt to apprentice workers (already alluded to) and, far more important, of a very ambitious and largely successful effort to take English workers to France. This was the brainchild of John Law, the Scots financier so influential under the Orleans Regency. His brother William and the watchmaker Henry Sully were essential intermediaries. Law's operation was certainly not a trivial one. About 70 watchmakers were recruited and established in Versailles and Paris, at least 14 glass makers and over 30 metal workers emigrated. The last group included lock- and file-makers, hinge-makers, grinders, and an important group of foundry workers who were established at Chaillot in Paris.

Most of the other workers in metals and glass were in Normandy, at Harfleur and Honfleur. A substantial colony of woollen workers was set up at Charlaval and on Law's recently acquired Norman estate, Tancarville. The main groups listed certainly do not include all the skilled workers involved. While we know of some shipyard workers (smiths and an anchorsmith, for instance) from the surviving listings, others have been found accidentally in other sources. They, or the odd tobacco worker, might be thought unimportant, but John May, who on his first visit took with him the technique of steam bending of ship's timbers, and subsequently returned to be the erector of the first French steam engine at Passy, is certainly significant. We have no good indication of the number of woollen workers. The total number of workers who emigrated through the Law scheme was probably over 150 and, since some took families with them, the final number of people going to France may well have been two or three hundred. The resultant panic, combined with worries about Russian workers learning English trades, led to a demand for legislation which was quickly provided.[20]

But the Russian problem was shelved, penalties against foreign apprentice-ship were not imposed, and the 1719 Act concentrated solely on the movement of workers. The main penalties were against their suborners, whether English or foreign, but there were consequences for workers too, particularly if, after emigration, they did not return when ordered to do so by British representatives abroad. The Act covered artisans in a particular group of industries: wool, iron, steel, brass and other metal trades, together with watchmakers and clockmakers – that is, it was fairly carefully aimed at the trades to which Law's scheme had been directed. The enticers could be fined £100 or imprisoned for three months, further offences could result in a year's jail. Enticers and enticed could be jailed until the next assizes if they could not produce bail. Those who were enticed but caught could be required to produce security against future offences. If any went abroad, but did not return home when warned, they could lose property rights and British citizenship. From 1750 enticers could be fined £500 per person suborned, £1 000 for a second offence; a prison sentence of a year or longer could be imposed.[21] There are instances of bails of £1 000 or even £4 000.[22] While, apart from the workmen in the indicated trades, efforts to entice abroad 'any other artificers or manufacturers' could be penalized, it is not clear to what extent the law was really applied, and whether at some time or other it was used against every trade where unauthorized emigration took place.

However much artisans were affected, the law was not used in some celebrated cases where entrepreneur-technologists sought to take up offers from abroad, or act as what we would now call industrial consultants. William Wilkinson's expensively rewarded efforts for the French government, in cannon production at Indret and coke smelting at Le Creusot, were not impeded, nor was Boulton's detailed advice on the hardware works at La Charité, then largely abandoned, which had been founded 30 years before by the émigré Birmingham industrialist, Michael Alcock. In a sense, then, the enforcement of the legislation might be regarded as class-biased, but perhaps the acid test would have been for Wilkinson and Boulton to have recruited men to work for foreign firms or governments. Would they then have been pursued

by the law, as Alcock's wife was when she recruited English workers for him?
There are certainly anomalies; for instance, English steam engine erectors do
not seem to have been prevented from working abroad.[23]

The concentration on preventing the emigration of workers as the best
means of preventing the export of technology was sensible, and reflected a
situation where skill was embodied in the worker, and where equipment was
often capable of being carried in a bag, or readily disposed in a few bales or
boxes and sent in several vessels. Where furnace industries were concerned,
however, the main plant could not be exported, and transference was dependent
on skilled men identifying the right raw materials to be worked on and the right
building materials, including refractories, in their new surroundings. The need
for the skilled man, and the inadequacy of descriptions or drawings, however
careful, are many times emphasized by key observers: 'the arts never pass by
writing from one country to another, eye and practice can alone train men in
these activities'; again, 'good information would make little impression on a
workman, stubborn in his system and habits, it is by example that one may
arrive at proving the true situation to him'; and again, 'even written materials
are a very feeble aid to the mechanical arts, they cannot impart the skill, one can
have it by work alone'. The carriage of machines to France was not enough
without the skilled men to accompany them... 'It is not with fine words that one
is able to get the advantages of machines, but with the rough hands that are used
to operating them'.[24]

However by 1730 it was already being queried by British officials whether
there should not be some wide prohibition of the taking abroad of machines as
well as people. The query was inspired by the use of a cloth-printing machine
of some kind by an Englishman working in French Flanders.[25] When the matter
was inquired into it was discovered that machines were not seizable, 'which is
a Defect in the said Laws'. Apart from the exception of stocking-frames, whose
export had been prohibited from 1696, the export of tools and machinery really
only began to be legislated against from 1750, when those in wool and silk
manufacture were forbidden. Such prohibitions tended to grow in a parcellated
and dislocated fashion. Tools for cotton and linen manufacture were included
in 1774, and this was extended to tools, machines, models and plans for wool,
cotton, linen and silk manufactures in 1781. Blocks and machinery for textile
printing were brought into the system in 1782. Forfeiting and sizeable fines
were the usual penalty. An Act of 1785 seems mainly to have been aimed at the
full range of equipment of the Birmingham hardware district, and this was
modified and extended the next year, and made permanent in 1795.[26]

What was the relevance and effect of this legislation? Given the centrality
of skills, the continuance of the 1719 legislation meant that almost any attempt
to transfer technology became in modern parlance industrial espionage, and
that those endeavouring to organize this on behalf of the French government

were industrial spies. The evidence is clear that the movement of English workers to France was not impossible, in fact hundreds went there. However the British government's actions against the Law scheme were remarkably effective. Workmen who had emigrated before the 1719 Statute was passed had to be treated exceptionally. The remarkable sum of £3 000 was allotted to bring them back home, and this, together with the financial difficulties in France, was surprisingly effective, with a lasting detrimental effect on French horology. The movement of workers to France was inhibited for some years. There was certainly some movement of workers in the 1730s and 1740s, but these decades have not been properly investigated. By the early 1750s, however, a former Manchester textile finisher and Jacobite officer, John Holker, had been seconded from a Scots regiment in the French army to assume an industrial role of great interest and significance. This had two elements: his own successful industrial enterprises in textiles and chemicals in Rouen and its environs, and his well-rewarded government post as 'Inspector-General of Foreign Manufactures'. This euphemistic job description concealed his real activities, which were those of industrial espionage in Britain, suborning of British workers, and some invigilation of their activities once in France. More conventionally, he toured the French provinces as an industrial inspector, frequently advising on those improvements which would be achieved by adopting British practice. He came back to Britain to recruit workers and establish agents, but he was also sometimes the contact point for British artisans who came independently to France.[27] Two important émigrés for whom Holker occasionally acted as intermediary with the French government were John Kay – awkward, only crudely literate, dissatisfied, but tolerantly treated by the French, who respected his genius,[28] and the Birmingham manufacturer, Michael Alcock. Alcock, formerly in a big way of business in Birmingham, possessed great technical gifts, but was moody, quarrelsome and violent. Nevertheless he and his sons, later established at Roanne, played a leading part in establishing 'quincaillerie anglaise' in France, and in his early years there he was able, with his wife's help, to bring a number of English workers over for La Charité and Saint-Etienne.[29] But Kay and Alcock themselves seem to have come to France without being recruited, prompted by difficulties in their British circumstances. Besides Holker and Alcock, many others took part in the recruitment of British workers. Often the suborners were French agents or industrialists. To give some prominent examples, the engineer Le Turc took English naval block makers to L'Orient to establish that manufacture on new and partly mechanized lines; it was later copied at Brest and Toulon. Another engineer, De Saudray, employed by the French foreign office, spied upon and sketched Boulton's hardware machinery in Birmingham, and then took two batches of West Midlands workers to France, but with little result.[30] The Orsel brothers, one of whom had been a merchant in Birmingham, brought over workers from the

same area for their Paris and other works.[31] Lambert and Boyer, endeavouring
with more energy than expertise to set flint-glass manufacture going at Saint-
Cloud, had to come to England in wartime in order to recruit the right
workmen.[32] Cutting short the long narrative of cotton technology transfer, it
can be said that, while some British textile experts brought the new machinery
in its early or its developed form to France apparently on their own initiative,
some of them made a bee-line for Holker at Rouen. Others were recruited by
earlier immigrants or by existing French companies, sometimes companies
which had previous British connections. After the interruptions of the French
Revolutionary War, there was a strong inflow of textile workers during the
peace of Amiens. Some volunteered their skills, others were suborned, but the
outcome was that a considerable colony, of whom a high proportion were
mechanics, was carried over into the Napoleonic Empire. Bauwens, operating
cotton mills in France and Belgium, made 32 journeys to England and brought
over more than 40 workers to his concerns.[33] Apart from the considerable immigration of cotton experts, a large colony, consisting of a couple of hundred
persons of British origin, was employed at the great copper-working plant at
Romilly before the Revolution.[34]

The point has sufficiently been made that, whatever the legal position, large
numbers of British workers went to France in the eighteenth century. Does this
mean that no one in Britain much minded, or that the legislation was wholly
ineffective, that there were no effective 'counter-espionage' efforts, official or
private? Such a view would go too far. Certainly those who tried to stop the
movement had some headaches. The English worker had a propensity to move
when it suited him, as Eden pointed out in the 1790s.[35] The English police system
was of the sketchiest, there was no *maréchaussée* to send in pursuit, no *lettre
de cachet* to obtain, as was once obtained for an errant English girl worker in
France. There was a customs service, but an overstretched one, and particularly
in the bustle of the river and quays at London it was easy for a few people to
slip through. As Holker pointed out, it was not possible to search everything
with equal rigour; ships for Holland were inspected less than those for France,
and it was possible to get people, tools or machines to France more safely by
sending them by another European country.[36]

The process of recruiting workers for France was not unhindered. When the
Alcock's underground route was interrupted because a girl courier refused to
take too many people at once, some workers got left behind and were seized,
and Mrs Alcock was imprisoned for a time and only released on bail of £1 000.
Local celebrations when she got off suggest that such arrests by the authorities
were not always popular. But the success of the Alcocks' suborning process
seems to have fallen off afterwards, considerable numbers of Birmingham
workers being prevented from leaving. A Frenchman of English origin who
was a manager of the works Alcock had formerly run at La Charité came to

Birmingham in search of a gilding expert. He got the man he needed, but had to run for it and exchanged pistol shots in a bizarre incident.[37] Albert, a Frenchman from Alsace, did some successful recruiting but was seized with a group of workers in 1791 and was put in jail for five years. An Englishman trying to get the puddling process for French employers was imprisoned and was not released until his fine could be paid at the Peace of Amiens. Bauwens got away with much recruiting, but his associate Paul Harding was caught and went to jail. Lambert and Boyer carried out audacious industrial espionage in wartime, but their hapless interpreter committed suicide in an English jail. Once their English workers reached Saint-Cloud they were got at by British embassy officials, who gave them notice to return under the 1719 Act and plied them with drink to reduce their usefulness to their French masters. On another level, those British industrialists who felt they had much to protect made expensive efforts to provide protection. The Prestonpans sulphuric acid works was surrounded by a high wall, as was the plate glass works at Ravenhead; even the access of British investors to the latter was restricted. An ingenious chemical manufacturer near London imported Welsh-speaking workers as a means of guarding his process. In a different kind of counter-espionage the British government made several approaches and highly favourable offers to John Holker to persuade him to return to England.[38]

We know that much British technology was transferred to France by the most effective means, that of moving skilled workers, but it is certain that counter-measures, legal and managerial, slowed down the process, as did the frequent wars. French suborners and their British accomplices counted, of course, on the British workers' particular characteristics. Drink was a general and besetting weakness; initially plied with drink in taverns to get their interest, many probably saw high pay in a cheaper country as the means to more drink. Their skills were matched by independence, unruliness and a lack of deference that made them easier to detach. Dupont de Nemours contrasted them with German workers: 'one can keep the secrets of a German works because German workers are docile, wise and content with little. But English workers are haughty, quarrelsome, risk takers and greedy. There is nothing easier than to suborn them ...'.[39]

This naturally raises the question of the quality of those who entered French service, and how well they settled into French society. There were paragons of dedication and proficiency at different levels, like the government official Holker, or the West Midland artisan Tinsley, who served successive managements at La Charité for over 30 years. Many were less satisfactory. Sometimes this could be blamed on the suborners and their agents; workers did not always understand that they were being expatriated in order to teach their skills to Frenchmen and thus rapidly lose their own scarcity value. The Orsels proved harsh and unjust masters and their men deserted to others, including the

Alcocks. De Saudray and his partners mishandled things and hardware tradesmen, surrounded by mud and poverty and without proper job safeguards, went home. Life in a different culture, with a different religion – Holker advised recruiting Catholics whenever possible – a different language, a different diet, in a society of dirigisme and bureaucracy (though both were creaking and crumbling in their ancien régime form) was not always congenial. Certainly some emigrants felt dissatisfied, alienated and unwelcome; it may have been a minority who returned, but it must have been a sizeable minority. Nor would the selection of workers have been perfect. On the one hand the dissatisfied, the disaffected, the indebted would have been readiest to go. On the other hand the selection would have been difficult because it was not easy for outsiders to know the range of skills required, and workers would often present their expertise in too favourable a light.

The export of machines was not so fraught an issue as the emigration of men until about 1780. The French then seized, with great fervour, on the possibilities of acquiring machines. Some seem to have been impelled by the apparent ease of reducing the matter to one of abstract principle: the English had machines which saved labour and helped the division of labour – gain the machines and the French would be their equals, an argument strong with those who advocated the Eden/Vergennes treaty. By none was it put more clearly than that *homme de systèmes*, Du Pont de Nemours: 'when a new machine produces some gain for English industry the French Government can always be master of it in six months for a small outlay'.[40] While British inventors were certainly in search of new standards of industrial efficiency, recent research into 'inventing the industrial revolution' would suggest that, however important its social consequences, inventors did not particularly have saving labour as a goal in itself.[41] To get the textile machines in their original forms was not too difficult; the early jenny, brought in by Holker's son in 1771, was a very small affair, and readily concealed when disassembled; Le Turc could send stocking-frame parts in the bottoms of earthenware crates, even a single water-frame, from which a millful could be copied, was not massive. But once gained, machines had to be imitated, maintained, installed in mills in some cases. Hence the large number of mechanics and millwrights who accompanied them, many capable of building machines from scratch in France. Yet the results were generally poorer than the best English practice, improvements did not accrue in France as they did in England, and continual updating was needed. With cotton machinery, as with the steam engine, the French after the interruption of the wars found themselves where English infusions had left them before the break.[42]

Most of the historical discussion on the utility of the legislation against machinery export concentrates on the contemporary debate after 1815, but there was great scepticism in some quarters before. The Lancashire magistrates, censuring workers for resisting the spread of technology, declared in 1779, 'it is impossible to restrain the force of ingenuity, when employed in the Improvement of Manufactures. That any Machines, that have been found, to effectuate that Purpose, become the property of the World...'[43] In 1789, Richard Crawshay, the iron merchant and ironmaster, currently applying 'R & D' to Cort's inventions, wrote to Lord Hawkesbury that

> The Tool Act from its first commence[ment] was opposed by the Traders in Ironwares of London and all the Outports that have a foreign Trade, on a general principle that every prescriptive law is a check and injury to the National Export Trade, as it prevents the Assortment of Goods wanted by every Country or individual, of course, the Orders will go to Germany or some other of our Competitors ... or lead them to habits of manufacture themselves, and thereby become our Rivals.

He said Matthew Boulton of Birmingham authorized him to state his agreement and affirmed that '99 men in every 100 who are in Trade throughout the Kingdom, are of the same Opinion'.[44]

The number of French visitors to England in the eighteenth century was obviously large, but many of course confined themselves mainly to London, with some incursions into the provinces to visit resorts, particularly Bath, and to stay in the houses of people to whom they had been recommended. Those who came to view industry very often came with a specific commission from government or, if with the benefit of a particular business firm in mind, the express consent and encouragement of government. If industrial espionage was involved, they would sometimes claim that the risks taken constituted a claim for government bounty to their firm or even a pension or the award of nobility to themselves. Among the more significant visits were those of Tiquet, who wrote home in 1738 to the Academician Hellot who had a special commission concerning coal and an interest in steel; Hellot himself; the inspector of industry Morel, who enlisted the aid of Holker for French manufactures; Gabriel Jars, another Academician with metallurgical interests in the 1760s, was required to spy where necessary, assuming the disguise of a naturalist. The artillery officer De La Houlière persuaded William Wilkinson to come to France in the 1770s; De Wendel and De Givry, with their interests in munitions industries, came in the early 1780s; Perier made several visits in pursuit of the Watt engine and the technology to build it; De Saudray was directly dispatched as an engineer officer in the French foreign office to spy on Boulton's works; Le Turc had some commissions from individuals and a whole series of commissions from the Bureau of Commerce and the Marine which extended from knitting machines to naval blockmaking. Faujas de Saint-Fond certainly travelled as a scientist and mineralogist, but his panegyrics on coal may be connected with his membership of the inspectorate 'des bouches à feu', charged with the conversion of French industries to coal.[45] Finally we may mention two men, Hurand and Rabasse, whom the Chamber of Commerce of Normandy commissioned to visit and report upon England at the time of the Eden Treaty, and who concentrated on Manchester as the main competitor in cottons. 'Manchester may be considered for England what Rouen is for France', they wrote, and they reported on the readiness with which Englishmen could be recruited if French firms got the proper encouragement from government.[46]

What kind of reception did these visitors receive from British industrialists? The answer is not a simple one. We have already mentioned the precautions some took to conceal their processes from all-comers, native and foreign. The Boulton and Watt circle frequently corresponded to warn each other of potentially dangerous foreign visitors. But, even while some members of that circle, like Wedgwood, were very touchy on the subject, and gave their workers printed pamphlets warning of both the legal and the personal problems of being suborned, others, like the Wilkinsons and the copper magnate Thomas Williams, seem to have taken the view that they were so far in the lead that it was unimportant who saw their works.

The case of France illustrates many of the general points to be made about the nature and timing of the transfer of British technology abroad during the eighteenth century. The divergence of British technology from that on the Continent, because of its progressive adaptation to the energy obtainable from coal, meant that processes like cementation or crucible steelmaking or the coal firing of the more sophisticated kinds of glass furnace transferred not at all, or very poorly, and this was largely true of coke-iron making. Birmingham-type hardware manufacture, with a more limited dependence on heat sources, did much better. The steam engine was transferred, but apart from the limited sites where coal was economically available it did not gain much ground before 1800, nor did it evolve once transferred. French ingenuity was not wanting, the engineering equipment and skill was. The preponderant method of acquiring British technology was the obtaining of skilled British workers, and intense efforts were put into this; written descriptions and drawings of equipment and machinery were acknowledged to be of little use. While the assessment of the introduced technology by commissioners of the Academy of Sciences may have sometimes rejected the spurious, it was often done without proper comparative materials, in circumstances which could not be exactly paralleled under working conditions, or by examining specimen products which had been made with an uneconomic expenditure of time and skill.

The Law scheme for technological transfer, though not followed up by schemes of comparable scale until mid-century, was a remarkable demonstration that there was already a series of trades in which there was English superiority, and that the technological balance between the two countries had shifted. Had it succeeded and been followed up, French deficiency in foundry work, the horological industries, flint-glass, steel production and file making might not have been so continuously deplored over the rest of the century. The legislative consequences of the Law scheme strongly identified technological transfer with illegality, and with industrial espionage. Such transfer was frequently attempted, primarily through the movement of workers, but its illegality probably added elements of precariousness and haste, and adversely affected the choice of available skilled men. At the same time the very considerable movement of men (including some managers) as well as machines showed that many of the industrial community in Britain, at every level, were not convinced supporters of the measures on the statute book which seemed to condemn much of the transfer of technology. There were some biases fed into the nature of transferred industry because a powerful military state was able to give special emphasis to the securing of techniques valuable to its forces, the solid boring of iron cannon, the production of coke iron for that purpose, the making of naval blocks, or the techniques needed to copper warships.

But from the elder Trudaine in the 1740s to Tolozan in the early 1790s the ancien régime possessed enlightened commercial administrators who perceived the existence of some British technological superiorities and set themselves to correct them, by espionage, by protecting and subsidizing immigrant processes, by finding financiers to invest in them. The aims were frequently defeated by an imperfect understanding of the essential features of the British advances, over-reliance on scientific advice, dependence on recruited immigrants without the right technical or character attributes, or the problems of bringing in financial backers who had influence, but had no grip on the real commercial or industrial problems of the relevant product. These administrators are often much more deserving of respect than of a superficial scorn; one may well ask if any British minister, indeed any contemporary British economic thinker, had any serious understanding of the reasons for, or the facts of, his nation's increasing technological preponderance. French ministers and scientists in a period before the means of industrial planning, or the application of science to industry (beyond its first infancy) were available, were trying artificially to catch up on an organic growth of technical change in the rival state, which its own intelligentsia seem to have understood no better, if as well, as they did.

NOTES

*The writer wishes to thank the Nuffield Foundation for their help in support of part of the research which is incorporated in this paper.

1. W. O. Henderson, *Britain and Industrial Europe 1750–1870* (Liverpool, 1954; Leicester, 1965) is still the best broad general account. There are, however, some excellent papers which should be mentioned, especially Eric Robinson's 'The International Exchange of

Men and Machines, *Business History*, **1** (1958); Peter Mathias, 'Skills and the Diffusion of Innovations from Britain in the Eighteenth Century', *Trans. Royal Historical Society*, 5th Series, **5** (1965) and David J. Jeremy, 'Damming the Flood: British Government Efforts to Check the Outflow of Technicians and Machinery, 1780–1843', *Business History Review*, **51** (1977). The writer has looked at the skills issue in relation to transfer in 'Skills, Coal and British Industry in the Eighteenth Century' in *History* **61** (1976) subsequently cited as 'Skills Coal'. There is a good account of those transfers which took place from Europe to Britain in this period in A. E. Musson, 'Continental Influences on the Industrial Revolution in Britain', *Britain and Her World 1750–1914, Essays in honour of W. O. Henderson*, ed. B. M. Ratcliffe (Manchester, 1975).

2. Particularly by N. F. R. Crafts, 'Industrial Revolution in England and France: Some Thoughts on the Question "Why was England First?"', *Economic History Review*, **30**, 3 (1977).

3. For instance, Mathias, 'Skills and Diffusion', quotation, p. 96.

4. For the evolutionary case see especially George Basalla, *The Evolution of Technology* (Cambridge, 1988).

5. J. N. Nef, *The Rise of the British Coal Industry*, 2 vols (1932) second impression (London, 1966), vol. I, part II, chs III and IV.

6. A. E. Wrigley, *Continuity, Chance and Change*, (Cambridge, 1988) p. 115.

7. The first statement of this view was in *Industry and Technology in the Eighteenth Century: Britain and France* (published lecture, Birmingham University 1973); it was developed in 'Skills, Coal' (see above) and in 'The Rise of Coal Technology', *Scientific American* **231**, No. 2 (1974); these papers form the basis of the succeeding pages.

8. D. J. Jeremy, *Transatlantic Industrial Revolution* (Cambridge, Mass., 1981).

9. C. Ballot, *L'Introduction du Machinisme dans l'Industrie Française* (1923).

10. F. Crouzet, *De la Supériorité de l'Angleterre sur la France* (Paris, 1985).

11. For the invigilation of British industry by Swedish observers see A. Birch, 'Foreign Observers of the British Iron Industry during the Eighteenth Century' *Journal of Economic History* (1955) pp. 22–3; for Triewald see L. T. Rolt and J. Allen, *The Steam Engine of Thomas Newcomen* (Hartington, Derbyshire, 1977) pp. 46, 76–7 and *passim*; Svante Lindqvist, 'The Work of Martin Triewald in England', *Trans. Newcomen Soc.* **50** (1978–9) pp. 165 ff and his *Technology on Trial* (Upsalla, 1984). For other observers see M. W. Flinn, 'The Travel Diaries of Swedish Engineers of the Eighteenth Century as a source of Technological History', *Trans. Newcomen Soc* **XXX** (1957–9) pp. 95–109, and his edition of *Svedenstierna's Tour of Great Britain (1802–3), the Travel Diary of an Industrial Spy* (Newton Abbot, 1973); for Schroderstierna, 'Dagbok', Kugliga Biblioteket MS X 303 (extracts seen by courtesy of Dr. Gunnar Kjellin); for Bengt Fermer, A. P. Woolrich (ed.), *Fermer's Journal 1759–60, An Industrial Spy in Bath and Bristol*, (Eindhoven, n. d.); for Robsahm, K. C. Barraclough, *Steelmaking before Bessemer: 2: Crucible Steel* (London, 1984) pp. 82–3, 184–6, 202–4.

12. *Commons Journals*, 27 January 1719.

13. A. G. Cross, *'By the Banks of the Thames'*, *Russians in Eighteenth-Century Britain* (Newtonville, 1980), especially ch. 6, 'On British Ships and in British Yards' and ch. 7, 'Learn from the British'; M. J. Okenfass, 'Russian Students in Europe in the Age of Peter the Great' in J. G. Garrard, *The Eighteenth Century in Russia* (1973); Eric Robinson, 'The Transference of British Technology to Russia 1760–1820: a Preliminary Enquiry', in *Britain and Her World* (ed. B. Ratcliffe, 1975) ch. 1; R. P. Bartlett, 'Charles Gascoigne in Russia, A Case Study in the Diffusion of British Technology, 1786–1806' in A. G. Cross (ed.), *Russia and the West in the Eighteenth Century* (Newtonville, 1983), pp. 354 ff.

14. H. Freudenberger, 'Technologischer Wandel in 18 Jahrhundert', *Wolfenbuttler Forschungern, Band 14*, (Wulfenbuttel, 1981) p. 105.

15. W. O. Henderson, 'The Influence of British Entrepreneurs on the Industrial Revolution in Belgium, 1750–1850', *Britain and Industrial Europe*, pp. 102 ff. (Leicester, 1965); G. J. Hollister-Short, 'A New Technology and its Diffusion: Steam Engine Construction in Europe, 1720–80', *Industrial Archaeology* **13**, nos 1 and 2 (1978).

16. The paragraph is partly based on the excellent paper of Dr. R. P. Amdam, 'Industrial Espionage and the Transfer of Technology to the Early Norwegian Glass Industry', recently read to the T.I.C.C.I.H. History of Glass Conference in Portugal, for access to which I am deeply indebted to him. See also Caros Barros, 'O Vidro an Portugal do seculo xv ao seculo xix' in *O Vidro em Portugal* (Lisbon, 1989). I would also like to thank Mr. Ole Pein for his correspondence about his ancestor Joseph Pyne as a Bristol glassmaker who contracted to join a Norwegian glass works in 1755.

17. A recent general discussion of industrial transfer from Britain to France in the eighteenth century is J. R. Harris, 'The Transfer of Technology Between Britain and France before the French Revolution', in C. Crossley and I. Small, *The French Revolution and British Culture* (Oxford, 1989) pp. 156 ff, later cited as 'Transfer of Technology'.

18. For transfer of textile technology there are many sources, but C. Ballot, *L'Introduction du Machinisme dans L'Industrie Française* (Paris and Lille, 1923) esp. ch. II 'Le Coton', pp. 41 ff; A Rémond, *John Holker, Manufacturier et Grand Fonctionnaire en France* (Paris, 1946), *passim*; J. Vidalenc, 'Quelques Remarques sur le Rôle des Anglais dans la Révolution Industrielle en France, particulièrement en Normandie de 1750 à 1850, *Annales de Normandie* 8, No. 1, Jan 1958; X. Linant de Bellefonds, 'Les Techniciens Anglais dans L'Industrie Française au XVIIIᵉ Siècle' (thesis, Faculté de Droit, Paris, 1971), part II, chs 1–6; Henderson, *Britain and Industrial Europe* pp. 10–26, together give a basic coverage.

19. 'Transfer of Technology', pp. 165–75.

20. A detailed account of Law's scheme and its effect on the legislation of 1719 will appear in I. Blanchard, A. Goodman and J. Newman (eds), *Industry and Finance in Early Modern Europe* (forthcoming, 1990).

21. For Acts see 5 Geo. I cap 27; 23 Geo. II cap 13; 14 Geo. III c. 71; 21 Geo. III c. 37; 22 Geo. III c. 60; 25 Geo. III c. 60; 26 Geo. III c. 79 and 89; 35 Geo. III c. 38.

22. J. R. Harris, 'Industrial Espionage in the Eighteenth Century'. *Industrial Archaeology Review*, VII, 2 (1985) p. 129 (subsequently 'Industrial Espionage').

23. 'Transfer of Technology', p. 176; J. R. Harris, 'The Diffusion of English Metallurgical Methods to Eighteenth-Century France', *French History*, vol. 2, no. 1 (1988) pp. 34 ff (subsequently 'Metallurgical Methods'); and 'Michael Alcock and the Transfer of Birmingham Technology to France Before the Revolution', *Journal of European Economic History*, vol. 15, no. 1 (1986) pp. 19–20, 48–9 (subsequently, 'Birmingham Technology').

24. 'Industrial Espionage', pp. 130, 134; Archives Nationales, F12 677C.

25. Public Records Office, State Papers Domestic, Geo. I 36, 20 fol. 354–7.

26. See above.

27. For Holker, see Rémond, *John Holker, passim*; Henderson, *Britain and Industrial Europe*, pp. 14–24; A. P. Wadsworth and Julia de L. Mann, *The Cotton Trade and Industrial Lancashire* (Manchester, 1931) pp. 195–207.

28. Wadsworth and Mann, *Cotton Trade*, pp. 456–64.

29. 'Birmingham Technology', pp. 1–41.

30. Archives Nationales F12, 677C, 1316. There is a great deal in French archives on Le Turc and De Saudray, which is now being worked on; a preliminary paper on them was read to the S.H.O.T. conference, Sacramento, 1989, J. R. Harris, 'French Industrial Espionage in the Eighteenth Century : Two Engineers'.

31. 'Birmingham Technology', pp. 39, 53.

32. 'Industrial Espionage', pp. 134–5.

33. 'Transfer of Technology', pp. 173–8.

34. 'Metallurgical Methods', pp. 37–8.

35. Sir F. M. Eden, *The State of the Poor* (London, 1797) I, pp. 297–8. 'Though man, in a civilised society, loses much of his character as a loco-motive animal, I believe there is no country in Europe where he changes his residence so often as in England.'

36. 'Industrial Espionage', pp. 130–1.

37. 'Birmingham Technology', pp. 42–3.

38. 'Industrial Espionage', pp. 132, 134–5.

39. Ibid., p. 136.

40. Ibid.
41. 'Transfer of Technology', pp. 177 ff; Christine MacLeod, *Inventing the Industrial Revolution* (Cambridge, 1988) pp. 159 ff.
42. S. Pollard, *Peaceful Conquest* (Oxford, 1981), pp. 85, 110, 143–6; F. Crouzet, *op cit*, pp. 289–91, 321–3.
43. Lancashire Record Office, Preston. Quarter Sessions Papers, 1779.
44. Crawshay Letter Books, Glamorgan C.R.O.: R. Crawshay to Lord Hawkesbury, 10 July 1789.
45. The above cases are included in 'Industrial Espionage', pp. 130–6.
46. Archives Departementales Seine Maritime, C. 1092.

3. Transfers between Culturally-Related Nations: The Movement of Textile and Railroad Technologies between Britain and the United States, 1780–1840

David J. Jeremy and Darwin H. Stapleton

INTRODUCTION

In the early nineteenth century textile and railway technologies, along with metallurgical technologies, stood at the technical heart of the industrialization process in Britain and the USA. The transatlantic transfer of these technologies, part of a larger movement of technical interchange which helped to transform the two nations into first-rank industrial powers, is therefore of great significance. This chapter considers textile and railway transfers in two case studies.

Although they were developing along somewhat different political and social paths, technological transfer between the USA and Great Britain was relatively quick and effective, presumably because they were closely related culturally shared language, legal and economic systems; and they enjoyed a common technical heritage. The technological synergy between these nations needs to be better understood in our age when the circumstances of international technological transfer are closely related to a communication revolution which relies on the shared knowledge of computer language and scientific methodology.

The history of early British–American technology transfer may be briefly summarized in order to set the scene for the case studies. The transfer of technology was almost exclusively one-way until the 1780s; as Americans devoted their energies to subduing a quarter of a continent, they relied heavily on the British homeland for the necessary skills, tools and ideas. Some technologies were necessarily modified for the circumstances of a virgin and nearly vacant land: the water-powered sawmill, for example, was early found to be far more useful in America than it had been in Britain.[1] But during most of the first two centuries of the European settlement of coastal North America few industrial technologies found a fertile soil there.

In the last two decades of the eighteenth century there were certain signs that American technology was developing its own innovative qualities and that the American economy was becoming increasingly hospitable to and supportive of invention. This is clear in particular examples of British–American migration. William Weston, for example, went to the infant USA in the 1790s to ply his trade as a civil engineer and found his services in demand in Pennsylvania, Virginia, New York and Massachusetts. John Isaac Hawkins went at the same time to study medicine, but turned to mechanical pursuits there (working on a copying device with Charles Wilson Peale) and returned to England as an inventor. James Smallman, an engineer with Boulton and Watt, emigrated to help establish the first steam engine foundry in the USA in 1797, and remained there to take a leading role in the first two decades of American engine manufacture.

In some areas of technology a broadly supportive infrastructure of skills was still lacking in the USA even in the early phases of industrialization. When Marc Brunel was a French refugee in America in the 1790s (before re-migrating to Britain and undertaking his famous collaboration on the Portsmouth pulley-block machines) he worked on the construction of a steamboat with Chancellor Livingston (prior to Livingston's more successful association with Robert Fulton). Brunel found that there were no workmen in New York City at the time who could make the metal fittings he required.[2] Into the 1820s a few of the most inventive Americans, such as John C. Dyer (a textile machine builder) and Jacob Perkins (a machinist) found Britain to be more hospitable to the exercise of their imaginations.[3]

Generally, however, as early as the 1780s the USA began to exhibit a pattern of developing valuable innovations. There arose in the first half of the nineteenth century a transatlantic fraternity of English-speaking technicians, an ebb and flow of craftsmen and industrial workers who emigrated, temporarily or permanently, bringing the latest technical knowledge from one side of the Atlantic, and observing and seeking to understand the innovations on the other.[4] This flow was abetted by the development of regular ocean travel and by economic fluctuations which brought alternating prosperity to Britain and America such that in some industries it was not uncommon for workmen (usually British) to emigrate and return several times.[5]

OBSTACLES TO TRANSFER

While the transfer of textile and railroad technologies between Britain and the USA during the period we are considering took place in a rich social environment, we cannot ignore the considerable obstacles which had to be overcome. Obstacles to the outward flows of technology from Britain operated at three levels before the 1840s. There were government prohibitions; cultural barriers; and manufacturers' idiosyncrasies. Together they slowed down to some extent the acquisition of new technology by foreign rivals. However, it proved impossible to protect Britain's reservoir of new knowledge with an hermetically tight seal.

Government prohibitions, enacted between the 1690s and the 1780s, in response to pressures from the woollen and later the cotton manufacturers, checked both men and machines. By the 1780s it was illegal for skilled artisans or manufacturers to emigrate with a view to carrying on their trades; conviction incurred loss of nationality and property. Recruiting agents were subject to fines of £500 per migrant sent abroad and twelve months' imprisonment. The export or attempted export of implements and machines relating to textile manufacture (and also to metal, leather, paper and glass making, and clockmaking) was punishable with a £200 fine, forfeiture of equipment and twelve months' imprisonment.[6]

These laws proved impossible to apply effectually. Customs never had enough staff to monitor a collection of islands with a 7 000-mile coastline. Nor were their staff sufficiently familiar with the technology. Relatively simple technology could be memorized and carried abroad in the artisan's head. More complex machines could be broken into a multitude of components and smuggled abroad as unrecognizable parts. Eventually, in 1824, as part of the shift to free trade, the restraints on emigration were lifted. Prohibitions on machinery export remained until 1843, however, with a range of equipment deemed innocuous being exportable under Board of Trade licence. The licensing system failed to deter the middlemen in the illegal export trade. Their success is indicated by the decline in insurance premiums offered to machinery smugglers: in 1825 these stood at 30–45 per cent of the equipment's value; by 1841 they were 10–25 per cent. In 1841 a witness before the Parliamentary Committee investigating the laws on machinery exports reliably reported the situation: 'all prohibited machinery known in England is taken to the continent; ... I once asked a respectable man if he could get me a certain machine out, and I said to him, "The packages are very large", and his reply was, "I will get you Edinburgh Castle out, if you like."[7] No wonder free machinery export came soon after.

Buttressing the prohibitory laws was the shambolic organization behind the British patent system. Before 1830 no more than a quarter of British patents were published and indexes were not published until the 1850s. Searchers therefore had to go to the original specifications and drawings, recorded on vellum sheets, sewn together in rolls and scattered over three different locations in London. By 1829 a copy could cost anything between two and 40 guineas. Foreign acquisitors might not have been deterred, given the well-stocked nature of Britain's technological shelf.[8] Between 1790 and 1830 nearly 4 000 patents were registered in Britain; of these over 300 related to textile technology. Before 1800, as Christine MacLeod has shown, these patents were designed to save capital rather than labour.[9]

The other sorts of obstacles can be briefly noticed. At a cultural level there were strong regional technical traditions. Manifested most obviously in diverse technical vocabularies and nomenclatures these regional traditions could also be seen in measuring systems (in which units had dimensions varying with regions[10]) and in different ways of organizing work (for example with much greater independence allowed the artisan in Yorkshire than in the West of England). These technical habits perplexed and vexed foreigners visiting Britain's textile districts in search of new knowledge. In addition, as a West of England woollen dyer recorded, when immigrants from different British districts were employed together they would give differing opinions about equipment or processes: 'I cannot conceive a more uncomfortable situation', he noted, but it was one under which he knew some managers laboured in the USA.[11]

Manufacturers' idiosyncrasies, particularly their individual attitudes to sharing new knowledge with foreigners, played a part that cannot be quantified in delaying international transfers. Generally speaking, Lancashire manufacturers tended to be more secretive than their Glasgow counterparts; but exceptions may be found in contemporary diaries and parliamentary reports. By the 1820s, Lancashire, now the most advanced of the cotton textile districts, was attempting to guard its technical secrets to the extent of suppressing the publication of works outlining the operating rules by which the new technology could be mastered.

TEXTILES: THE DOMINANCE OF SKILLED ARTISANS AS TECHNOLOGY CARRIERS

Starting from the insights of sociologists and economists, one of us has argued that the westward transatlantic transfer of textile technologies in the early industrial period exhibits certain salient features.[12] The most prominent are the following: surmountable obstacles in Britain, the initiating country; the dominance of skilled artisans as international technology carriers; the establishment of pilot plants in the receptor country by combinations of immigrant artisans and indigenous capitalists; and diffusion and modification in the receptor country in accordance with local economic and social circumstances. In this chapter we briefly comment on each of these in turn.

Under the weight of emigration, westward and eastward, Britain's reservoir of technical secrets split open. Between the 1770s and the 1820s the numbers of workers with textile and machine-making skills annually emigrating from Britain to the USA (earlier, the American colonies) trebled. From around 170 a year in the 1770s and on the eve of the war of 1812, the rate shot up to over 600 in the late 1820s. Before the 1820s two-thirds of these immigrants were weavers.

Generally such workers were carriers of obsolete skills. Not all were, however. One, Joseph Hague of Hayfield, Derbyshire, in 1775 built the first spinning jenny seen in the colonies. Another, William Gilmour from Dunbarton, Scotland, introduced the Horrocks power loom to Rhode Island manufacturers after he arrived in New England in 1815. These men were highly exceptional.

By the late 1820s a higher proportion of machine makers was emigrating: 20 per cent of the annual rate of 600, in contrast to the 11 per cent of the 170 annual rate of the mid 1770s. Indeed the proportion of those with new industrial skills was evidently on the increase. Numbers of spinners, for example, quadrupled between the 1800s and the 1820s.

The importance of emigrants as technology carriers in the early days of the mechanized cotton industry is illustrated by the first attempt to export a spinning mule to America, in 1783. Broken down at Liverpool into unrecognizable components packed in casks labelled 'Queen's Ware pottery', it parted company from its owner when he fell ill at Cork. He returned to Liverpool, where he died, but the mule parts reached Philadelphia in the custody of his son. For four years, local mechanics struggled to make sense of the parts. In the end they packed the lot up and sent them back to England.[13] By 1793, however, machinists could be found in New York to build all kinds of textile machines, including mules.

The other major piece of spinning technology taken to America was Arkwright's water-frame. Credit for this is usually given entirely to Samuel Slater, who had been apprenticed to Arkwright's partner Jedidiah Strutt before emigrating to the USA in 1789. In fact there were multiple efforts to acquire Arkwright's technology in the late 1780s, when its commercial value was unquestioned and well-known. Tench Coxe, Philadelphia merchant and publicist of economic nationalism, in 1787 sent a secret agent to England to procure Arkwright models. The effort failed and the agent was deported after paying a fine. Another merchant, William Pollard, secured a US patent for Arkwright's water-frame but encountered fatal cash-flow problems when he tried to set up an Arkwright-type factory. The truth is that Slater was moving on a crowded stage. To him, however, must be given credit for achieving the essential combination of both technical and commercial success.[14]

Once cotton spinning factories were set up, power loom weaving and, later, mechanized calico printing were transferred from Britain to the USA: in each case illegally (by British law) and in many instances by British immigrants. William Gilmour took knowledge of Horrocks's variable batten speed motion (patented 1813) which, in allowing larger shuttles and incurring fewer warp breakages than earlier, cruder power looms, was the first commercially viable power loom in Britain. So pleased were they that the cotton manufacturers of southern New England in 1817 presented Gilmour with $1 500.[15] During the 1820s three powerful New England firms (the Merrimack Manufacturing Co. of Lowell, Massachusetts; the Dover Manufacturing Co. of Dover, New Hampshire; and the Taunton Manufacturing Co. of Taunton, Massachusetts) competed to secure the latest calico-printing technology from Lancashire. In each case they sent to England an agent whose instructions included the hiring of skilled printers and machinists as well as the purchase of printing machines.

IMMIGRANT ARTISANS AND INDIGENOUS CAPITALISTS COMBINE TO ESTABLISH PILOT PLANTS IN TEXTILE MANUFACTURING

Almost certainly Slater would not have succeeded without the support of American capitalists. With some difficulty he solved the technical problems presented in setting up a water-frame factory near Providence, Rhode Island. Those problems related to the design and operation of the new equipment. Under his direction a local blacksmith, Orziel Wilkinson, built the carding, drawing, roving and spinning machines required. Under his direction they were operated by children, as in England.[16] But it was the Providence merchant, Moses Brown, the merchant firm of his son-in-law, William Almy, and his cousin, Smith Brown, who supplied the capital for Slater to build his machines; to secure an old fulling mill and then to build a purpose-built factory; to pay wages; to pay for shipments of raw cotton; and to finance sales of yarn and then handwoven cloth along marketing networks already established.[17] One social reinforcement underlying the Almy & Brown network was the Quaker connection.[18]

The same combination of American capital and immigrant skill can be traced with the establishment of calico-printing works. John Dynley Prince was brought from Manchester to Lowell in 1825 and over the next 30 years was responsible for building up one of the largest and most important printeries in the United States, the Merrimack Print Works. Lowell's rivals, at Taunton and Dover, were much less fortunate in their choice of British printer. Taunton's made no great impact. Dover's recruit, Peter Bogle from Chorley, turned out to be either secretive or incompetent and 'highly pernicious' to the interests of the New Hampshire firm.

The exception to the pattern was the development of power loom weaving by Boston capitalists. One of their number, Francis Cabot Lowell, visited Britain, got into Scottish factories and took back to New England clear ideas about the power loom which he then developed with a local mechanic, Paul Moody.[19] There was a link with immigrant experience again, however, for Moody had trained with the Scholfields (see below).

Immigrants as technology carriers tended to be more successful if they migrated as a group, rather than going solo. Slater left much to chance until, early in 1790, he moved from New York to Providence, Rhode Island, where he found the backing of Quaker capitalists, and married into a family of Quaker blacksmiths and machine workers. Much less risky, in commercial, technical and social terms, was the migration of the Scholfields, a family of woollen clothiers from Saddleworth, Yorkshire, who emigrated to Boston in 1793. Initially two brothers, with their wives and children, plus a spinner and weaver, migrated as a group. They found local backing from a wealthy Newburyport merchant, William Bartlett. With his support they built a woollen factory housing carding machines, jennies and handlooms and finishing equipment. Three more brothers came over from the West Riding and within 20 years they had fanned out across New England, setting up carding and spinning mills. Their major technical achievement was the introduction of the British woollen carding machine into the USA.

Immigrant machine makers, in the Philadelphia region at least, played an important role in the internal diffusion of the imported new technology. By their numbers and competition for contracts, they lowered prices of machines and machine parts. They spread the use of cast iron in machine frames. They trained young Americans. And by selling key metal components (rollers, spindles, flyers, gears, guides, plates, levers and the like) they furthered the spread of their Lancashire machine-making methods.[20]

INTERNAL DIFFUSION AND MODIFICATION IN ACCORDANCE WITH LOCAL ECONOMIC AND SOCIAL CIRCUMSTANCES IN TEXTILE MANUFACTURING

Immigrants played a major part in diffusing new textile technology internally in the USA. Slater, his English and American kin and his former employees spread English spinning technology through southern New England. The Scholfields served woollen carding similarly. English machine makers played a key part in the Philadelphia region. Later, in the 1830s, James Montgomery, the Glasgow cotton mill manager who emigrated to work for the York Manufacturing Co. at Saco, Maine, in 1836, wrote extremely informative and influential books about early cotton technology and in one made the first exact and reliable comparison of British and American manufacturing costs.[21]

Not all immigrants were such effective diffusers of new technology, however. Secretiveness, excessive drinking, a propensity to unionize: these practices clashed head-on with American industrial values in which were bound awareness of nature's abundance, the Puritan work ethic and dreams of rags to riches. More generally, the technologies brought by the immigrants did not always fit American circumstances. For example, British equipment was designed for producing high- as well as low-quality products (yarns or cloth): Americans were more interested in lower qualities, suited to the nature of local demand. British equipment tended to be built to last; Americans relied more on wood than metal in their early machine building and became accustomed to shorter replacement periods, which had the added asset of permitting a faster rate of innovation. Above all, British equipment was relatively labour-intensive and skill-intensive in its operation; Americans, faced with a relative labour scarcity, found this inappropriate to the combination of factors of production (land, labour, capital) they possessed. Their great advantage over their British counterparts was that for a given outlay they could afford to buy much better grades of raw cotton and, with these, they had the ability to manufacture with cruder technologies.

Out of this divergence came a variety of American modifications to the imported technology. In cotton manufacturing the most important emerged from the so-called Waltham system of manufacturing set up by Boston merchant capitalists in 1813 and moved to Lowell on the Merrimack River in 1822.[22] The Waltham-Lowell system was characterized by vertically integrated spinning, weaving and finishing; large-scale production; a highly respectable female work-force recruited from New England farming families; and standardized products for mass markets with low disposable incomes. Technically the results were, in one direction, power-hungry and cruder machines (dead spindle, power loom), in the other, more sophisticated labour-saving devices (stop motions on the power loom, warper, dresser and filling frame). Equally important was the organization of the factory community, utilizing youthful, educated female labour and, in New England, publicly at least, aspiring to a new, more elevating vision of industrialization.[23]

In Rhode Island the industrial patterns laid down by Slater directed modifications towards high as well as low quality of product, towards family labour and small-scale operations. Versatility of equipment became important. Out of these considerations developed a series of roving frames (for preliminary spinning), the highly important cap and ring spindles, the power looms for weaving twill and fine cloths. The spindles were slow to be adopted. In the long term one of the most important innovations was the application of the differential gear to the roving frame by Aza Arnold, a mechanic who had served his apprenticeship under Slater. Curiously, the differential gear had been known since antiquity, so this was a case of re-invention.[24]

In America woollen manufacturing innovations were also directed at labour-saving goals. The most important devices were the rotary cloth shear (developed in the 1790s) and the woollen condenser which, attached to the delivery end of the carding machine, produced a continuous slubbing ready for spinning.

These, then, were the main characteristics of the westward transfer of textile technologies from Britain. It should not be forgotten that a number of American improvements were brought back to Britain, some very quickly (within six months), some in a decade or more. By the middle of the nineteenth century flows of technical and commercial information moved across the Atlantic in both directions far more efficiently than they had during the previous century.

THE ORIGIN AND DIFFUSION OF BRITISH RAILROAD TECHNOLOGY

The transfer of railroad technology from Britain to the USA was a more abrupt and demanding process than the transfer of mechanized textile technology. With the textile industry it was possible to mechanize one step of the process while retaining a handiwork technology in another step. Modern railroads, however, came as a package: they required trained engineers, graded ways, rails and ties, locomotives and cars, inclined planes (in the early years) and stations and other freight-handling facilities. While some experimentation was necessary and desirable, potential transferors generally had to promote the adoption of an entire complex of new technologies.

Railroad technology in its modern form is a British invention. Most historians agree that its roots lie in an older pan-European mining technology, but that its conversion to a general transportation system occurred fairly rapidly in Britain in the first quarter of the nineteenth century, and that the opening of the Stockton and Darlington (1825) and the Liverpool and Manchester (1830) railroads, and their technological and commercial success, are the starting-points for the beginning of the railroad era.

Americans were well aware of these developments, both because their interest in transport technology was raised to a fever pitch by the enormous success of the Erie Canal (begun in 1817 and opened fully in 1825) and because the vastness of their nation had turned many minds to the problem of overland transportation.[25] Literate Americans had many opportunities to learn about railroads by reading imported British newspapers and books, but must have found reports by their own countrymen particularly fascinating. The New York chemistry professor, John Griscom, for example, published in 1823 an account of his travels abroad which included the tantalizing remark that 'the most novel and singular application of steam, which I have yet observed, is in the transportation of coal from the mines to the border of [Leeds], upon an iron rail-way, by means of a steam wagon'.[26] The most influential account by an eye-witness was William Strickland's *Reports on Canals, Railways, Roads and Other Subjects* (1826). Strickland was a trained civil engineer working in the Philadelphia region who was sent to Britain by the Pennsylvania Society for the Promotion of Internal Improvement, a group of Philadelphia merchants who wanted to improve their city's connections to its economic hinterland. Strickland's book contained brief but explicit descriptions of the Stockton and Darlington railroad and others, as well as excellent drawings of railroad technology.[27]

The initial steps in the adoption of railroad technology were all taken by companies that hired American engineers who, like Strickland, had travelled to Britain to gain first-hand acquaintance with the technology. Without exception the Americans were able to visit the railroads freely and in some cases the visiting engineers became close friends with their British counterparts.[28] Between 1825 and 1840 at least 15 American engineers visited Britain to study railroads, and they returned to build the vast majority of early American railroads.[29] The transfer of an entire technological system was undertaken enthusiastically by Americans, but certainly required trials and errors. For one thing, the modern railroad form – with steam locomotives, steam-powered inclined planes and iron rails – was still a recent and evolving technology in Britain. The engineers and promoters of the Liverpool and Manchester Rail-road, for example, carried out well-publicized experiments on steam locomotives and tried out several different kinds of rail and track.

In a parallel manner, early American railroads, such as the Baltimore and Ohio (Maryland) and Mohawk and Hudson (New York), tested several types of motive power and laid down wooden, iron and stone rails in order to try out 'American' materials and technology.[30] A committee of the directors of the Mohawk and Hudson railroad summarized this approach early in 1829 as follows:

> Although the great principles of railway motion are the same, still every line of railway has features peculiar to itself, both in the nature of the traffic, and in its levels. Every railway therefore ought to have conveying machines adapted to it. To attain this important advantage, a temporary railway is usually erected, upon which the engineer can try the experiments upon the practical scale. This is usually done in Great Britain, and has been done in this country, upon the Hudson and Delaware Railway, as well as upon that at Baltimore.[31]

While trial-and-error was perhaps a learning experience, those immediately successful early railroads, such as the Boston and Lowell (Massachusetts),

Columbia and Philadelphia (Pennsylvania) and Camden and Amboy (New Jersey), were those which copied British technology as closely as possible, importing rails and locomotives from British manufacturers.[32] During the following decade American engineers gradually modified the British system to create what became recognized as an American version. Some elements of the system long remained dependent on British technology, other elements were quickly 'Americanized'.

RAILROADS: THE EVOLUTION OF AN IMPORTED TECHNOLOGY

The human element, the engineers, rapidly became independent. Americans who were trained by apprenticeship on the massive state canal projects of the 1820s or at the United States Military Academy (West Point), where civil engineering was a regular element of the curriculum, were able to acquire a sufficient knowledge of railroad technology through a visit to Britain. The three engineers sent there by the Baltimore and Ohio railroad in 1829 returned home to report confidently (in the third person) that

> A careful investigation of the subject committed to them, under circumstances so favorable to correct conclusions, has resulted in their entire economical means of conveyance, and that the completion of the work in which this company has embarked, in the manner and on the principles which have so far governed its location and construction, will, in their opinion, fulfill the most sanguine expectations of the company, and of the public.[33]

This statement of confidence was thoroughly vindicated by the later achievements of the small circle of American engineers who visited Britain. So far as can be determined, this select group dominated American railroad construction until the late 1830s, and then bequeathed the direction of most later lines to their assistants and associates.[34] For example, in 1835 the Long Island (New York) Railroad was formed and sought an engineer: three or four candidates were either visitors or their former assistants. The company's choice was one of those who had gone to Britain seven years earlier for the Baltimore and Ohio, and not, incidentally, the engineer with the most experience in railroad construction.[35] The Long Island Railroad was laid out and put into operation without any technical difficulties.

Newly-formed railroad companies which could not immediately obtain the services of one of the visitors (who worked almost entirely in the Atlantic Coastal states), or their *élèves* (students), often struggled to get coherent technical information. The board of directors of the Little Miami, an early Ohio railroad in the Cincinnati, Ohio, area founded in 1837, at first hired Ormsby M.

Mitchel – a West Point graduate who had taught mathematics but did not have engineering experience[36] – to survey and estimate the cost of building the first 16 miles of their route, then a year later turned briefly to a self-styled expert, 'R. H. Fountleroy, engineer', for another opinion. Finding the Fountleroy estimate twice Mitchel's, the directors' survey committee noted that it was 'unable to determine, which of these estimates [is] most to be relied upon'. The directors were so lacking in access to information about railroad construction that they were 'unable fully to satisfy their own minds upon the subject' or the appropriate salary for an engineer. Fifteen months after they had begun to plan their railroad the directors finally hired an engineer who could be relied on because he had just completed construction on the pioneering railroad in the Midwest, the Mad River and Lake Erie (Ohio).[37] As this contrast between the Long Island and Little Miami railroads suggests, the availability of engineers who carried the authority of experience made an enormous difference in initiating a railroad project.

While Americans generally were able to obtain the know-how to lay out, build and operate railroads through direct observation of British examples, there were certain elements of railroad technology which American industry could not immediately supply, namely locomotives and rails.

It took about a decade for American mechanical engineers to develop sufficient expertise, first to compete effectively with British locomotive manufacturers and then to drive them out of the American market. Certainly the American engineers who visited Britain greatly admired the locomotives they saw and often recommended importing them. Company minutes show that the directors relied heavily on their engineers' advice in the arcane matter of selecting a locomotive.

The Mohawk and Hudson directors, for example, first requested in 1829 that their engineer make drawings of locomotives 'upon the most approved plans now practiced in England' and a year later began the process of purchasing two engines by receiving their engineer's report on the subject. Subsequently they resolved to order a British locomotive immediately, but indicated the uncertain status of locomotive manufacture in the USA by noting only that they 'were taking measures to obtain another in this country'.[38]

In fact several American manufacturing firms were initiating a commitment just about the time the Mohawk and Hudson began its search. Manufacturers such as Mathew Baldwin (Philadelphia), William Norris (Philadelphia), Ross Winans (Baltimore) and the Locks and Canals Co. (Lowell, Massachusetts) quickly adapted British designs to American conditions. Thus, although Americans purchased numerous British locomotives up to 1841, when the last one was imported, by an informed estimate only about one-fourth of all locomotives on American railroads were British-made at that time.[39]

American importation of British locomotives may have been somewhat prolonged by the American reliance on the British capital market in the late 1830s and early 1840s. During those years American internal improvement promoters (both public and private) found British investors willing to provide vast infusions of capital needed to construct both canals and railroads. In one of the earliest instances, the Philadelphia and Reading Railroad sent its engineer, Moncure Robinson, to England in the winter and spring of 1837 to sell the company's bonds and stock; he was not only successful in obtaining outright sales, but also found that he could purchase rails and locomotives with the securities as well as the proceeds of his sales. Robinson's lines imported numerous locomotives in the next two years when most American railroads had turned to domestic products.[40] Other American railroads tried to follow Robinson's lead in raising capital in Britain, but with varying degrees of success.[41]

Americans relied upon imported rails from Britain into the 1850s. The British iron industry developed rapidly in the late 1700s and far outstripped American pig-iron production until Americans began to institute the use of coal for fuel in the 1840s. The British also had large rolling mills in operation well before the Americans, and could easily accommodate orders for miles and miles of rails in the 1830s and 1840s, when only a few pioneering rail mills were opened in the USA. Only after mid-century did the American rail industry become the major supplier to American railroads.[42]

American railroads were therefore forced to import British rails and associated hardware, such as spikes and bolts. They generally did so through established Anglo-American commission merchants. The Mohawk and Hudson turned to W. & J. Brown in Liverpool for its first order of 400 tons of rails in 1830, for example. In 1832 the Allegheny Portage Railroad, a project of the state of Pennsylvania (where about 50 per cent of American iron production was located) contracted with A. & G. Ralston, Philadelphia importers, for all of its rails.[43] An engineer on the Allegheny Portage noted that the design of the rail was intended to be 'that used on the best English railways made *since* the Liverpool and Manchester', indicating that Americans were trying to import rails with the latest improvements.[44]

Very soon Americans began to impose their technical requirements on the British producers by employing American inspectors at British rail mills. A. & G. Ralston regularly employed one by 1836, and in that same year both the Baltimore and Port Deposit Railroad (Maryland) and the Philadelphia, Wilmington, and Baltimore Railroad had an agent in Britain to 'superintend the manufacture and forwarding [of] the rails for shipment'.[45] In 1840 the Philadelphia and Reading Railroad insisted on having an inspector in Britain who was 'competent, faithful & industrious in our service, & as exclusively devoted to our interest as can be wished'.[46] These agents became sources of informa-

tion, not only on British railroad technology, but also on the British iron industry. One agent had a role in the transfer of anthracite iron technology to the
USA, and others may have been important in the transfer of rolling mill
technology.[47]

In the early 1840s some American railroads began to purchase rails from the
earliest American rail mills, and then it was usually Midwestern roads for
whom the high costs of inland shipment made the higher-cost domestic sources
competitive. The engineer of the Little Miami (Ohio) Railroad was directed to
go to 'New York or Europe' to buy iron in 1841, but after going to New York
chose to make a contract with the new Great Western Iron Co., a new works
north of Pittsburgh, Pennsylvania, which had blast furnaces and a rolling mill
on the same site.[48] In 1846 the Madison and Indianapolis (Indiana) Railroad
without hesitation made a contract for rails in Cincinnati, Ohio.[49] But two years
later the Mohawk and Hudson, an Eastern line, was still purchasing British
rails.[50]

In the myriad other elements of railroad-related technologies American
engineers were usually able to turn to American precedents. In bridge design,
for example, the railroads could employ masons and wooden-bridge builders
with experience in crossing the major Atlantic coast rivers. The Baltimore and
Ohio Railroad's masonry Thomas Viaduct was built in 1833–5, for example,
and remains in use over a century-and-a-half later. But most railroads built
wooden bridges, even for long spans, an innovation that was much admired by
foreign observers, such as French engineer, Michel Chevalier; German engineer, Paul C. Denis; and Austrian engineer, Karl von Ghega.[51]

It is worthwhile noting here that Chevalier and von Ghega were not alone
in their admiration. By the latter 1830s there came to the USA a steady stream
of European engineers to examine the railroad technology which seemed in a
fair way towards conquering a continent. Numerous publications recorded
their travels and observations and promoted American railroads as cheaper and
more adaptable to varying geographic conditions than British railroads.[52] As
a result, in various areas of Germany and Austro-Hungary, the American model
was followed in preference to British technology. In Russia, American engineers were actually given the direction of the Moscow–St Petersburg line.[53]

CONCLUSION

We recognize that there are many differences between the transfer of textile
technology and that of railroad technology from Britain to the USA. Textile
technology was typically transferred by artisans, of which there was a sizeable
community of the more or less skilled and more or less innovative. They tended
to take their skills to the particular mills and shops in which they were

employed. In many cases the transferred innovations were incremental because the underlying knowledge of the technology – textile spinning and weaving – was fairly widespread. Innovations in textile technology could confer considerable advantages on those who exploited them and kept the knowledge from others. Railroad technology, however, was the property of a tiny group of highly-trained professional engineers who acted as consultants to several projects at the same time. The technology was new and systemic, requiring an all-or-nothing choice for adoption. It was not site-oriented, but involved tying together distant geographic centres, and its ideal application required the creation of a continental network of railroads. Sharing the knowledge of railroad technology was therefore advantageous.

However one understands these differences, the broad similarities in these case studies as we have reviewed them suggest that, at least in the case of culturally similar nations, some generalizations are possible about the interrelationships of donating and receiving nations. First, even in the case of transoceanic communication by ship, critical technical information flows readily and can be acted on quickly. Skilled immigrants and trained visitors are both excellent conduits. Second, successful transfers are accompanied by rapid adaptation of the new technology. Native techniques and materials are infused into the techniques in such a way that they begin to take on a new character. Finally, there comes a time when the recipient nation, if it chooses to industrialize, becomes a new source of innovation, so that its version and adaptation of the technology may become a model for other industrializing nations. In the case of Britain and the USA, the latter had established a recognizable version of a textile industry by the 1820s, and of railroads by the 1840s.

NOTES

1. Darwin H. Stapleton, *The Transfer of Early Industrial Technologies to America* (Philadelphia, 1987) p. 6.
2. Stapleton, *Transfer of Early Industrial Technologies*, pp. 50–9; Edward C. Carter, John C. Van Horne, and Lee W. Formwalt (eds), *The Papers of Benjamin Henry Latrobe* (New Haven, Conn., 1984–8) 1, pp. 143–4n, 304–5, 321n; 2, pp. 809–10, 845–6, 904–5; Nathan Reingold (ed.), *The Papers of Joseph Henry* (Washington, 1972–in progress) 3, pp. 281–3.
3. Stapleton, *Transfer of Early Industrial Technologies*, pp. 12, 17.
4. The similar term to transatlantic fraternity, 'international fraternity of mechanicians', was coined, so far as we are aware, by Anthony F. C. Wallace in *Rockdale* (New York, 1978) pp. 211–19.
5. Rowland T. Berthoff, *British Immigrants in Industrial America, 1790–1950* (Cambridge, Mass., 1953) p. 52, notes that English, Welsh and Scottish miners moved freely between the USA and Britain in the nineteenth century.
6. David J. Jeremy, 'Damming the Flood: British Government Efforts to Check the Outflow of Technicians and Machinery, 1780–1843', *Business History Review* 51 (1977) pp. 1–34.

7. *Parliamentary Papers* (Commons) 1841 (201) VII, 55.
8. Textile patenting 1790–1830 is analysed in David J. Jeremy, *Transatlantic Industrial Revolution: The Diffusion of Textile Technologies between Britain and America, 1790–1830s* (Cambridge, Mass., 1981) pp. 54–64; a broader analysis is H. I. Dutton, *The Patent System and Inventive Activity During the Industrial Revolution, 1750–1852* (Manchester, 1984).
9. Christine MacLeod, *Inventing the Industrial Revolution: The English Patent System, 1660–1800* (Cambridge, 1988) pp. 160, 172.
10. David J. Jeremy, 'British and American Yarn Count Systems: An Historical Analysis', *Business History Review* 45 (1971) pp. 336–68.
11. William Partridge, *A Practice Treatise on Dying* [sic] (New York, 1823; 1973 reprint) p. 20.
12. David J. Jeremy, *Transatlantic Industrial Revolution.*
13. David J. Jeremy, 'British Textile Technology Transmission to the United States: The Philadelphia Region Experience, 1770–1820', *Business History Review* 47 (1973) pp. 24–52.
14. Anthony F. C. Wallace and David J. Jeremy, 'William Pollard and the Arkwright Patents', *William and Mary Quarterly* 34 (1977) pp. 404–25.
15. William R. Bagnall, *The Textile Industries of the United States* (Cambridge, Mass., 1893) p. 550.
16. Barbara M. Tucker, *Samuel Slater and the Origins of the American Textile Industry, 1790–1860* (Ithaca, NY, 1984) ch. 3.
17. Caroline F. Ware, *The Early New England Cotton Manufacture: A Study in Industrial Beginnings* (New York, 1931; reprinted 1966) ch. 7.
18. Mack Thompson, *Moses Brown: Reluctant Reformer* (Chapel Hill, NC, 1962).
19. Robert F. Dalzell, Jr., *Enterprising Elite: The Boston Associates and the World They Made* (Cambridge, Mass., 1987) ch. 1.
20. David J. Jeremy, 'Immigrant Textile Machine Makers along the Brandywine, 1810–1820', *Textile History* 13 (1982).
21. This was his *A Practical Detail of the Cotton Manufacture of the United States of America … Contrasted and Compared with that of Great Britain* (Glasgow, 1840); see also David J. Jeremy, *Technology and Power in the Early American Cotton Industry* (Philadelphia, 1990).
22. George Sweet Gibb, *The Saco-Lowell Shops: Textile Machinery Building in New England, 1813–1949* (Cambridge, Mass., 1950).
23. Thomas Dublin, *Women at Work: The Transformation of Work and Community in Lowell, Massachusetts, 1826–1860* (New York, 1979).
24. David J. Jeremy, 'Technological Diffusion: The Case of the Differential Gear', *Industrial Archaeology Review* 5 (1981).
25. Stapleton, *Transfer of Early Industrial Technologies*, pp. 35–71.
26. John Griscom, *A Year in Europe, Comprising a Journal of Observations*, 2nd edn (1st edn. 1823) 2 vols (New York, 1824) 2, pp. 190–1.
27. William Strickland, *Reports on Canals, Railways, Roads and Other Subjects* (Philadelphia, 1826). See also William Strickland, 'A Description of the Hetton Rail Road, in England', *Franklin* [Institute] *Journal* 1 (1826) pp. 15–16, plate.
28. Stapleton, *Transfer of Early Industrial Technologies*, p. 123. Strickland, for example, named one of his sons Hartley Strickland after Jesse Hartley, a British engineer whom he had met in 1825.
29. Darwin H. Stapleton, 'The Origin of American Railroad Technology, 1825–1840', *Railroad History* 139 (Autumn 1978) pp. 65–77.
30. John H. White, Jr., 'Tracks and Timber', *IA: The Journal of the Society for Industrial Archeology* 2 (1976) pp. 35–43; John H. White, Jr. and Robert M. Vogel, 'Stone Rails Along the Patapsco', *IA* 4 (1978) pp. 1–14.
31. Minutes, 17 February 1829, Mohawk and Hudson Rail Road Co., box 39, Conrail Papers, Manuscripts Division, New York Public Library, New York, N.Y.
32. Stapleton, *Transfer of Early Industrial Technologies*, pp. 146, 156–8.

33. Jonathan Knight, Wm. G. McNeill and G. W. Whistler to the Baltimore and Ohio Railroad Co., 25 May 1829, *Niles Register* (Baltimore, Md.) 20 June 1829.
34. Stapleton, 'The Origin of American Railroad Technology', pp. 67–8, 76–7.
35. Ibid., pp. 71, 72, 74; minutes, 18 June 1835, Long Island Railroad Co., reel 58, acc. 1807, Hagley Museum and Library (HML), Wilmington, Del. The four engineers were Isaac Trimble, Walter Gwynn, William G. McNeill (the B&O engineer) and Andrew Talcott. All were Army officers and graduates of West Point. Talcott was a member of the Army's Corps of Engineers, officers of which were at the time often given leave to work for private canal and railroad companies. It cannot be determined whether Talcott had done so, or whether he served under a visitor. George W. Cullum, *Biographical Register of the Officers and Graduates of the U. S. Military Academy* (Boston, 1891) 1, pp. 186, 280, 285–6.
36. Clark A. Elliott, *Biographical Dictionary of American Science: The Seventeenth Through the Nineteenth Centuries* (Westport, CT and London, 1979) pp. 179–80.
37. Minutes, 24 August 1837–10 December 1838, Little Miami Rail-Road Co., vol. 311, Accession 1807, HML. Robert M. Shoemaker was the engineer finally hired by the Little Miami; he is identified as the resident engineer of the Mad River and Lake Erie Railroad in the account of a travelling engineer: Franz Anton Ritter von Gerstner, *Der Innern Communicationen der Vereinigten Staaten von Nordamerica* (Vienna, 1843) 1, p. 352. Shoemaker worked under chief engineer James H. Bell on the Mad River and Lake Erie; Bell's background and training is unknown: *American Railroad Journal* 5 (1836), p. 626.
38. Minutes, 21 July 1829, 11 November 1830, 8 January 1831, Mohawk and Hudson Railroad. The company soon ordered a locomotive from the West Point Foundry, Cold Spring, N.Y.: ibid., 21 March 1831.
39. John H. White, Jr., *American Locomotives* (Baltimore, 1968) p. 7.
40. Stapleton, *Transfer of Early Industrial Technologies*, pp. 161–2; Gowan & Marx to Moncure Robinson, 20 January 1837, and Gowan & Marx to R. P. Lardner, 23 April 1837, box 42, Acc. 1520 HML.
41. See, for examples, the success and failure of two Eastern railroads: minutes, 12 June 1838, 14 August 1838, 14 May 1839, 9 October 1839, 12 May 1840, 23 January 1843, Philadelphia, Wilmington, and Baltimore Railroad, Acc. 1807, HML; minutes, 30 November 1840, 15 December 1840, 26 January 1841, 14 September 1842, Long Island Railroad.
42. Charles K. Hyde, *Technological Change and the British Iron Industry, 1700–1870* (Princeton, NJ, 1977) pp. 106–9, 166–8; Peter Temin, *Iron and Steel in Nineteenth-Century America: An Economic Inquiry* (Cambridge, Mass., 1964) pp. 46–50, 114–21. See also Robert W. Fogel, *Railroads and American Economic Growth: Essays in Econometric History* (Baltimore and London, 1964) ch. 5.
43. Minutes, 27 September 1830, Mohawk and Hudson Rail Road; 'Articles of Agreement', 2 May 1832, vol. 4, box 2, Contracts, Allegheny Portage Railroad, Divisional Records, Board of Canal Commissioners, William Penn Archives, Harrisburg, Pa. It is interesting to note that Gerard Ralston was known as a public advocate of railroads: Nicholas Wood, *A Practical Treatise on Railroads* ed., George W. Smith, (2nd edn, Philadelphia, 1832) p. ix.
44. Solomon W. Roberts to Josiah White, 10 April 1832, Charles Roberts Autograph Collection, Haverford (Pa) College Library (emphasis in original).
45. *American Railroad Journal* 5 (1836) p. 433; minutes 16 May 1836, Philadelphia, Wilmington, and Baltimore Railroad, Acc 1807, HML. The wisdom of employing such inspectors was confirmed by reports taken from the British press that inferior iron was incorporated into rails: e.g., *American Railroad Journal* 13 (1841) pp. 343–7, citing *Railway Magazine*.
46. Elihu Chauncey to W. H. Keating, 11 January 1840, letterbook, Philadelphia and Reading Co., box 17, acc. 1520, HML.
47. Stapleton, *Transfer of Early Industrial Technologies*, p. 178.
48. Minutes, 3 November 1841, 20 October 1842, Little Miami Railroad.
49. Minutes, 6 November 1846, Madison and Indianapolis Railroad, Acc 1807, HML.
50. Minutes, 5 October 1848, Mohawk and Hudson Railroad.

51.   Stapleton, *Transfer of Early Industrial Technologies*, pp. 151–3; s.v., 'Karl von Ghega',
      and 'Paul Camille Denis', *Neue Deutsche Biographie* (Berlin, 1953–85) 3, p. 599; 6, pp.
      364–5.
52.   See, for example, von Gerstner (above, n. 37); Karl Ghega, *Die Baltimore-Ohio-Eisenbahn
      über das Allegheny-Gebirg mit Besonderer Berücksichtigung der Steigungs-und
      Krümmungsverhältnisse* (Vienna, 1844); Michel Chevalier, *Histoire et Description des
      Voies de Communication aux États-Unis, et des Travaux d'Art Qui en Dépendent* (Paris,
      1840) with plates.
53.   Darwin H. Stapleton, 'Neither Tocqueville nor Trollope: Michel Chevalier and the
      Industrialization of America and Europe', in Robert Weible (ed.), *The World of the In-
      dustrial Revolution: Comparative and International Aspects of Industrialization* (North
      Andover, Mass., 1986) pp. 21–34; Richard Mowbry Haywood, *The Beginnings of Railway
      Development in Russia in the Reign of Nicholas I, 1835–1842* (Durham, NC, 1969);
      Dionysius Lardner, *Railway Economy: A Treatise on the New Art of Transport* (New York,
      1855, reprinted, New York, 1968) pp. 396–405.

PART 2

Western Industrial Nations before 1914

4. Iron and Steel Technologies moving between Europe and the United States, before 1914

Charles K. Hyde

During the period extending from the mid-eighteenth century to the First World War, Great Britain led the world in developing new technologies for producing pig iron, wrought iron and steel. Benjamin Huntsman (1704–76), working in Sheffield in the early 1740s, developed the crucible process for making high-quality steel and this remained the dominant steelmaking technology worldwide for more than a century.[1] Abraham Darby (1678–1717) successfully used coke instead of charcoal in the blast furnace in 1709, but the rest of the British iron industry did not begin to use mineral fuel to produce pig iron until the 1750s. Still, by the end of the eighteenth century, coke had superseded charcoal in smelting.[2] Similarly ironmasters developed new technologies to replace charcoal with coke in the production of bar or wrought iron, starting in the 1760s. But in 1783–4, Henry Cort (1740–1800) developed the 'puddling and rolling process', which diffused rapidly and dominated the refining sector by the end of the Napoleonic Wars.[3]

British iron and steel makers retained their technological leadership through most of the nineteenth century as well. By pre-heating the blast to the furnace, an innovation introduced by James Beaumont Neilson (1792–1865) in 1828, building larger furnaces and through other innovations in blast furnace machinery and practice. British ironmasters made substantial productivity gains in the middle decades of the nineteenth century.[4]

In the mid-1850s, Henry Bessemer (1813–98) introduced a new process that revolutionized steelmaking in Britain and in the rest of the western world. Much of this chapter will examine the international diffusion of Bessemer's process in detail. Shortly after Bessemer's breakthrough, William Siemens (1823–83), a German who spent most of his life in Britain, and the Frenchmen Pierre and Emile Martin, in 1861–5 developed the open-hearth method for making steel, commonly known as the Siemens–Martin process. By 1867, both Siemens and the Martins were producing steel commercially with the new process.[5] A decade later, in 1877–9, two English cousins, Sidney G. Thomas

51

(1850–85) and Percy C. Gilchrist (1851–1935), enabled steelmakers to use phosphoric pig iron in Bessemer converters and open-hearth furnaces by adding a basic furnace lining and a lime-rich (basic) slag.[6] Sheffield producers then led the world steel industry in introducing new alloy steels between the 1880s and the First World War, including manganese, silicon, high-speed and stainless steel.[7]

Historians have often portrayed the American iron and steel industry as technologically under-developed during the eighteenth and most of the nineteenth centuries, threatened by cheap, high-quality products from Europe that would have swamped American manufacturers without protective tariffs. Histories of the British iron and steel industry recognize the importance of the USA as a market for British products, but dismiss the American iron industry as technologically backward.[8] Even James Swank, viewing American progress in iron and steel from the perspective of 1891, emphasized America's remarkable lack of technological sophistication in coke-smelting and crucible steel production and its reliance on high tariffs to avoid competition from cheaper European iron and steel.[9]

The American iron and steel industry may have appeared to be technologically 'backward' compared with its European counterparts. The transfer of European iron and steel technologies to the USA occurred in a halting and uneven fashion because of significant differences in economic conditions on both sides of the Atlantic. For instance, the protracted use of charcoal iron technology in America, particularly in smelting, long after its passing in Britain reflected the relative abundance and low cost of charcoal in North America, which removed most of the economic incentive to use coal technology.[10]

But when American ironmasters could realize substantial savings with coal technology, by adopting puddling furnaces and rolling mills, they quickly adopted the new techniques.[11] Beginning in 1817, for example, a pair of puddling furnaces and adjoining rolling mill went into operation in western Pennsylvania, and the puddling and rolling processes diffused quickly.[12] Similarly, later British improvements in puddling that reduced wastage of pig iron, primarily the use of cast iron bottoms in the furnace (1818) and the *wet puddling* or *pig boiling* process (c. 1830), spread quickly to America and aided the adoption of puddling and rolling.[13] In Pennsylvania, which in the 1840s and 1850s accounted for more than half of American iron production, the proportion of wrought iron manufactured in rolling mills rose from 80 per cent in 1849 to 95 per cent in 1856, with virtually all of it puddled iron.[14] Finally the hot blast spread quickly from Britain to America, where ironmasters used it in charcoal furnaces and in furnaces fired with anthracite coal and bituminous coke.

In several important instances, American iron and steel producers not only adopted new technologies quickly, but then surpassed European practice in short order. American ironmasters began producing pig iron with anthracite coal in 1838, immediately after the process was first successful in South Wales, and by the mid-1850s surpassed European producers in terms of output and productivity.[15] Bessemer steel technology diffused quickly in the USA, starting in the mid-1860s, only about five years after the process was commercially successful in Europe. By the late 1870s, American Bessemer steel producers had easily surpassed their European counterparts in terms of mechanization, productivity and costs.[16]

The uneven pace of technology transfer and diffusion of European iron and steel technology in the USA before the First World War reflected transatlantic differences in the costs of labour, resources and capital, as well as variations in entrepreneurial vision, technical competence and craft skills. This chapter uses five case studies to examine the variations in the transfer of iron and steel technologies in the nineteenth and early twentieth centuries: the manufacture of anthracite pig iron, bituminous coke pig iron, crucible steel, open-hearth steel and Bessemer steel. Together the case studies exemplify the wide range of forces that influenced technology transfer.

The detailed histories of iron and steel technologies that successfully migrated from Europe to the USA in the nineteenth century reveal much about the process of technology transfer. Large differences in production costs and in the quality of the product achieved in Europe and America, using the same technology, can explain most of the observed variations in the rates of adoption of European techniques in the USA. High transportation costs in America, especially before the coming of the railroad, significantly slowed technology transfer. In most of the cases where transfer occurred, foreign workers and managers played a critical role, bringing the new technology in their hands and heads. Both foreign and native-born iron and steel manufacturers were quick to modify the original European technologies to better suit American conditions, especially in the cases of anthracite pig iron and crucible steel manufacturing.

ANTHRACITE PIG IRON

Although many British ironmasters had produced pig iron with coke since the late 1750s, American iron producers first used coal in the blast furnace in the late 1830s. The coal technology first transferred was that of smelting pig iron with anthracite coal and the hot blast, which had just achieved commercial success in South Wales in 1837, rather than the well-established method of smelting with coke from bituminous coal. The chronology of adoption reflected the facts of American economic geography – anthracite was the only coal east of the Appalachian Mountains and therefore readily accessible to ironmasters. Starting in the late 1820s, Pennsylvania ironmasters experimented with anthracite coal in the production of wrought iron with the puddling process. Success came in the mid-1830s and, by the early 1840s, ironmasters commonly used anthracite in puddling furnaces in eastern Pennsylvania.[17]

Dr Frederick W. Geissenhainer, a Lutheran clergyman of New York City, experimented with smelting iron using anthracite coal and a hot blast in 1830 and 1831, and received a patent for his process on 19 December 1833. He built the Valley furnace in Schuylkill County, Pennsylvania, and in August and September 1836 succeeded in making pig iron exclusively with anthracite coal as the fuel. After Geissenhainer's death in 1838 following a prolonged illness, George Crane, who had patented the same process in Britain in September 1836, purchased Geissenhainer's American patent.[18]

The Pennsylvania anthracite iron industry developed quickly, with a cluster of new furnaces built in the late 1830s. Between August 1838 and August 1841, nine anthracite furnaces went into blast. The firm of Boughman, Guiteau & Co. erected the first, near Mauch Chunk, Pennsylvania, which went into blast on 27 August 1838. The second, the Pioneer furnace at Pottsville, first smelted with anthracite on 10 July 1839, and by the following spring a half-dozen furnaces in eastern Pennsylvania were using anthracite.[19]

American ironworks successfully made pig iron with anthracite coal less than five years after British ironmasters had done so, which reflects the lack of significant information barriers. The actual transfer was the direct result of the migration of people who had worked with the new process. A Welsh ironmaster, Benjamin Perry, managed a furnace at Pottsville, Pennsylvania, when it began a second trial with anthracite coal on 26 October 1839. Because the Pottsville furnace remained in blast for 90 days, the owners collected a $5 000 prize offered by a group of Philadelphians to anyone who could accomplish that feat.[20] Between April and July 1840, four new furnaces began smelting iron with anthracite and Benjamin Perry put two of them into operation. However none of these pioneer efforts was both technically and commercially successful.[21]

The Mauch Chunk furnace was in blast three times in 1838 and 1839, but the longest blast lasted only three months and yielded only about 100 tons of pig iron. According to Johnson, the blowing apparatus at Mauch Chunk was defective and the quality of pig iron generally inferior.[22] By September 1840 the firm was bankrupt and the property was disposed of by a sheriff's sale.[23] Although the Pottsville furnace collected a prize for remaining in blast for 90 days, it also had an inadequate heating apparatus for the blast and produced pig iron of indifferent quality.[24] The blowing apparatus Thomas built for Lehigh Crane provided more than twice the volume of air to the furnace than was the case at the five furnaces that predated his.[25] James M. Swank also credited Thomas with the initial success of anthracite smelting in the USA:

because the furnace built under his directions at Catasauqua and blown in by him was the first of all the early anthracite furnaces that was completely successful, both from an engineering and a commercial standpoint.[26]

The Lehigh Crane Iron Co. achieved the first entirely successful application of anthracite coal in smelting, in both technical and commercial terms, during the summer of 1840 at its furnace at Catasauqua, Pennsylvania.[27] The key figure in the transfer of anthracite technology was David Thomas (1794–1882), who had worked in iron works in South Wales, beginning at age seventeen. He was the manager of the Yniscedwyn Ironworks in early 1837, when the firm pioneered smelting with anthracite coal and the hot blast. In November 1838, the Lehigh Coal and Navigation Co. sent Erskine Hazard to observe anthracite smelting at Yniscedwyn. This firm, which operated the Lehigh Canal and owned extensive coal deposits in the Lehigh Valley of eastern Pennsylvania, wanted to promote anthracite iron to stimulate canal traffic and coal sales. In April 1839, Hazard and other prominent stockholders of the Lehigh Coal and Navigation Co. formally established the Lehigh Crane Iron Co. to pursue smelting with anthracite.[28]

Hazard had hoped to induce George Crane, the owner of the Yniscedwyn works, to come to America, but Crane instead recommended David Thomas to superintend the construction and operation of an anthracite ironworks in Pennsylvania. Thomas was initially reluctant to leave South Wales, but an ambitious wife and a generous contract convinced him. He and his family arrived in America in May 1839, but more than a year elapsed before the Lehigh Crane Iron Co. works at Catasauqua smelted with anthracite.[29]

Thomas had bought the blowing apparatus in Britain, but the 60-inch diameter blowing engines never arrived because the hatchway of the vessel contracted to deliver them was too small to receive them. No American manufacturer had previously bored a cylinder of that size, but Merick and Towne's foundry in Philadelphia took on the task and delivered the cylinders in May 1840. Finally, on 4 July 1840, the furnace at Catasauqua successfully made pig iron with anthracite coal.[30] In sharp contrast with the modest outputs achieved by the other anthracite pioneers, Thomas produced 1080 tons during the last half of 1840 and, in an uninterrupted 'campaign' extending from May 1841 to August 1842, the Catasauqua furnace yielded 3316 tons of high-quality pig iron.[31]

The rapid adoption of anthracite coal smelting in the USA was the result of indirect, but nevertheless significant government assistance, combined with efficient networks of distribution. The state of Pennsylvania enacted legislation in 1836 allowing firms who smelted with mineral fuel to incorporate, a valuable privilege.[32] Even after Thomas's success, anthracite smelting did not spread without some difficulties. William Henry, an experienced American ironmaster, failed in his efforts to put a new anthracite furnace, at Scranton, Pennsylvania, into operation in late 1841. The furnace finally worked in January 1842, but only after a Welsh ironmaster, John F. Davis, took control.[33]

American producers modified anthracite iron technology after transplanting it to the USA. The first anthracite blast furnace of the Lehigh Crane Iron Co., which David Thomas built in 1840, was larger than contemporary anthracite furnaces in South Wales, developed higher blast pressures, and used a larger volume of air. Thomas and others built even larger furnaces in Pennsylvania in the 1840s, establishing new milestones for the American iron industry. The third furnace built at Lehigh Crane (1846) used waste heat from the furnace to produce steam to power the blowing apparatus, an innovative design.[34]

Much of the diffusion of anthracite iron technology in the 1840s and 1850s was the result of David Thomas's efforts. He built five anthracite furnaces for the Lehigh Crane Iron Co. by 1850, making the firm's works at Catasauqua a magnet for ironmasters interested in smelting with anthracite. The Lehigh Coal and Navigation Co. encouraged the adoption of anthracite smelting in order to increase canal traffic and coal sales. Thomas supervised the building of furnaces for the Thomas Iron Co. at Hokendauque, Pennsylvania, starting in 1854. His son Samuel built an anthracite furnace at Boonton, New Jersey in 1848 and then managed the Thomas Iron Co.[35]

David Thomas had such enormous influence in part because eastern Pennsylvania was the home of most of the anthracite iron industry. Pennsylvania had all six anthracite blast furnaces working in the country in 1840 and by 1846 the state had 40 in blast. In 1856, when the USA had a total of 121 anthracite furnaces, 93 were in Pennsylvania.[36]

The remarkable rate of adoption of anthracite smelting in the 1840s and 1850s cannot be emphasized too much. By 1854, the first year with reliable output figures, anthracite pig iron output was about 300 000 tons, just under half of the national total. Output reached about 420 000 tons in 1860 and then climbed to 830 000 tons a decade later, when anthracite pig iron still accounted for half of total output.[37]

BITUMINOUS COKE PIG IRON

The American anthracite iron industry grew rapidly between 1840 and 1870, but the older and more-established technology, smelting with coke made from bituminous coal, was not significant in the USA until after the Civil War. In 1854, pig iron made with coke was less than 8 per cent of American output, while charcoal and anthracite coal accounted for the rest, in roughly equal amounts. Pig iron smelted with coke did not exceed that made with charcoal until 1869 and did not surpass anthracite pig iron until six years later.[38]

The persistence of charcoal iron technology in the USA suggests American technological backwardness. As late as 1859, about 450 charcoal blast furnaces produced one-third of American pig iron output.[39] Swank noted that American charcoal pig iron production continued to expand during the second half of the nineteenth century. Charcoal ironmasters produced 703 000 tons of pig iron in 1890, only 7 per cent of total output, but twice the output levels of the mid-1850s.[40]

American ironmasters who continued to use charcoal were simply responding in an economically rational way to American raw materials costs and market conditions. Charcoal remained a cheaper fuel in much of the country, especially where coal had to be transported great distances. Schallenberg and others have shown that charcoal blast furnace operators survived through the nineteenth century because they lowered production costs and increased efficiency through technological advances, including the use of taller blast furnace stacks and the hot blast.[41] To some extent they survived because buyers of pig iron were willing to pay a premium for iron smelted with charcoal.[42]

Two of the early successful efforts to use bituminous coal in the blast furnace involved British ironworks managers who emigrated to the USA. William Firmstone, who had managed the Lays works in England's Black Country, moved to the USA in 1835 and in the same year made pig iron with coke at the Mary Ann furnace in Pennsylvania.[43] John Crowther, manager of seven blast furnaces in Staffordshire, emigrated in 1844 and initially managed coke-fired furnaces at Brady's Bend Iron Works, north-west of Pittsburgh. Crowther then ran the Mahoning furnace in north-east Ohio, where in 1846 he successfully introduced the use of raw bituminous coal in the blast furnace.[44]

Coke made from bituminous coal was not extensively used to smelt iron until the late 1850s because the known and accessible bituminous coal deposits contained sulphur and phosphorous and the resulting pig iron was (rightly) viewed by consumers as inferior to iron made from charcoal or anthracite coal. The reduced price that coke pig iron fetched in the market made smelting with bituminous coal unprofitable.[45]

The discovery and development of the high-quality bituminous coal of the Connellsville region of western Pennsylvania in the 1850s tipped the economic balance in favour of bituminous coal technology. The first blast furnace to use Connellsville coke exclusively began working in Pittsburgh in 1859 and was a great success.[46] The resulting pig iron was roughly the same quality as that made with charcoal and anthracite coal, but could be produced at a lower cost. Bituminous coke pig iron output, barely 100 000 tons or roughly one-tenth of total output in 1860, increased sharply to 570 000 tons in 1870, one-third of the US production. By the early 1880s, coke pig iron output exceeded two million tons a year, roughly half of national output.[47]

CRUCIBLE STEEL

Huntsman's crucible steel process, which diffused quickly in Sheffield in the 1740s and 1750s, was not successfully adopted in the USA until the 1860s, easily the longest delay in the transfer of iron and steel technology. Starting in 1818, more than a dozen producers failed in their efforts to make crucible steel in the USA.[48] A breakthrough came when three new works opened in Pittsburgh in 1861–3 and produced high-quality crucible steel.[49] By the late 1870s, Pittsburgh had a dozen crucible steel works in operation, with seven producing more than 5 000 tons a year each.[50] When American crucible steel output exceeded 50 000 tons in 1879, the domestic industry was supplying nine-tenths of American demand.[51]

Significant inhibiting forces in Britain, such as industrial secretiveness, did not slow the transfer of crucible steel technology. Benjamin Huntsman and other Sheffield steel producers attempted to keep secret their techniques for making the clay crucibles used in Huntsman's process, but by the late eighteenth century all the elements of crucible steel technology were common knowledge.[52]

A substantial number of transplanted Sheffield steelworkers carried crucible steel technology across the Atlantic in the nineteenth century. The first documented attempt to make crucible steel, at Valley Forge, Pennsylvania, involved two transplanted Englishmen. The Adirondack Iron & Steel Co. employed English immigrants during their failed attempt to make crucible steel in 1848–53 at their Jersey City, New Jersey works. English-born workers found in the Pittsburgh crucible steel industry at the 1870 Census included melters, refiners, hammermen, foremen and managers.[53]

The slow adoption of crucible steel technology before 1860 reflected shortages of raw materials as much as the failure of American steel manufacturers to use the technology properly. They had great difficulty producing crucibles from American clays, because none were equivalent to the Stourbridge clay used by the Sheffield steelmakers. McKelvy & Blair, a Pittsburgh firm that made crucible steel in 1852–4, imported their clay from England. Joseph Dixon's graphite crucibles, manufactured in Jersey City, New Jersey, starting in 1847, relieved American producers of that barrier.[54] Similarly American producers had difficulty in finding American charcoal iron equal to the best Swedish iron used in Sheffield.

The greatest barrier to the diffusion of crucible steel production was the perception that American producers could not match the *consistent* high quality of Sheffield steel. Throughout the nineteenth century, steelmakers only imperfectly understood the chemistry and metallurgy of the crucible steel process, which remained an art. Producers could not identify the sources of impurities in the metal, the cause of most complaints about quality, well enough to guarantee crucible steel without defects.[55] Even the Sheffield product was occasionally substandard, but American customers preferred it because the Sheffield producers also offered excellent service and technical advice.[56] The most important development for the American crucible steel industry was the passage of the Morrill tariff (1861), which gave the industry substantial protection from foreign steel and permitted steelmakers to improve quality.[57]

Crucible steel technology underwent substantial changes during the 20 years after its adoption in the early 1860s. The plumbago (graphite) pots used by American producers were larger than the clay crucibles used in Sheffield and were superior heat conductors as well. American crucible steel makers mechanized most of the handling of raw materials and finished product, operated their furnaces around the clock, six days a week, and had more heats per furnace between repairs than their Sheffield counterparts. In order to take advantage of plentiful gas supplies in the Pittsburgh region, steel manufacturers adopted Siemens regenerative gas furnaces in the mid-1870s and the new technology entirely replaced coke-fired furnaces by the late 1880s. American crucible steel production technology was ideally suited for high output, though the original Sheffield technology remained unsurpassed where quality was the prime requirement. Sheffield melters and metallurgists retained a leadership position by developing new alloy steels.[58]

OPEN-HEARTH STEEL

The Siemens–Martin (open-hearth) process for making steel was the last major European steel technology to cross the Atlantic before the First World War. American adoption came fast on the heels of commercial success in France (1866) and Britain (1867). Frederick J. Slade built a Siemens–Martin open-hearth furnace in 1868 for the New Jersey Steel and Iron Co. at Trenton, New Jersey, owned by the firm of Cooper, Hewitt & Co.[59] The Trenton furnace operated intermittently for two years, but was not a commercial success. That distinction belonged to the Bay State Iron Works in South Boston, Massachusetts, which made open-hearth steel in 1870 in a furnace built by Samuel T. Wellman.[60]

The open-hearth process was not widely used until after 1885, mainly because it was a more costly technology than the Bessemer process. Labour-intensive methods used to load open-hearth furnaces, and the need to replace furnace linings often, made open-hearth steel considerably more costly than Bessemer steel. Costs declined in the 1890s to rough parity with Bessemer technology, giving open-hearth steel an advantage because of its reputed superior quality.[61] The share of American steel production made by the open-hearth process remained under 10 per cent until 1887, then climbed to one-third in 1900, and on the eve of the First World War accounted for two-thirds of the total.[62]

The well-documented transfer of open-hearth technology was simple and direct. Abram Hewitt toured the steelworks of Europe while serving as a US commissioner to the Paris Exhibition of 1867. After viewing samples of Martin steel at the exhibition, Hewitt visited several steelworks that used the open-hearth process and immediately acquired the Martin patent rights for the USA. Hewitt then sent Frederick J. Slade to France to study the process and Slade in turn supervised the erection of the first American open-hearth steel works at Trenton, New Jersey.[63]

The adoption of open-hearth steel technology went slowly following the initial transfer embodied in the works at Trenton (1868) and South Boston, Massachusetts (1870). Samuel T. Wellman was the key figure in the diffusion of open-hearth technology in the USA. He built a Siemens regenerative gas furnace for the Nashua Iron Co. in 1866 and served as an engineer for many Siemens furnace installations, beginning with the Cooper, Hewitt & Co. plant in Trenton. Wellman, who built the first two open-hearth works, then designed plants for the Nashua Iron Co. in Nashua, New Hampshire (1872), the Otis Iron and Steel Co. works in Cleveland (1874), and most of the other open-hearth plants that opened in the 1870s.[64]

Crucible steel producers from Pittsburgh were among the pioneering firms to adopt the open-hearth process in the 1870s and 1880s. This was a logical and natural choice, given their familiarity with the Siemens gas furnaces used in the process, their emphasis on high-quality steel, and the difficulty in obtaining a licence for Bessemer steel. The pioneers included the largest Pittsburgh crucible steel firms: Anderson & Woods (1873): Park, Brother & Co. (1881): Singer, Nimick & Co. (early 1880s); and Hussey, Howe and Co. (1886). They were anything but conservative in choosing techniques.[65]

Open-hearth steel output remained less than one-tenth the production of Bessemer steel until 1887, but quickly caught up as the cost advantage of Bessemer steel narrowed.[66] By the First World War, the cost of manufacturing open-hearth steel had fallen below Bessemer steel costs. Steel producers preferred open-hearth steel because the process allowed tighter control over quality than the Bessemer process. Consumers also believed open-hearth steel to be stronger than Bessemer steel when subject to stress. During the quarter-century before the First World War, demand for steel rails declined, while most of the growth in demand for steel was in the areas where consumers preferred open-hearth steel – for structural steel, wire, rods and sheets.[67] By the early 1910s, open-hearth steel accounted for two-thirds of American output and Bessemer steel only one-third.[68]

BESSEMER STEEL TECHNOLOGY

Bessemer's revolutionary process for manufacturing steel passed cold air through molten pig iron in an open-topped converter, which burned off silicon, carbon and other impurities in the metal, yielding large quantities of cheap steel. The transfer of Bessemer steel across the Atlantic started slowly because the process initially worked poorly in Britain. After Bessemer's discoveries of 1855–6, the first group of patentees was unable to produce saleable metal.[69] Bessemer steel was brittle when hot ('red-short') because of the presence of excess oxygen in the metal. Robert Forester Mushet (1811–91) discovered in late 1856 that introducing *spiegeleisen*, a compound containing manganese, iron and carbon, into the converter removed the excess oxygen and simultaneously added enough carbon to the molten metal to produce steel. Bessemer used *spiegeleisen* in secret until 1860, when Mushet's patent lapsed.[70] However Mushet's method of recarburization was not unique. Bessemer was able to use other manganese compounds to yield similar results.[71]

The other major source of trouble was phosphorous, which resulted in metal that was brittle when cold ('cold-short'). In his initial experiments, Bessemer had inadvertently used pig iron that was free of this contaminant. The first group of British patentees was not as lucky and produced worthless steel. However, in July 1858, Bessemer's Swedish patentee, Göran Fredrik Göransson, identified phosphorous as the cause of these problems, after producing good steel from charcoal pig iron.[72] With some help from these two inventors, Bessemer eliminated the two major causes of failure for his process.

The transfer of Bessemer steel technology to the USA generated much conflict and controversy over Bessemer's claim of originality. In the 18 October 1856 issue of *Scientific American*, William Kelly (1811–88), who operated the Suwanee Iron Works in Eddyville, Kentucky, claimed to have made wrought iron by passing air through molten pig iron since late 1851, some four years before Bessemer's work. Kelly applied for an American patent on his 'pig-boiling process' in early 1857, in an effort to overturn Bessemer's patent application of 11 November 1856. Kelly presented a large body of evidence to support his claim, including testimony from many who worked at or visited his ironworks that he had used the 'pneumatic process' as early as 1847. The US Patent Office recognized Kelly's priority and awarded him a patent on 13 April 1857, while Bessemer kept the patents covering the tilting converter and its machinery.[73]

The significance of Kelly's process will remain in dispute without new evidence to throw more light on the controversy. As might be expected, British historians of the steel industry have either ignored Kelly or rejected his claims out of hand.[74] Similarly, American historians have emphasized Kelly's originality. In his classic history of the iron and steel industry, James M. Swank credited Kelly with discovering the principle of blowing air through molten pig iron before Bessemer, but pointed out that Kelly produced wrought iron, not steel, and in small quantities.[75] Of course Bessemer also did not produce steel initially. Alexander Holley, who built most of the early Bessemer steel plants in the USA, testified in 1870 in support of Kelly's claim of priority.[76] Herbert N. Casson, writing nearly four decades later, came to the same conclusion.[77] Kelly had little technical and no commercial success with his process until he used Bessemer's converter design.[78]

The most flagrant effort to praise Kelly and discredit Bessemer was John N. Boucher's *William Kelly, A True History of the So-called Bessemer Process* (1924). Boucher 'documented' Kelly's claim that two English puddlers observed his process at his Kentucky works in 1851 and carried the information to Bessemer. One version holds that Bessemer himself was one of the industrial spies. Boucher's main source of information, Mrs Mildred A. Kelly, the ironmaster's widow[79] was hardly an unbiased source. Bessemer visiting Kelly's works in person is unlikely because Bessemer suffered from violent seasickness and as a result rarely left England.[80] Besides, he was pursuing a prolific career as an inventor, exhibited at the Crystal Palace Exhibition in 1851 and, in 1852–3, patented 12 mechanical inventions.[81] Kelly and his heirs probably fabricated all these allegations, given their implausibility.

The adoption of the Bessemer/Kelly process began along two distinct lines, originating with the two inventors, although the two paths finally merged in 1865, with the pooling of the patents. During the pivotal year of 1857, William Kelly lost his Kentucky ironworks through bankruptcy, received a patent for his discovery, and began experiments with his process at the Cambria Iron Works in Johnstown, Pennsylvania, at the invitation of the works superintendent, Daniel J. Morrell. Kelly conducted several sets of trials at Cambria Iron Works from 1857 to 1862, with mixed results until 1861, when he imported a tilting converter of the Bessemer type from Europe.[82]

In May 1863, five men established the Kelly Pneumatic Process Co. to manufacture steel: Daniel J. Morrell, the Cambria Iron Works superintendent; Eber Brock Ward, a Detroit ironmaster; Zoheth S. Durfee, a technical expert on steel making processes; James Park, Jr., a Pittsburgh crucible steel manufacturer and William M. Lyon, a Pittsburgh ironmaster.[83] Eber Brock Ward (1811–75) was the central figure in the Kelly Pneumatic Process Co. He had organized the Eureka Iron Co., which operated a furnace in Wyandotte, Michigan, south of Detroit in 1855, and established the North Chicago Rolling Mills Co. in Chicago in 1857. Ward acquired Kelly's patents in 1861 and in that same year sent Zoheth Durfee to Europe to investigate the Bessemer process and to buy the rights to use it in the USA. Durfee failed in his effort, but in a later trip, in 1864, acquired the American rights to Mushet's patents for the use of *spiegeleisen* in the converter.[84]

Ward hired William F. Durfee, Zoheth Durfee's cousin, to build an experimental converter at the Eureka Iron Works in Wyandotte before he had secured the Bessemer patent rights. William Durfee, using only Bessemer's patent drawings and some published descriptions of the process as a guide, built a tilting converter by the end of 1862, only to discover that the negotiations with Bessemer had failed. He also built a blowing engine in 1863 to provide the air for the process and in early 1864 built a stationary converter, in an effort to avoid infringing Bessemer's patents, but the results were never satisfactory. William Durfee finally had some successful trials after his cousin brought Llewellyn Hart, who had experience with a Bessemer converter in France, to Wyandotte in the spring of 1864. When Durfee finally made steel in quantity with the pneumatic process at Wyandotte, on 6 September 1864, he used a two and a half ton tilting converter. Following the pioneer manufacture of Bessemer steel at Wyandotte, Ward rolled the first steel rails in the USA on 24 May 1865 at his North Chicago Rolling Mill.[85]

The direct transfer of Bessemer technology to the USA began at the Rensselaer Iron Works in Troy, New York. Alexander Lyman Holley (1832–82), an engineer and technical publisher, visited Europe in 1862–3 to study the manufacture of ordnance and armaments, and during the journey saw Bessemer's Sheffield steel plant in operation. After his return Holley had a meeting with two Troy iron makers, John F. Winslow and John A. Griswold, who wanted to manufacture Bessemer steel. They dispatched Holley to England, where he spent the autumn and early winter of 1863 negotiating for the American rights to Bessemer's patents, while simultaneously studying the process at the Sheffield works. Bessemer granted a licence on 31 December 1863 to the Troy group to manufacture steel on a royalty basis, but with an option to buy the patent rights outright. When Holley returned to Troy, in early 1864, he was a partner in the firm of Winslow, Griswold & Holley. He immediately began building the Bessemer works at Troy, equipped with a two and a half ton converter. The owners viewed this plant as an experimental operation only, as had been the case at the Eureka Iron Works in Wyandotte.[86]

The Troy works finally made its first Bessemer steel on 16 February 1865, after a year of construction and trials. By July 1865 the process was unquestionably successful and Winslow, Griswold & Holley started negotiations with Bessemer to buy the patents outright, reaching an agreement on 7 December 1865. The two groups making steel, at Wyandotte and Troy, were on a collision course by mid-1865, headed for the courts to resolve their conflicting patent claims. Neither group could make steel without using the other group's patents and in the early part of 1866 the parties reached an out-of-court agreement to pool the Kelly, Mushet and Bessemer patents. The two groups agreed to split the royalties from the combined patents, with 70 per cent to the Troy group and 30 per cent to the Wyandotte group. The relative success at Troy compared with

Wyandotte helps explain the royalty split. Daniel Morrell, who negotiated for the Kelly Pneumatic Process Co., agreed to this split in part because he wanted to avoid long and costly litigations. The two parties established 'The Trustees of the Pneumatic or Bessemer Process of Making Iron and Steel', with Winslow, Griswold and Daniel Morrell serving as trustees. The patent pool, which became the Pneumatic Steel Association, renamed the Bessemer Steel Association in 1875, and the Bessemer Steel Co. in 1877, licensed 11 new producers in the first decade of operation.[87]

With the patent controversy put to rest, Holley built a commercial Bessemer plant in Troy for Winslow and Griswold. The new plant began production in early 1867 with two five-ton converters.[88] Holley was the key figure in the diffusion of the new technology in America. He either designed or consulted in the design of 11 of the 12 plants built in 1865–76 and, until his death in 1882, was the premier technical advisor to the American Bessemer steel industry.[89] Besides providing plans for new plants, Holley often supervised construction and managed new plants during their first months of operation. The Pennsylvania Steel Co., for example, received a licence in January 1866 for a plant to be built near Harrisburg and hired Holley to bring the plant into production. They built a house for his use and paid off his debts of $20 000 to Winslow and Griswold.[90] Holley not only served as consulting engineer to the Pneumatic Steel Association, but several member firms in the association also retained him as a consultant.[91]

The owners of the combined patents tried to promote their use in the United States. Licensees had to pay royalties of five dollars a ton for ingots rolled into rails and ten dollars a ton for ingots used for other products. For a fixed fee of $5 000 the licensee also received a complete set of plans for the plant to be built, technical information on all the machinery and processes involved, and the right to have two men observe Bessemer steelmaking at the Troy plant for a maximum of two years.[92] To promote the sale of licences, Holley tested hundreds of samples of pig iron at Troy for their suitability in the Bessemer process.[93]

A small group of men, many trained by Holley, managed the initial diffusion of Bessemer steelmaking in the 1860s and 1870s. They learned the process together, and with their lieutenants, managed the first generation of plants. Robert Hunt, who had worked for the Cambria Iron Co. in Johnstown, Pennsylvania, managed the Wyandotte works for nearly a year, starting in May 1865, before returning to Cambria. He was instrumental in rolling steel rails at Cambria from the Pennsylvania Steel Co. plant, the first new Bessemer plant after Troy. Hunt ran Cambria's Bessemer plant for two years, beginning with its first blow in 1871, but in 1873–5 he managed the Troy works.[94] Besides Holley and Hunt, three other managers played key roles in the diffusion of the new technology – John Fritz, his brother Geoorge Fritz, and Captain William Jones.

The Fritz brothers each managed the Cambria Works. John Fritz served as works manager for the Bethlehem Iron Co. and Jones became manager of the Edgar Thomson Steel Works in 1875, after serving an apprenticeship with George Fritz at Cambria. The five men met periodically to discuss common problems and new developments in Bessemer technology, while remaining fierce competitors at their respective Bessemer works.[95]

Holley and the other technical experts and managers worked in a steel industry with very few, large-scale producers that earned enormous profits in a tightly-regulated market. Capitalists from the American railroad industry founded most of the Bessemer steel firms to manufacture steel rails, which remained their principal product until the 1880s. The Bessemer producers, in combination with the railroad men who were their owners and dominant customers, operated as a pool, setting production levels and prices for the industry. The American steel industry also enjoyed the benefits of high protective tariffs that virtually excluded British rails from the market. The economic stability that resulted from the structure of the industry produced sustained high profit levels that encouraged the huge investments required for larger and more efficient plants and enabled producers like Carnegie to reap healthy profits. During the generally depressed years of 1876–8, Carnegie's Edgar Thomson Steel Co. earned profits of 25, 20 and 30 per cent respectively on invested capital, which nearly doubled over those years.[96] The firm earned over $2 million in 1880 and its profits of $1.6 million in 1881 represented a return of 130 per cent on invested capital.[97] In 1879 the Pennsylvania Steel Co. earned profits of 200 per cent on invested capital.[98]

The railroads and their leaders played pivotal roles in the emergence of the Bessemer steel industry. Many of the Bessemer innovators had previously served as railroad presidents; they included Ward, Winslow, D. J. Morrell and Erastus Corning, a partner in Winslow's Troy steel operations, while Holley had written about American railroad practices.[99] In 1865 railroad men and others with railroad ties founded the Pennsylvania Steel Co., the first major Bessemer enterprise begun after the Troy works, for the express purpose of manufacturing steel rails. Even before the works included a rail mill, the Cambria Works rolled some of its steel into rails in July 1867. The founders included Edgar Thomson, president of the Pennsylvania Railroad; Samuel Felton, president of the Philadelphia, Wilmington and Baltimore Railroad; Nathaniel Thayer from the Baldwin Locomotive Works; and William Sellers, a prominent Philadelphia machine tool manufacturer.[100] The firm was in effect a subsidiary of the Pennsylvania Railroad, which provided $600 000 in capital and immediately gave the new enterprise a $200 000 contract for steel rails.[101]

Investors built all ten Bessemer plants that began operations between May 1868 and September 1876 at an existing iron rail mill site or included a new rail mill as part of the facility.[102] Perhaps the Edgar Thomson Works, located near

Pittsburgh and completed in September 1875, is the best example of the links between the railroad and the Bessemer steel industry. Railroad men were the chief planners and investors in this rail plant, named after the president of the Pennsylvania Railroad. The most important investor was Andrew Carnegie, who had served as superintendent of the Western Division of the Pennsylvania Railroad in 1859–65. William Shinn of the Allegheny Valley Railroad, became secretary–treasurer of the works and eventually manager. Shinn brought railroad cost accounting techniques to the Edgar Thomson plant. Designed by Holley and located on the Pennsylvania and the Baltimore and Ohio Railroad lines, this fully-integrated plant of blast furnaces, Bessemer converters and a rail mill epitomized American steelmaking practice.[103]

With only 11 Bessemer firms in operation after 1869, with output limited almost exclusively to rails purchased by a few large customers, restricting the market was a strong temptation. The first effort to pool the sale of rails came out of the formation of the Bessemer Steel Association in 1875 and apparently failed. However, in October 1877, the steel producers vested the existing patents in the Bessemer Steel Co., restricted any new entrants into the industry, and developed an effective pooling arrangement. The original Bessemer and Mushet patents had expired in 1870 and the Kelly patent, renewed once, would expire in 1878, but the pool owned more than a dozen later patents for various improvements in machinery and equipment, most of these developed by Holley. The Bessemer Steel Co. licensed no new plants in 1877–9, a time of severe depression in the industry. When the Vulcan Works in St Louis, Missouri was about to go bankrupt in late 1878, the Bessemer Steel Co. closed the plant, but assumed the mortgage payments to avoid bankruptcy proceedings and thus prevented anyone else from operating it.[104]

Controlling the market for steel rails was possible because the railroads planned their purchases once a year and a small number of them dominated the market for rails. The Pennsylvania Railroad bought most of the output of the three Bessemer works on its main line, the Pennsylvania Steel Works, the Cambria Works, and the Edgar Thomson Works. The members of the pool collectively set rail output and prices for each of the 11 member firms.[105] High tariffs on imported rails, supported by the railroads, further restricted competition. In 1870, a specific duty of 28 dollars a ton placed on imported rails amounted to about 45 per cent *ad valorem*. But in the mid-1870s, Bessemer steel prices fell sharply, so that by 1877 the effective duty had increased to 100 per cent.[106]

During the decade ending in 1867, 11 new plants came into service. Bessemer steel output, a mere 3 000 tons in 1867, skyrocketed to 561 000 tons by 1877, and stood at 1.2 million tons in 1880, slightly above British output. A decade later the USA produced 4.1 million tons, roughly twice British production. Most of the growth in 1867–77 occurred in the second half of the period, when the largest and most successful new plants went into production. The initial spurt of adoption was not without problems. Two Bessemer plants closed permanently in 1869 – the Wyandotte works and the Freedom Iron and Steel Works in Mifflin County, Pennsylvania. The Freedom works, the only early plant not designed by Holley, operated for only a year, a victim of the high-phosphorous pig iron produced there.[107]

The ability of the Bessemer producers to restrict output by limiting entry into the industry diminished in the 1880s. Ten new Bessemer plants began operating in 1881–5, but half of these made products other than rails. Another 18 opened in 1886–9, by which time the Bessemer Association was largely ineffective.[108] The mix of products changed quickly in the late nineteenth century, further weakening the Bessemer steel pool. Throughout the 1870s rails consistently accounted for roughly 80 per cent of Bessemer steel output, but this share fell sharply to under 50 per cent by the start of the 1890s, reflecting the increased use of structural steel and other steel products.[109] Finally Andrew Carnegie's disruptive and energetic influence on the steel industry ended in 1901 with the formation of the United States Steel Corporation.[110]

Within a decade of the initial transfer of Bessemer steel technology to the USA, American Bessemer plants were decidedly superior to British plants, in terms of output levels and productivity. As early as 1878, American Bessemer converters produced an average of 37 000 tons a year, while their British counterparts produced only about 13 000 tons. By 1890, British converter production had increased to 25 000 tons, but American output had also risen, to 49 000 tons.[111] American superiority was largely the result of Alexander Holley's work in modifying and improving the original technology. By the late 1870s, a distinct American Bessemer practice had emerged.

Holley introduced modifications in plant equipment and layout in the original Bessemer experimental plant at Troy in 1865–6. Although he began melting pig iron in a reverberatory furnace, the usual practice in Britain, he changed to a cupola furnace in the first months of operation. Holley provided the cupola with duplicate bottoms that could be changed rapidly without loss of production. He placed the ladle in which molten pig iron accumulated on scales, so that the weight of every charge could be documented.[112] The typical floor plan of British Bessemer plants had two converters facing each other, separated by a deep pit containing the ingot moulds which received the molten steel from the converters. Holley tried several other arrangements, including the placement of the converters side by side.[113] His most important improvement was the Holley Vessel Bottom (1874), which allowed rapid replacement of a failed converter bottom without significant cooling of the converter proper, thus minimizing any production losses.[114]

By the time Holley designed his tenth steel plant, the Vulcan Iron Works in St Louis, Missouri, which began operating in 1876, he had created a distinct American design for Bessemer steelworks. He placed the converters side by side and eliminated the deep pit by elevating the converters well above ground level. Holley also introduced cheaper top-supported hydraulic cranes for moving ingots, increased their number from two to three, and arranged all the cranes and vessels in order to operate them from a single point. The Vulcan Works and most other American Bessemer plants by that time used his removable converter bottom.[115]

American Bessemer steelmaking technology had surpassed British practice by the mid-1870s, when significant reverse flows began between the USA and Great Britain. George Snelus at the West Cumberland Bessemer steelworks successfully used Holley's removable converter bottom in 1875 and it diffused quickly to the rest of the industry in Britain. Bolckow Vaughan & Co., one of the leading iron and steel manufacturers, used the 'American plan' for laying out their new plant in 1876. Similarly, in 1878, Brown, Bayley and Dixons (Sheffield) followed the American arrangement of cranes in the converter house. By the late 1870s, British Bessemer steel producers recognized that 'best-practice' technology was operating in the USA, rather than in Europe.[116]

American Bessemer steel plants out-produced their British counterparts by the 1880s, but this lead was not simply the result of superior hardware or plant layout. Instead, the resourcefulness of a few dozen works managers, spurred on by personal and corporate competition, led to 'hard driving' of Bessemer steel plants to yield the maximum output. The principal works managers, including John Fry at Cambria, Robert Forsyth at the North Chicago Works, Robert Hunt at Troy, and William R. 'Bill' Jones at the Edgar Thomson Works, consciously strove to establish new production records and took great delight in beating their rival managers and friends.[117]

Production records were not simply the result of driving the men to the breaking point, as some European steelmakers suspected. Most of the gains came from achieving more nearly continuous running of Bessemer plants than in Europe. By improving the flow of materials within the plant, American steel managers reduced wasted movements for men and machines. In brand-new integrated plants, such as the Edgar Thomson Works, the plant design reflected the effort to achieve an optimal work flow within the entire steelworks.[118] By minimizing equipment breakdown and repairs during normal operating shifts, works managers similarly reduced idle time for men and machines. At the Edgar Thomson plant, for example, management made a great effort to prolong the lives of converter linings until the end of the work week, when repairs would not reduce output.[119]

At several meetings of the Iron and Steel Institute, the British trade association, managers of American Bessemer plants made presentations that trumpeted the superiority of American practice over that of the European steelmakers. Captain W. R. Jones, superintendent of the Edgar Thomson Works, delineated the performance of his plant in great detail in 1881, while, nearly a decade later, Henry M. Howe did the same for the entire American Bessemer industry. Both men discredited the claims that 'hard driving' of Bessemer plants, which produced production records, resulted in poor-quality steel, undue strain on the men and equipment and increased costs. Although none of the European participants in these meetings directly confronted Jones or Howe on the drawbacks of 'hard driving', many of them remained sceptical, at least in private. Both Americans emphasized the importance of competition among the plant managers in achieving greater efficiency in operations, along with production records.[120]

Once the American Bessemer steel industry became the world leader, in terms of machinery and equipment, 'hard driving' practices and output, the industry retained that position well into the twentieth century. To be sure, some of the hardware innovations, such as the Holley Vessel Bottom, found their way back to the steel industries of Europe, but the other key ingredients in the recipe for American success in steel were not transferable. American steelmakers enjoyed a large and expanding internal market protected by tariffs and enormous supplies of high-quality coal and iron ore to complement their technological prowess. Tariff protection was more important to the American steel industry than is usually recognized. Faced with considerably higher labour costs than their European competitors, American producers did not surpass them in terms of total costs and productivity until the early twentieth century.[121]

SOME GENERAL OBSERVATIONS

The five examples of technology transfer considered in this chapter – anthracite pig iron, bituminous coke pig iron, crucible steel, open-hearth steel and Bessemer steel – had many common features. Industrial secretiveness did not inhibit the transfer of these technologies, with the possible exception of crucible steel. The transfer of technology often took place via the migration of artisans or managers experienced in using the technology, as was the case for anthracite pig iron, coke pig iron and crucible steel. For Bessemer and open-hearth steel, where patent agreements were in force. Americans such as Hewitt and Holley gained an understanding of the processes by studying the technology in use in various European plants. Even with a licence in hand and free access to the new process, establishing experimental plants in the USA was still a necessity.

The modification of transplanted technologies to fit American conditions and thus accelerate diffusion seemed to take place rapidly and systematically when a dominant promoter/patron of the technology emerged – David Thomas for anthracite pig iron, Alexander Holley for Bessemer steel and Samuel Wellman for the open-hearth process. Government support was also critical in most of these cases. The State of Pennsylvania's special incorporation laws encouraged the anthracite pig iron industry, while Federal tariff protection after 1861 helped all the infant steel industries survive and mature in the second half of the nineteenth century. Finally reverse flows of American technology to Europe is most evident for Bessemer steel, where British and Continental producers began to copy American 'best-practice' techniques by the 1880s.

NOTES

*Robert B. Gordon of Yale University and Bruce E. Seely of Michigan Technological University offered valuable comments on an earlier version of this chapter. I am solely responsible, however, for any errors of fact or interpretation.

1. T. S. Ashton, *Iron and Steel in the Industrial Revolution* (Manchester, 2nd edn, 1951) pp. 24–59 and M. W. Flinn and Alan Birch. 'The English Steel Industry Before 1856, With Special Reference to the Development of the Yorkshire Steel Industry', *Yorkshire Bulletin of Economic and Social Research*, Vol. 6 (1954) pp. 78–84. See also Kenneth C. Barraclough, *Steelmaking before Bessemer* (2 vols, London, 1984).

2. Charles K. Hyde, *Technological Change and the British Iron Industry, 1700–1870* (Princeton, 1977) pp. 23–41, 53–75.

3. Ibid., pp. 76–116 and R. A. Mott, *Henry Cort: The Great Finer* (London, 1983).

4. Hyde, *Technological Change*, pp. 146–65.

5. Alan Birch, *The Economic History of the British Iron and Steel Industry, 1784–1879* (London, 1967) pp. 371–8; James M. Swank, *History of the Manufacture of Iron in All Ages* (Philadelphia, 1892) pp. 419–20; and Jeanne McHugh, *Alexander Holley and the Makers of Steel* (Baltimore, 1980) pp. 274–83.

6. Birch, *Economic History of the British Iron and Steel Industry*, pp. 378–86.

7. Geoffrey Tweedale, *Sheffield Steel and America: A Century of Commercial and Technological Interdependence, 1830–1930* (Cambridge, 1987) pp. 57–83.

8. Ibid., pp. 227–8, 279.

9. Swank, *Iron in All Ages*, pp. 366–94, 494–501, 532–40.

10. H. J. Habakkuk, *American & British Technology in the 19th Century: The Search For Labour-Saving Inventions* (Cambridge, 1967) pp. 157–8.

11. Ibid., p. 96.

12. Swank, *Iron in All Ages*, pp. 217. 227–9.

13. Hyde, *Technological Change*, pp. 142–3, 168; and Peter Temin, *Iron and Steel in Nineteenth-Century America: An Economic Inquiry* (Cambridge, MA, 1964) pp. 18, 100, 102. According to Darwin H. Stapleton, *The Transfer of Early Industrial Technologies to America* (Philadelphia, 1987) p. 20, pig boiling was used in Pittsburgh in 1837.

14. Temin, *Iron and Steel in Nineteenth-Century America*, pp. 100–1, 280.

15. Stapleton, *Transfer of Early Industrial Technologies to America*, pp. 169–210, *passim*.

16. McHugh, *Alexander Holley and the Makers of Steel, passim*.

17. Walter R. Johnson, *Notes on the Use of Anthracite in the Manufacture of Iron* (Boston, 1841) pp. 11–12; and Alfred D. Chandler, Jr., 'Anthracite Coal and the Beginnings of the Industrial Revolution in the United States', *Business History Review*, Vol. 46 (Summer 1972) p. 160. David Brody, *Steelworkers in America: The Non Union Era* (Cambridge, Mass, 1960).

18. Swank, *Iron in All Ages*, pp. 354–7.

19. Johnson, *Notes on the Use of Anthracite*, pp. 28–31 and Swank, *Iron in All Ages*, pp. 359–61.
20. W. Ross Yates, 'Discovery of the Process for Making Anthracite Iron', *Pennsylvania Magazine of History and Biography*, vol. 98 (April 1974) pp. 207–8, 219–20.
21. Ibid., p. 220.
22. Johnson, *Notes on the Use of Anthracite*, pp. 32–8.
23. Stapleton, *Transfer of Early Industrial Technologies to America*, p. 172.
24. Johnson, *Notes on the Use of Anthracite*, pp. 38–41.
25. Ibid., pp. 28–9.
26. Swank, *Iron in All Ages*, p. 361
27. Stapleton, *Transfer of Early Industrial Technologies to America*, pp. 172–4, 181–4.
28. Ibid., pp. 172–4, 180–1.
29. Samuel Thomas, 'Reminiscences of the Early Anthracite-Iron Industry', *Transactions of the American Institute of Mining Engineers*, vol. 29 (1899) pp. 905–7.
30. Ibid., pp. 910–14.
31. Ibid., pp. 915–16.
32. Stapleton, *Transfer of Early Industrial Technologies to America*, p. 179.
33. Ibid., pp. 186–7.
34. Ibid., pp. 188–91.
35. Ibid., pp. 195–9.
36. Swank, Iron in All Ages, p. 362.
37. Temin, *Iron and Steel in Nineteenth-Century America*, pp. 266–8.
38. Ibid., p. 268
39. Richard H. Schallenberg. 'Evolution, Adaptation, and Survival; The Very Slow Death of the American Charcoal Iron Industry', *Annals of Science*, vol. 32 (July 1975) pp. 341–7.
40. Swank, *Iron in All Ages*, pp. 352–3, 376.
41. Richard H. Schallenberg, 'The Very Slow Death of the American Charcoal Iron Industry', pp. 341–58; Richard H. Schallenberg and David A. Ault, 'Raw Materials Supply and Technological Change in the American Charcoal Iron Industry', *Technology and Culture*, vol. 18 (July 1977) pp. 436–66; Bruce E. Seely, 'Blast Furnace Technology in the Mid-19th Century: A Case Study of the Adirondack Iron and Steel Company', *IA: The Journal of the Society For Industrial Archeology*, vol. 7 (1981) pp. 27–54; and Robert B. Gordon, 'Materials for Manufacturing: The Response of the Connecticut Iron Industry to Technological Change and Limited Resources', *Technology and Culture*, vol. 24 (Oct. 1983) pp. 602–34.
42. Swank, *Iron in All Ages*, p. 366; Louis C. Hunter, 'The Influence of the Market Upon Technique in the Iron Industry in Western Pennsylvania Up to 1860', *Journal of Economic and Business History*, vol. 1 (Feb. 1929) pp. 265–7; and Gordon, 'Materials For Manufacturing' p. 631.
43. Swank, *Iron in All Ages*, pp. 367–8.
44. Ibid., pp. 373–4.
45. Temin, *Iron and Steel in Nineteenth-Century America*, pp. 74–80. Previously, Louis C. Hunter had argued that the adoption of coke smelting followed and reflected a shift in the demand for iron products away from high quality wrought iron, which required smelting with charcoal. See Hunter, 'The Influence of the Market Upon Technique', pp. 241–81.
46. Nathan Rosenberg, *Perspectives on Technology* (New York, 1976) p. 185 and Swank, *Iron in All Ages*, p. 231.
47. Swank, *Iron in All Ages*, p. 378.
48. Tweedale, *Sheffield Steel and America*, pp. 13–15; Swank, *Iron in All Ages*, pp. 384–90; and Bruce E. Seely, 'Cast Crucible Steel Making', in Paul F. Paskoff, (ed.), *Encyclopedia of American Business History and Biography: Iron and Steel in the Nineteenth Century* (New York, 1991) p. 80. In the same volume, Seely catalogued the failures at the Cincinnati Steel Works (1832–7), the Adirondack Iron & Steel Co. (1848–53), and at Singer, Nimick & Co. (1853–63) on pp. 145, 8–10 and 312, respectively.
49. Swank, *Iron in All Ages*, pp. 391–4.
50. Tweedale, *Sheffield Steel and America*, pp. 16–18.

51.   Ibid., p. 25.
52.   Birch, *Economic History of the British Iron and Steel Industry*, pp. 305–7.
53.   Ibid., pp. 378–94; Tweedale, *Sheffield Steel and America*, pp. 13–18; and Seely, 'Adirondack Iron & Steel Company', in Paskoff (ed.), *Encyclopedia of American Business History and Biography*, p. 9.
54.   Swank, *Iron in All Ages*, pp. 391–2; and Tweedale, *Sheffield Steel and America*, p. 15.
55.   Swank, *Iron in All Ages*, pp. 391–4; Tweedale, *Sheffield Steel and America*, pp. 19–26; and Seely, in Paskoff, (ed.), *Encyclopedia of American Business History and Biography*, pp. 9–10, 80, 144, 183, 270 and 312.
56.   Robert Gordon and Geoffrey Tweedale, 'Pioneering in Steelmaking at the Collins Axe Company, 1826–1924', *Historical Metallurgy*, 24, No. 1 (1990), pp. 1–11.
57.   Swank, *Iron in All Ages*, pp. 393–4.
58.   Tweedale, *Sheffield Steel and America*, pp. 19, 37–42.
59.   Swank, *Iron in All Ages*, pp. 420–2.
60.   McHugh, *Alexander Holley and the Makers of Steel*, pp. 290–1.
61.   Temin, *Iron and Steel in Nineteenth-Century America*, pp. 140–1.
62.   Ibid., pp. 272–3.
63.   Swank, *Iron in All Ages*, pp. 421–2; and McHugh, *Alexander Holley and the Makers of Steel*, pp. 187–8.
64.   Victor Windett (ed.), *The Open Hearth: Its Relation to the Steel Industry* (New York, 1920) pp. 35–43; and David B. Sicilia, 'Samuel Thomas Wellman', in Paul Paskoff (ed.). *Encyclopedia of American Business History and Biography*, pp. 359–61.
65.   Bruce E. Seely, in several contributions on the crucible steel industry in Paskoff (ed.), *Encyclopedia of American Business History and Biography*, pp. 81, 184, 217, 313.
66.   Temin, *Iron and Steel in Nineteenth-Century America*, p. 270.
67.   Ibid., pp. 145–52, 224–30.
68.   Ibid., p. 273.
69.   Birch, *Economic History of the British Iron and Steel Industry*, pp. 321–8; J. C. Carr and W. Taplin, *A History of the British Steel Industry* (Cambridge, Mass., 1962) pp. 19–23; and McHugh, *Alexander Holley and the Makers of Steel*, pp. 100–5.
70.   McHugh, *Alexander Holley and the Makers of Steel*, pp. 151–62.
71.   Philip W. Bishop, 'The Beginnings of Cheap Steel', *Contributions From the Museum of History and Technology*, Bulletin 218 (Washington, DC, 1959) pp. 37–41.
72.   Ibid., pp. 35–41.
73.   McHugh, *Alexander Holley and the Makers of Steel*, pp. 112–16.
74.   Birch, *Economic History of the British Iron and Steel Industry*, p. 322; and Carr and Taplin, *History of the British Steel Industry*, p. 42.
75.   Swank, *Iron in All Ages*, p. 399.
76.   McHugh, *Alexander Holley and the Makers of Steel*, p. 130.
77.   Herbert N. Casson, *The Romance of Steel: The Story of a Thousand Millionaires* (New York, 1907) pp. 6–9.
78.   Bishop, 'Beginnings of Cheap Steel', pp. 44–5.
79.   John Newton Boucher, *William Kelly: A True History of the So-Called Bessemer Process* (Greenburgh, Pennsylvania, 1924) pp. 19–27, 86–90.
80.   McHugh, *Alexander Holley and the Makers of Steel*, pp. 121–2.
81.   Henry Bessemer, *Sir Henry Bessemer, F.R.S.: An Autobiography* (London, 1905) pp. 124–9.
82.   McHugh, *Alexander Holley and the Makers of Steel*, pp. 124–8.
83.   Ibid., pp. 128–9.
84.   Thomas Jay Misa, 'Science, Technology and Industrial Structure: Steelmaking in America, 1870–1925', PhD thesis, University of Pennsylvania, 1987, p. 27.
85.   McHugh, *Alexander Holley and the Makers of Steel*, pp. 174–5, 178–82, 186; and William F. Durfee, 'An Account of the Experimental Steel Works at Wyandotte, Michigan', *American Society of Mechanical Engineers, Transactions*, vol. 6 (1885) pp. 40–60. Durfee's account, written 20 years after the fact, is the only surviving description of the Wyandotte experiments. He faced serious opposition while at Wyandotte from the so-

called 'iron men' in the region and from Eureka Iron Works employees, who sometimes resorted to sabotage to undermine his efforts.

86. McHugh, *Alexander Holley and the Makers of Steel*, pp. 172, 190–1.
87. Ibid., pp. 197–200.
88. Ibid., pp. 203–5.
89. Misa, 'Science, Technology and Industrial Structure: Steelmaking in America, 1870–1925', pp. 34–5, 47–50.
90. Elting E. Morison, *Men, Machines, and Modern Times* (Cambridge, Mass., 1966) pp. 164–5.
91. McHugh, *Alexander Holley and the Makers of Steel*, p. 295.
92. Ibid., p. 199; and Temin, *Iron and Steel in Nineteenth-Century America*, pp. 132–4.
93. Robert W. Hunt, 'A History of the Bessemer Manufacture in America', *Transactions of the American Institute of Mining Engineers*, vol. 5 (June 1876) p. 205.
94. Hunt, 'History of the Bessemer Manufacture in America', pp. 202–7.
95. Temin, *Iron and Steel in Nineteenth-Century America*, p. 133.
96. Ibid., p. 172.
97. Ibid., p. 178; and Alfred D. Chandler, Jr., *The Visible Hand: The Managerial Revolution in American Business* (Cambridge, MA, 1977) p. 269.
98. Morison, *Men, Machines, and Modern Times*, p. 175.
99. Ibid., pp. 152–3.
100. McHugh, *Alexander Holley and the Makers of Steel*, p. 211.
101. Misa, 'Science, Technology and Industry Structure: Steelmaking in America, 1870–1925', p. 36.
102. Swank, *Iron in All Ages*, pp. 411–12.
103. Misa, 'Science, Technology and Industrial Structure: Steelmaking in America, 1870–1925', pp. 36–40.
104. Temin, *Iron and Steel in Nineteenth-Century America*, pp. 174–7.
105. Morison, *Men, Machines, and Modern Times*, pp. 172–4.
106. Temin, *Iron and Steel in Nineteenth-Century America*, pp. 173–4.
107. Swank, *Iron in All Ages*, pp. 411–14.
108. Ibid., pp. 179, 183.
109. Ibid., pp. 270, 274–5.
110. Ibid., pp. 189–93.
111. Carr and Taplin, *History of the British Steel Industry*, pp. 154–5.
112. Robert W. Hunt, 'The Original Bessemer Steel Plant at Troy', American Society of Mechanical Engineers, *Transactions*, vol. 6 (1885) pp. 61–2.
113. Temin, *Iron and Steel in Nineteenth-Century America*, p. 135.
114. McHugh, *Alexander Holley and the Makers of Steel*, p. 263.
115. Hunt, 'History of the Bessemer Manufacture in America', pp. 214–15.
116. Duncan Burn, *The Economic History of Steelmaking, 1867–1939: A Study in Competition* (Cambridge, 1961) pp. 47–8.
117. McHugh, *Alexander Holley and the Makers of Steel*, p. 258.
118. Ibid., p. 253.
119. Ibid., pp. 360–2.
120. Captain W. R. Jones, 'On the Manufacture of Bessemer Steel and Steel Rails in the United States', *Journal of the Iron and Steel Institute*, vol. 18, part 1 (1881) pp. 129–45; and Henry M. Howe, 'Notes on the Bessemer Process', *Journal of the Iron and Steel Institute*, vol. 37, part 2 (1890) pp. 95–161.
121. Robert C. Allen, 'International Competition in Iron and Steel, 1850–1913', *Journal of Economic History*, vol. 39 (December 1979) pp. 924–34.

5. Shipping Industry Technologies

Simon Ville*

The nineteenth century witnessed the replacement of the wooden sailing ship of centuries past by the metal steamship. The leading maritime nation, Britain, was also the cradle of most of the new technology which spread thence to the USA, France, Germany, Japan and most other maritime nations by the eve of the First World War. The new technology was introduced into receiver countries in different ways, particularly by shipowners buying new and second-hand vessels from overseas and by the dissemination of knowledge through shipbuilders, engineers and naval architects. For an industry of such international mobility there existed many vehicles for the transfer of technology and few means of protecting new ideas in spite of inter-firm and inter-port rivalry. Delays in the diffusion of new technology had much more to do with its relative economic feasibility for particular regions and trades than with knowledge of the discovery itself. The experience of the shipping industry confirms the view of technological change as a gradual process of incremental improvements, 'a cumulation of minor improvements, modifications and economies, a sequence of events where, in general, continuities are much more important than discontinuities'.[1] Most often the early invention is highly imperfect, requiring a process of continual modification and adaption of the original idea, fashioned by local needs or personal experience and expertise.

TECHNOLOGICAL DEVELOPMENTS

The introduction of iron and steam technology involved four principal changes: the development of the marine engine and its complementary boilers, the alliance of these to effective propulsive devices and consequent changes in the hull design. Early steamshipping was regarded as two separate technologies: the shipyard construction of hull and fittings and the engineering provision of engines, boilers and paddles. Progress laboured against the absence of a scientific basis for steamshipping and the absence of standardization of engines, boilers and paddles.

Steam offered greater speed and regularity than sail. While most sailing clippers could travel as fast as most cargo steamers, they were more subject to delay in port and at sea during adverse winds and plotted longer routes to pick up windstreams. Experiments with steam-powered river boats on the Clyde around 1800 soon spread to the Humber, Mersey and Thames as steam found its earliest use in river craft and tugs. By the 1820s and 1830s larger engines and more efficient paddles brought steam into the coastal trade. Early steamship firms, such as the General Steam Navigation Co., operating in the British coastal and near trades, battled to keep their vessels fully employed in order to cover high capital and coal costs.[2] The adoption of the tubular boiler in the 1830s increased boiler pressures to around 20lb per square inch.[3] By the 1840s paddles were being replaced by the screw propeller, which acted upon a consistently large volume of water and was more efficient in rolling seas.

The introduction of the compound engine increased the power and efficiency of the steam engine. By this principle the steam generated was used more than once at reducing pressures in a series of cylinders. John Elder and Charles Randolph, Clyde shipbuilders, patented a compound engine in 1853 but its effective use had to await the introduction of higher-pressure boilers and surface condensers in the following decade. The surface condenser allowed sea water to be used through contact instead of injection. By the mid-1870s the compound engine accounted for three-quarters of the horsepower of the British shipping industry.[4] In the 1880s and 1890s triple and quadruple expansion engines further improved efficiency. By the 1880s pressures of 200lb per square inch were being generated.[5] Improvements in the quality and quantity of mild steel production, hastened by the work of Bessemer and Siemens, enabled the building of stronger boilers able to withstand the higher pressures.

Charles Parsons built the first steam turbine in 1884 and an improved version was used to power the *Turbinia* a decade later. Turbines were lighter and operated more smoothly than reciprocating engines, but only achieved sufficient advantage to offset their greater capital costs at high speeds and therefore found their earliest use in passenger and naval vessels. By 1909 reduction gearing had made the turbine more suitable for cargo vessels. In the years immediately prior to the First World War the internal combustion engine was introduced into shipping. The engine was smaller than coal-powered engines, required no boiler and its oil fuel was lighter, less bulky, easier to load and could be stored in the ship's double bottom, where it did not occupy cargo space. Engine improvements had reduced fuel consumption from 10lb per standard horsepower per hour in the early steam engines to 3.5lb with the early compound engines, 1.3lb for steam turbines and only 0.45 for the diesel engine. Diesel also benefited from the extraction of 40 to 50 per cent more calorific value from a ton of fuel.[6] Superheaters and forced draught also helped to reduce fuel consumption. Britain's advanced metallurgical industries helped her to dominate the use of iron in shipbuilding. Iron plates were used in construction from the 1840s. Falling prices and improved quality caused the output of iron vessels to exceed that of wooden by 1862 in Britain.[7] Vessels could now be built longer than about 300 feet and were stronger, lighter, more resistant to bad weather, safer from fire and more malleable for design purposes. Iron's greater strength permitted thinner hull walls and therefore savings in volume and weight, which permitted the carriage of more cargo.[8] While giving greater overall strength, local weaknesses could make iron vessels vulnerable to rocks or shot.[9] Armour plating, double bottoms, watertight compartments and sluice doors helped to provide the solution. The magnetic effect of iron upon compasses was the cause of several shipping disasters before shipowners learned to make an accurate allowance for magnetic deviation. The problem of fouling of iron hulls was overcome by anti-fouling paints and cargo sweating was mitigated by improved ventilation.

Steel began to replace iron in shipbuilding from the 1870s. The first ocean-going merchant steamer built of mild steel, the *Rotomahana*, came out of the yard of William Denny in 1879 and was sold to the Union Steamship Co. of New Zealand.[10] Steel offered further savings in cargo weight and its greater tensility enabled it to support more pitching and rolling in heavy seas and undergo extensive body repairs after an accident without damaging the quality of the steel. Only seven steel vessels were lost between 1878 and 1885, in spite of a rapid growth in the amount of tonnage built from less than 5 000 to above 130 000.[11] The greater tensility and malleability of steel encouraged the construction of more specialist vessels according to the needs of particular trades. In the north-east of England a range of 'well-deckers' and 'turret-deckers' were built for tramping, while Clydeside concentrated upon the production of liner vessels.[12] The most important new specialist vessel was the oil tanker. The geographical concentration of known oil sources meant a high shipment demand by the later nineteenth century. Twice the volume of oil could be carried in bulk than in containers, while loading and discharge time was reduced from days to a matter of hours. The *Vaderland,* built by Palmer's of Newcastle for a Philadelphia firm in 1872, was the first vessel designed specifically for the bulk carriage of oil.[13]

VEHICLES OF TECHNOLOGY TRANSFER

Contemporaries recognized the importance of emulating British shipbuilding technology. 'It must be cordially admitted that British shipbuilding has served from first to last as a splendid model, which the Germans have not hesitated to use on the greatest scale', noted Haack in 1889,[14] while Terano and Yukawa acknowledged 'the very large debt that Japan owes to the assistance of Great

Britain, without which the development of its shipbuilding industry could not have advanced so speedily and with such satisfactory results'.[15] British shipping predominated in the trade of many world ports, which gave shipowners first-hand evidence of the latest technology and shipbuilders and naval architects the opportunity to make sketches of vessels. In 1914, Britain carried more than half of the world's seaborne commerce and from 1883 more than half of her fleet had consisted of steamships (Table 5.1).[16]

Table 5.1   British share of entrances and clearances at foreign ports, 1890 (%)

Germany	35	United States	53
Argentina	42	Russia	53
France	44	Belgium	53
Chile	47	New Zealand	87
Italy	49	South Africa	88
Canada	52	India	88
Netherlands	52		

Source: Report of the Departmental Committee on Shipping and Shipbuilding, Parliamentary Papers 13 (1918) Cd. 9092, p. 75.

British vessels were mostly sold to maritime nations, particularly Norway, Greece, Italy, Spain, Germany, France, Belgium, Russia, Japan, Sweden, Austria-Hungary, Netherlands, USA, Australia and New Zealand. Overseas demand outpaced the expansion of the British fleet: 12 per cent of British shipbuilding output was sold overseas in the period 1869–83; this proportion had doubled by 1900–13. Second-hand sales also grew disproportionately: the tonnage sold overseas grew by a factor of 3.8 between 1875/84 and 1904/13, while the total amount of tonnage on the British register increased by only 75 per cent.[17] More than half the steam tonnage of many countries, including France, Russia, Spain, Netherlands, Belgium and Italy, was built in Britain.[18] Virtually the entire Hungarian shipping industry of the 1890s came from British yards; Swan Hunter of Wallsend, for example, sold a series of vessels to the Royal Hungarian Sea Navigation Co. of Budapest.[19] Japan's commercial expansion at the end of the nineteenth century was supported by ship purchases from the north-east of England by major companies such as TKK, OSK, NYK and Mitsui.[20] Overseas sales introduced technology into the receiver country while also initiating discussion of technology between shipbuilder and shipowner. The letter books of South Shields shipbuilders, Readheads, indicate discussions of the latest ship technology and advice on how best to achieve the required specifications. Plans, drawings and, sometimes, models were supplied. Repeated orders from the same shipowner enabled further vessels to be built to the previous design and incorporating any recent innovations.[21]

Some British shipbuilders worked hard to increase their overseas sales. William Gray of West Hartlepool encouraged technology transfer by offering favourable credit terms to foreign buyers. S. M. Kuhnele and Sons of Bergen were allowed eight years to pay for a vessel at 5 per cent.[22] Swan Hunter accepted a quarter of the payment for the *SS Cacouna* (of the Black Diamond Steamship Co.) of Montreal in 1884 in fully paid shares of the firm.[23] Denny's of Dumbarton also bought shares in foreign shipping companies. When the Otago Steamshipping Co. was formed in 1863, Denny's subscribed £3 000 of the initial capital and built their first vessel. Denny's became a major shareholder in the Union Steamship Co. of New Zealand after accepting part payment for two steamers in company shares and subsequently built 42 vessels for them. When the Irrawaddy Flotilla and Burmese Steam Navigation Co. was reformed in 1876, Peter Denny became its chairman and during the next 60 years Denny's built over 250 vessels for the Company.[24] Some shipbuilders sent out 'foreign emissaries' in search of business. From 1863, Stuart Rendel of Armstrong's filled this role very effectively and by 1870 almost a dozen foreign governments were regular customers.[25] The Japanese navy employed A. R. Brown, a former P & O navigator, to arrange the purchase of vessels from Britain. Glover Brothers of London ordered vessels for Mitsui, including the screw steamer, *Takosan Maru,* which was built on the self-trimming cantilever principle patented by its builder, John Priestman.[26] Some shipbuilders also acquired building capacity abroad, a trend particularly strong amongst warship builders: Vickers began building in Italy, Russia, Canada, Sweden and Brazil, Armstrong in Italy and Canada, John Brown in Canada and Russia and possibly Firth in Russia and the USA. Hawthorn-Guppy, from their base in Naples, designed and built engines for the Italian navy.[27]

Shipbuilders in the receiving countries imitated the latest designs. Visits to Britain enabled them to learn about the latest iron and steel steamships. American shipbuilder Charles Cramp and his chief engineer, J. Shields Wilson, went to England in the early 1870s to examine the compound engines being built by Elder and returned to the USA to build some of the earliest American examples.[28] In 1881 another American shipbuilder, J. Taylor Gause, visited English shipyards and circulated his notes to executives in the firm. Of Lairds he noted, 'the best work I saw on hulls anywhere was here, they are now using steel, mainly with tensile strain of 30 to 32 tons per square inch, both plates, angles, beams and rivets'.[29] In a similar fashion German architects and mechanical engineers visited British yards to study their equipment and organization. L. E. Bertin, the renowned French naval engineer, made an exploratory visit to Britain in 1884, while American naval representatives went to Glasgow and Greenwich.[30] J. Scott Russell noted that naval architects, surveyors of the navy, ministers of the marine, great admirals and great naval commanders came 'from all parts of the world to Portsmouth, and Plymouth, and Chatham and Woolwich, to search out and inform themselves in all that was most admirable in the design, construction, armament and equipment of ships of war'.[31]

Import substitution gradually developed from such transfers of technical knowledge. Armstrong's built many of the earliest cargo steamers for the German market but were gradually edged out by domestic firms. Foreign shipbuilders relied heavily upon British designs, materials and labour at first, before gradually increasing the value added domestically. The Kosmos Line of Hamburg imitated the quadruple expansion engines built by Wigram, Richardson & Co of Sunderland.[32] In France the Compagnie Générale Transatlantique ordered three new iron paddle steamers from Scotts of Greenock for their new run to New York from 1864. Subsequent orders, however, went to the Penhoët yard at St Nazaire, using French materials and Creusot engines but under the superintendence of Scotts and using a large number of skilled workmen from Greenock.[33] John Roach, a Delaware shipbuilder, initially bought compound engines from Randolph and Elder, before producing his own.[34] The adoption of Parsons' turbine by Mitsubishi is an interesting example of how the technology was transferred to enable import substitution. From 1906 Mitsubishi began to order turbines from Parsons. The agreement made provision for the training of Japanese engineers and indicated that the next model would be built in Japan to Parsons' design and subsequent ones would also be designed in Japan and simply require Parsons to check them.[35]

International cooperation between British and foreign shipbuilders was particularly important for the transition to steam in the Spanish shipbuilding industry. The Squadron Act of 1887 envisaged expansion of the Spanish navy. The government wished to give orders to Spanish firms but the absence of steam and steel technology prevented this option. The tender for three cruisers was won by an Anglo-Spanish group led by Martinez de la Riva and Charles Palmer. De la Riva provided the finance and Palmer, a naval architect from the Brown and Cammell yard, the know-how.[36] The Squadron Act of 1908 laid out a programme for naval reconstruction following the destruction of Spain's Cuban and Pacific fleets. Tenders came from a French industrial combine associated with Schneider et Compagnie, from an Italian group led by the shipbuilder, Ansaldo, and from an Anglo-Spanish consortium which included Beardmore and Palmer's. The successful tender was again an Anglo-Spanish group which included a range of Spanish industrial and financial concerns. The British participants included Vickers, Maxim, Brown and Armstrong who between them provided 40 per cent of the capital for the newly established firm, la Sociedad Española de Construcciones Navales (SECN). The terms of the agreement provided for British designs for three battleships, Spanish rights to the Parsons turbine patent and a high inflow of technical management into Spain.[37]

Import substitution could be accelerated by attracting skilled British shipwrights, architects and yard managers.[38] Many workers and foremen in French, German, Danish and Russian yards were British. In the 1880s men were often sent abroad on the initiative of the Boilermakers and Ironbuilders Society while Japanese yards employed European workers, including Dutch shipwrights, at Mitsubishi.[39] Readheads supplied onboard engineers with their new vessels.[40] The value of migrant workers to the transfer of ship technology is, however, open to question. While the wooden sailing ship industry had been a craft occupation learned on site, the building of iron steamships required an extensive training in the applied sciences, particularly mechanical engineering and naval architecture. This created a clear distinction between engineers, technicians and managers, on the one hand, and ordinary labour performing simple tasks, on the other. Thus the ordinary shipwright possessed only a limited knowledge to take with him. Foreign workers could cause instability amongst the work-force as Charles Cramp, a Philadelphia shipbuilder who hired foreign labour to help ease the transition of his yard from wooden to iron shipbuilding in the 1860s, noticed.[41]

Engineers and naval architects had much to offer foreign shipyards. The *Clermont*, one of the earliest ocean-going steamships, was built in 1817 by Robert Fulton, an émigré from Scotland to the USA. The Japanese shipbuilding expansion of the 1860s relied heavily upon French technical staff. A shipyard established at Yokosuka in 1864 had been planned by a French naval engineer. Many Italian firms drew upon British personnel: the 'Officine Meccaniche' was for long managed by Mr de Grave Sells from Britain. John Ericsson, a Swedish inventor, took his ideas on a screw propellor to the USA in the 1830s and built four coal-carrying screw-propelled steamboats for the Phoenix Foundry of New York.[42] Some foreign engineers came to Britain to improve their skills. Daniel Martens and Olaf Olsen, who formed the first specialist iron and steel steamship company in Norway, were both educated in Britain and worked in the Middlesborough shipbuilding industry before returning to Norway taking with them English workers and equipment.[43] German mechanical and naval engineers also came to Britain to gain shipbuilding experience before returning to Germany with some shipwrights to start a business.[44]

Foreign shipbuilders, naval architects and engineers all sought a formal education in Britain. A Royal School of Naval Architecture and Engineering was established at South Kensington in 1864 and was transferred to the Greenwich Royal Naval College nine years later. It took in students from British and foreign shipyards. In 1883 the University of Glasgow created the first Chair of Naval Architecture in the world and provided lectures and practical instruction in ship drawing, calculations and designs. Students attended from many countries, including the USA, Germany, Austria, Denmark, Japan, Netherlands, Norway, Peru, Rumania and Russia. Further chairs were created at Durham in 1907 and Liverpool in 1909.[45] Price, the General Manager at Palmer's, stated that 'almost all ... the best men in this employment in Germany and Denmark and Norway and Holland have been trained in this country'.[46]

Professional institutions complemented the role of the universities. The Institution of Naval Architects (INA) was established in 1860. Its regular meetings and annual transactions highlighted many of the latest developments in shipping technology. Many foreign shipbuilders, naval architects and marine engineers were among its members; they organized meetings in different countries and ensured a two-way flow of ideas. Bertin, C. Hemje, a naval architect from New York, and E. E. Goulaeff, Lieutenant of Naval Architecture in the Imperial Russian Navy, were all members. The INA served as a model for similar professional bodies in other countries and fostered international links between the different institutions. The Association Technique Maritime was founded at Paris in 1888, the American Society of Naval Architects and Marine Engineers at New York in 1893 and the Schiffbautechnische Gesellschaft at Berlin in 1899. All three included members who belonged to the INA. Similar bodies emerged in Japan, Italy and Sweden.[47]

The North East Coast Institution of Engineers and Shipbuilders was established in 1884. By the 1890s its members came from many ports of the world, including Paris, Bilbao, Hamburg, Genoa, Leghorn, Antwerp, Helsingfors, Bergen, Bremerhaven, Odessa, Constantinople, Trieste, New York, Washington DC, Boston, Philadelphia, San Francisco, Valparaiso, Bombay and Sydney. Some represented foreign shipbuilders, including Astilleros del Nervíon in Spain and Ansaldo in Italy. Overseas members benefited from hearing papers delivered at meetings and published in the Institution's transactions. In May 1898, for example, A. E. Long gave a paper entitled 'Some points of interest in the designing of cargo steamers'. The educative role of the Institution was reaffirmed by the establishment of a reference library in 1889 and a scholarship fund in 1907.[48]

Books, journals and newspapers were all further sources of international technology transfer. William Rankine (1820–72) Professor of Engineering at Glasgow University, wrote a series of important articles and books, including *Shipbuilding, Theoretical and Practical* in 1866. Many British books and journals were international in context and circulation. Lloyd's publications were consulted in many countries while individual treatises were often translated into several different languages. Reed's *Shipbuilding in Iron and Steel*, for example, was translated into French.[49] Ship plans could also prove helpful. The US cruiser *Charleston* was based upon designs bought from Armstrong's of Newcastle and previously used for Japanese, Italian and Chilean vessels.[50]

Consular officials and commercial agents also aided the transfer of technology. In 1886, R. Cattarns, general manager of the General Steam Navigation Co., noted how knowledgeable German, French and American consular officers were on commercial issues.[51] In 1918, the German consular service was again commended for 'the very complete form in which information is tabulated ... and placed at the disposal of German traders'. German commercial agents were likewise praised for their linguistic capabilities and their willingness to modify products.[52]

There was no clear pattern amongst the initial recipients of the new technology. In countries importing second-hand tonnage, such as Norway and Greece, early interest came from shipowners. In Germany shipbuilders, aware of the growing domestic market for new liners, were quicker to adopt the new technology. The change to iron and steam was sometimes made by existing shipbuilders such as William Cramp of Philadelphia, although the Bethlehem Shipbuilding Corporation's expansion into shipbuilding from iron production was more typical.[53] New steamship yards were sometimes adapted from several old sailing yards under new ownership. The Bremer Vulkan Maschinenfabrik built large steam freighters and oil tankers but was originally formed from four old wooden yards. Another German shipbuilding firm, Joh. C. Tecklenborg Aktien-Gesellschaft, manufactured wooden sailing vessels until 1879 and then turned to building in iron and steam.[54] Their corporate structure was similarly diverse. The Mitsubishi shipyard at Nagasaki was developed along a policy of large-scale vertical integration with an engine works, docks, building berths, experimental tanks and a technical school.[55] This was beyond the resources of many traditional wooden shipbuilders, who could only survive by buying in engines and other parts. Tecklenborg, for example, only built its own engine works in 1891 once the firm had become established as an important steamship builder. Firms with an existing large capital structure were attracted into the industry. The Bethlehem Corporation has already been mentioned. In Norway Fredrikstad Mekaniske Verksteder had been established in 1870 to repair and construct machinery for the mechanical wood pulp industry. In Spain Anglo-Spanish consortiums included firms with a variety of backgrounds such as banking and steelmaking.[56]

ADOPTION AND DIFFUSION OF TECHNOLOGY

Britain's dominance of steamshipping continued until the First World War, by which time she owned 42 per cent of the world steam fleet.[57] Her leadership in most trade routes, helped by a worldwide empire and the strength of her coal, iron, steel and engineering industries, ensured this predominance. A large and expanding coal export trade provided two-way trading for British shipowners on many routes and therefore made ship owning a more profitable occupation.

Table 5.2   Registered merchant steam tonnage, 1860–1910 (000 tons)

Country	1860	1870	1880	1890	1900	1910
UK	454(10)	1113(20)	2724(41)	5043(63)	7208(78)	10043(90)
Germany	23(3)	82(8)	216(18)	724(51)	1348(69)	2397(83)
Japan	–	–	41(46)	94(64)	543(63)[1]	1234(75)[1]
Norway	–	14(1)	58(4)	203(12)	505(34)	897(59)
France	68(7)	154(14)	278(30)	500(53)	528(51)	816(56)
Spain	15(4)	115(18)[2]	234(42)	408(66)	679(88)	745(94)
Italy	10(2)[3]	32(3)	77(8)	187(23)	377(40)	674(61)
Sweden	–	28(8)	81(15)	141(28)	325(53)	597(77)
USA[4]	97(4)	193(13)	147(11)	198(21)	341(41)	557(70)
Netherlands	10(2)	20(5)	64(20)	129(50)	268(77)	488(91)
Aust-Hung	21(6)[5]	50(15)	64(20)	98(42)	247(82)	478(94)
Russia	–	–	89(19)	–	364(58)	464(64)
Denmark	–	11(6)	52(21)	113(37)	250(61)	416(76)
Canada	26(5)	31(4)	100(8)	116(12)	164(26)	338(45)
Greece	0	5(1)	–	45(17)	143(45)	302(68)
Australia	12(9)	24(13)	59(28)	130(44)	190(57)	285(69)
Belgium	4(12)	10(33)	65(86)	72(95)	113(100)	188(98)
New Zealand	1(4)	6(22)	12(19)	38(52)	56(57)	113(75)
China	–	–	22(100)	30(71)	18(46)	89(86)
Brit. India	–	–	12(14)	25(36)	43(57)	87(81)
Finland	1(1)	6(2)[6]	11(4)	26(10)	54(16)	72(18)
Portugal	–	–	–	–	52(48)	70(61)

Notes: Several writers have calculated figures for 'effective tonnage' which takes account of the greater output of steam. However there is no reliable ratio because steam's relative efficiency varied widely according to time and trade. The table includes motor tonnage for later years. Percentage of total national tonnage in parenthesis.
– Indicates no evidence available.
[1] Gross tons.
[2] 1874.
[3] 1862.
[4] Excludes river, lake, coasting and fisheries traffic.
[5] 1861.
[6] 1872.

Sources: *Tables showing the progress of merchant shipping in the U.K. and the principal maritime countries*. Parliamentary Papers 76 (1912–13) Cd. 6180, pp. 48–51; B. R. Mitchell, *European Historical Statistics, 1750–1970*, (London, 1975) pp. 613–23.

In 1912 Britain was responsible for 70 per cent of coal exports.[58] British shipowners additionally benefited from the low price of bunker coal in Britain. Close links between British shipowners and shipbuilders, together with the strength of the components industry, also help explain Britain's leadership in the new technologies of metal and steam. (Tables 5.2 and 5.3).[59]

Table 5.3   The transition from wood to metal (000 tons)

Country	1886			1910		
	Wood	Iron	Steel	Wood	Iron	Steel
UK	959(13)	5680(80)	413(6)	69(1)	712(7)	10167(93)
Germany	674(56)	514(42)	16(1)	13(1)	128(5)	2645(95)
USA[1]	1708(88)	235(12)	1(0)	1115(51)	227(10)	845(39)
Norway	1364(94)	80(6)	7(1)	192(13)	424(30)	818(57)
France	278(34)	502(62)	28(4)	73(6)	178(14)	1016(80)
GB cols	1360(85)	194(12)	34(2)	201(21)	140(15)	605(63)
Italy	704(85)	120(15)	3(0)	126(14)	321(35)	482(52)
Japan	45(36)	30(24)	49(39)	49(7)	136(19)	539(74)
Neths	188(53)	133(37)	14(4)	3(1)	25(4)	608(96)
Sweden	340(81)	81(19)	–(2)	122(21)	175(29)	286(48)
Russia	271(72)	87(23)	18(5)	142(24)	112(19)	338(57)
Spain	161(39)	225(57)	9(2)	14(3)	107(23)	354(75)
Denmark	126(57)	88(40)	6(3)	48(11)	40(9)	368(81)

Notes: A small remainder are composite built. Percentage of total national tonnage in parenthesis.
– Indicates no data.
[1] Great Lakes tonnage included for steam, not sail.

Sources: *Lloyd's Universal Register, 1886* (London, 1886); *Lloyd's Universal Register, 1910–11)* (London, 1911); S. Palmer, 'The British Shipping Industry, 1850–1914' in L. R. Fischer and G. E. Panting (eds) *Change and Adaptation in Maritime History. The North Atlantic Fleets in the Nineteenth Century*, (Newfoundland, 1985), pp. 96–7.

    Most other maritime nations followed Britain's conversion to steam within a decade or so. By 1883 the majority of the British fleet was steam-powered. By the end of the decade the same could be said of Germany, Japan, France, Spain, Netherlands and New Zealand.[60] Sweden, Austria–Hungary, Russia, Denmark, Australia and British India had been added to this list by 1900. Only the Finnish fleet remained predominantly sail in 1914. The rate of transition to steam was most rapid in Germany, Spain, Netherlands and Austria–Hungary in the last two decades of the nineteenth century. In the USA, which was one of the pioneers of the steamship, the transition was more gradual, over half a century from 1860. France, Australia, Canada and New Zealand also adopted the steamship more gradually. The rate of adoption slowed or even halted in some years, particularly during the low freight rates of the mid-1880s. The construction of steam navies was conditional upon official policy such as the Japanese and Spanish decisions to modernize and rearm at the end of the nineteenth century. Adoption rates also fluctuated between ports. Stockholm and Gothenburg accounted for 55 per cent of Sweden's steam tonnage in 1891/ 5 but only 12 per cent of sail, while virtually all Danish steam tonnage was registered at Copenhagen in the 1870s. Bergen was similarly dominant in Norway and Helsinki in Finland.[61]

We know less about adoption rates for the use of iron and steel in shipbuilding. Figures provided by Lloyd's, though not comprehensive, give some indication of the trend. In the third quarter of the nineteenth century iron was widely adopted as the main construction material for shipbuilding. By 1886 less than half the tonnage registered in the UK, France, Japan and Spain was built of wood. Thenceforth the trend was towards steel construction; by the eve of the First World War steel shipbuilding was predominant in most countries except for Canada and the USA. Steam and metal were natural partners in ship construction and so it comes as little surprise to see their contemporaneous adoption. By the 1880s few wooden steamers were built, although steel sailing vessels remained important in France, Germany, the USA and Norway up to 1914.

Adoption rates resulted from rational behaviour by shipowners aware of the benefits of steam and steel. Neither insufficient knowledge nor prejudice played a significant role. Nor does the experience lend weight to the view of technological change as a logistic function where the probability of adoption is an increasing function of the number of firms already using it but a decreasing function of the size of the investment.[62] Gjolberg has shown that, of the years 1875, 1885, 1890, 1895, 1900 and 1905, steam was more profitable than sail in Norway in only 1890 and 1895, thus justifying the decision of many to remain with sail until the twentieth century.[63] Kaukiainen rationalizes the late adoption of steam in Finland where 'the opportunity cost of steam was relatively high, and therefore the "second-best technology" was much more competitive than in the leading west European nations'.[64] Trade patterns, the availability of finance, cost inputs, improvements in the existing technology and the structure of shipowning were among those factors bearing upon the diffusion of steel and steam.

Steam diffused first into the coastal and short sea trades and those voyages where speed or regularity was important, as in the carriage of passengers or perishable goods. Before about 1850, steamers were largely confined to short-haul trades within Europe where inefficient engines could be regularly refu-elled with cheap coal, thereby saving on fuel costs and cargo space. Most transatlantic passenger services changed to steam in the 1860s: in 1856, 96 per cent of passengers arriving in New York had come by sail; by 1862, 32 per cent arrived in a steamer, as did most travelling eastbound. The opening of the Suez Canal in 1869 and the development of compound engines provided opportunities for steam on more distant routes. Suez cut the voyage to India by half and to China by one-third.[65] This meant substantial savings of fuel and time on a route which was impractical for sailing vessels. The development of the international telegraph and liner operations produced more long-haul opportunities for steam in the later nineteenth century and gradually marginalized sail into trades where speed and regularity were of little importance and at ports where the volume of traffic was insufficient to justify the capital improvements required by steamships.

The long average hauls of American vessels and the large volume of low-grade cargoes carried (grain, coal, hides, jute, coffee, wool, oil) encouraged the continued use of sail. In commodity trades such as the Californian grain trade, freight rates and cargo volumes fluctuated greatly, and it was safer to cover such risks using the lower capital investment of sail. In effect, the vessels were used as grain warehouses and the cargo might be sold several times during the course of a voyage.[66] Finland's late adoption of steam can be partly explained by the carriage of cheap, bulk cargoes such as logwood from the Gulf of Mexico and Canada, nitrate from South America and grain from Australia. There was a heavy volume imbalance in Finnish trade; three times as much was exported as imported.[67] Many ballast passages and low capacity utilization made this trade inappropriate for the higher capital and running costs of steam. In contrast to the Scandinavian countries, Finland failed to move in the later nineteenth century into the major tramping cross trades, where freight rates and utilization were frequently higher. While in 1905, 64 per cent of the volume of goods carried in Danish vessels were moving between foreign ports, by the early 1920s only 10 to 15 per cent of Finnish shipping earnings were so derived. Less than a quarter of Denmark's cross-trading in 1905 was carried by sail.[68]

Sweden also suffered from an import–export imbalance, together with the seasonal interruption of ice. However the expanding ore trade gradually became large and profitable enough to attract steamshipping. The concentration of the ore trade upon Stockholm and Gothenburg helps explain why these ports adopted steam more rapidly than the rest of Sweden. Axel Brostrom built up a large fleet of steamships in the Gothenburg ore trade by 1914.[69] In Norway Bergen moved earliest into steamshipping, helped by its fish trade, to which speed was important. This expertise was turned to other perishable trades, especially the Mediterranean fruit trade in the 1870s and the North American fruit trade in the 1880s. Germany's rapid transition to steam concerned her concentration upon the passenger and cargo liner services of the north Atlantic, although opportunities for sailing vessels existed on the long hauls: Ferdinand

Laeisz built up a fleet of sailing vessels in the nitrate trade between Hamburg and Chile.[70]

The greater cost of steamships presented problems of finance. Shipowners had to be sure that profits would be sufficient to amortize steamer replacements. This encouraged a pattern of earlier steam adoption in wealthy countries and ports. The purchase of steamships was difficult in the backward and capital-deficient Finnish economy, where in the 1850s even sailing ship capital exceeded manufacturing investment. Norwegian shipowners benefited from financing provided by the Ship Mortgage Bank and several British and Dutch banks. In Sweden the Wallenburg financial group provided financial support.[71] The Scandinavian countries kept capital costs to a minimum by buying second-hand tonnage discarded by British shipyards. Building shipyards for steel and steamships required much more capital than for wooden sailing vessels and was unlikely to find a large domestic market. It was only in the years before 1914 that some new shipyards were built in major towns where finance and credit opportunities were better, which in Norway meant Bergen (Bergens Mekaniske Verksted), Oslo (Akers Mekaniske Verksted) and Fredrikstad (Fredrikstad Mekaniske Verksted). A more wealthy local economy and better sources of finance contributed to Stockholm and Gothenburg's domination of Swedish steam shipowning and building while several large Helsinki firms dominated Finnish steamshipping, particularly the Finnish Steamship Co. (F.A.A.) which owned 40 per cent of the country's steam fleet.[72]

Steamshipping was not always appropriate for a country's economic development. The slow transition to steam in Canada and the USA was a form of benign neglect as these economies moved away from their Atlantic maritime staples to westward manufacturing expansion.[73] Falling profits and the low demand for steamers in a localized shipping industry discouraged technological adoption by Canadian shipowners, who turned to investment in banking and new industries. The Canadian shipbuilding industry went into decline in the late nineteenth century as the British demand for wooden sailing vessels collapsed.[74] The interlocking economic structure of localized rural economies also hampered technological change in some countries. In southern Norway and northern Sweden, vertical integration of shipbuilding, timber production and sawmilling sustained the older technology. In Finland and Norway, peasants conducted seasonal shipping ventures to supplement their wages, using old, cheap wooden sailing vessels on local voyages. By marginalizing shipowning into a part-time and supplementary occupation they were unlikely to earn sufficient income to bear the amortization costs of a steamer. In Finland, in 1914, only 4 per cent of peasant tonnage was steam compared with 30 per cent of urban shipowning.[75] Canadian historians have rightly emphasized the important place of shipping within the Atlantic staple industries. High input and output ratios with such industries as timber, sawmilling and merchanting

made for low costs and help explain why 'both the rise and decline of shipping
... can be explained by the rise and relative decline of the staples'.[76] The absence of a heavy industrial base discouraged the adoption of the steel steamer.

Construction costs influenced technological diffusion. Germany's powerful iron and steel industry encouraged the rapid development of steel shipbuilding, though not as early as in Britain, where the heavy industries were
fortuitously located near the coast and major ports. By the 1880s, German steel
was reckoned to be cheaper than British, and Krupps was rapidly becoming a
major supplier in many countries.[77] Italy also benefited from the rapid growth
of her iron and steel industry. France lacked good supplies of coal and iron and
had to resort to imports. Norway imported its iron and steel but benefited from
low homeward freights. Sweden had a good but expensive domestic supply of
iron. The USA developed its iron and steel industry towards the end of the
nineteenth century. Tariff policies, monopolistic practices, the unfavourable
localization of the industry and increased domestic transport costs associated
with the Pittsburgh basing point system,[78] however, served to make American
steel more expensive at home than abroad. The highest steel prices were found
in Canada, the USA and Scandinavia, where timber was also cheapest, thereby
emphasizing the cost differentials.

Continual improvements in the efficiency of the sailing vessel also affected
diffusion rates. As American sailing ship sizes rose to around 3 000 tons by the
1890s, labour costs rose less than proportionately, designs were substantially
improved and sailing times reduced.[79] The American industry also had to bear
wage rates up to 50 per cent higher than in Europe, although more and better
equipment (steam-driven sawing machinery and lathes) meant higher labour
productivity levels. Canadian sailing vessels remained cheap, designs improved and the use of lightweight spruce permitted up to 25 per cent more cargo
weight than was possible in oak ships although their lifespan was much shorter
than that of hardwood vessels.[80]

Many governments encouraged technological adoption through preference
policies which included shipping and shipbuilding subsidies, reduced rail rates
and the refund of shipping dues. The French concentrated upon a subsidy
policy and by the terms of a law of 1881 offered generous bounties to
shipbuilders and subsidies to shipowners. In Japan the Shipbuilding Encouragement Act of 1896 offered a subsidy of 12 yen per ton for iron and steel
vessels of 700 to 1 000 tons and 20 yen for larger vessels. The German
government offered preferential railway rates for goods destined for export,
immigration control stations and the removal of import duties on shipbuilding
materials. Direct subventions on some routes benefited steamshipping. In 1885
the government reached an agreement with Norddeutscher Lloyd of Hamburg
to carry mail to the Far East and Australia. Nationalism and imperialist
ambitions encouraged the expansion of the navy. William II declared, 'Unsere

Zukunft liegt auf dem Wasser' ('Our future is on the waves') which was reinforced by the nationalist propaganda of the 'Flottenverein' (Navy Society) for the sea, the navy and the colonies.[81]

Similar sentiments were reflected by A. T. Mahan in America, where tariff barriers protected shipbuilding. Naval policy was important in modernizing Spanish shipyards. Finnish governments offered interest-free loans to purchase steam vessels and paid subsidies to steamers operating in early winter: during 1897–8 loans accounted for 25–30 per cent of steamshipping investment.[82] The Italian government subsidized shipbuilding output from 1885 and allowed raw materials into the country free of duty.

Public policy, however, was of limited importance to the diffusion of shipping technology, being often ill-conceived and ill-directed. It was not until laws passed in 1893 and 1902 that French subsidies excluded sailing and foreign vessels. In Germany only 4 per cent of net tonnage received direct subventions and much of this was concentrated upon the African and Australasian services, which continued to be unprofitable.[83] The Deutsche Levant-Linie, however, expanded its fleet of steamers from 10 to 59 between 1898 and 1914, after being given shipment rights over materials for the Baghdad railway. A shipbuilding subsidy of 30 pesetas per ton was introduced by the Spanish government in the 1850s, but applied only to vessels over 400 tons making an initial voyage to America or Asia and therefore excluded most Spanish shipping.[84] A further problem concerned the dichotomy between shipbuilding and shipowning interests. The mail agreement between Norddeutscher Lloyd and the German government stipulated the use of German-built steamers and thereby prevented the company using British vessels. In the USA, Congress protected domestic shipbuilders with tariff barriers which served to weaken an already dwindling interest in shipowning.

TECHNOLOGICAL MODIFICATIONS AND REVERSE FLOWS

Imported technology may require modifications. Jeremy has shown how British textile technology was sometimes of too high a quality for the American market, which needed simple machinery to deal with coarse fabrics.[85] British shipping technology was of a highly variegated nature, ranging from large first-class passenger liners to smaller and simpler tramp steamers. Individual vessels could be built to the purchaser's specifications and a large second-hand market offered further quality and cost options. Thus, while many British owners were operating large, modern steamers, Scandinavians frequently opted for smaller and older vessels. Sometimes individual vessels were modified according to local conditions. America's long and wide but shallow rivers encouraged the modification of several imported British vessels. The *Robert F. Stockton*, built by Lairds in 1839, was sailed across the Atlantic and fitted with a screw for use as a tug on the Delaware River and Raritan Canal.[86] Production methods were also modified in some regions. Many American and German firms adopted a more capital-intensive structure than in Britain because of the relative shortage and high cost of skilled shipyard workers.[87]

Most new shipping technology flowed out of Britain in the nineteenth century; exceptionally Frenchmen Tellier and Carré developed refrigerated ships while William Denny III and John McAusland brought back further knowledge of river navigation from Burma in the 1870s.[88] Ferdinand Carré perfected an ammonia-compression refrigeration machine and in 1877 the vessel *Paraguay* brought frozen mutton to Le Havre from San Nicholas. British shipbuilders, however, quickly followed suit in building 'reefers' – Dennys, for example, built *Ruahine* for the New Zealand Shipping Co. in 1891 as the boom in frozen meat exports from the Antipodes began to set in.[89] As late as the 1880s few British owners bought foreign because British vessels were regarded as the best. The position began to change shortly before 1914 as Britain's competitive advantages waned. Britain's coalmining industry and coal export trade were central to sustaining maritime leadership. Coal was gradually replaced by oil and its by-products, which provided no comparative advantage and acted as a disincentive to British shipbuilding. Much of the early development of the motor ship was provided by the Danish firm of Burmeister and Wain, who produced a flow of technology back to Britain by establishing links with Harland and Wolff in Belfast and, in 1914, acquiring a shipyard on the Clyde. British shipbuilders also lost ground in the development of oil tankers by the early twentieth century: many tankers were built at Motala in Sweden. British shipbuilders were benefiting from German know-how in the construction of liners by 1914 and engineers now came to Britain to instruct rather than to learn.

The new technologies of steam and steel originated largely from the British shipping industry in the nineteenth century and were transferred to most other maritime nations in the half-century up to 1914. The vehicles of transfer were many and resulted from overseas trading, foreign ship sales, international migration and visits by shipbuilders, naval engineers and mechanical engineers, the work of learned societies, professional organizations and educational institutions, along with the information contained in printed works. The rate of adoption of the new technology varied between different receiver economies according to economic dictates, particularly trade routes, the availability of financing, construction and operating costs, government policy and the appropriateness of metal steamships to the country's economic structure. Receiver modifications were limited by the wide product choice. Reverse flows of technology back to Britain were rare until shortly before 1914, when she began to lose the comparative advantages which had made her the industry's leader throughout the world.

NOTES

* The author would like to thank Dr P. N. Davies (University of Liverpool), Professor F. Broeze (University of Western Australia), Associate Professor S. R. H. Jones (University of Auckland), Dr K. E. Jackson (University of Auckland) and Mr D. Topliss (National Maritime Museum) for their helpful comments and advice.

1. N. Rosenberg, 'Factors Affecting the Diffusion of Technology', *Explorations in Economic History*, **10** (1972) p. 7. The alternative viewpoint can be found in J. E. Schumpeter, *The Theory of Economic Development* (Cambridge, Mass., 1934).

2. S. Palmer, '"The Most Indefatigable Activity": The General Steam Navigation Co., 1824–50', *Journal of Transport History*, 3rd ser., **3** (1982).

3. S. Palmer, 'Experience, Experiment and Economics: Factors in the Construction of Early Merchant Steamships', in K. Matthews and G. Panting (eds), *Ships and Shipbuilding in the North Atlantic Region* (Newfoundland, 1979) p. 241.

4. A. Slaven, 'The Shipbuilding Industry' in R. Church (ed.), *The Dynamics of Victorian Business* (London, 1980) p. 111.

5. G. S. Graham, 'The Ascendancy of the Sailing Ship, 1850–85', *Economic History Review*, new ser., **9**, (1956–7) p. 88.

6. G. Henning and K. Trace, 'Britain and the Motorship: a Case of the Delayed Adoption of a New Technology', *Journal of Economic History* **35** (1975) pp. 365–8; M. E. Fletcher, 'The Suez Canal and World Shipping, 1869–1914', *Journal of Economic History*, **18** (1958) p. 557.

7. Slaven, 'Shipbuilding Industry', p. 113; *The Construction Materials of Vessels placed on the U.K. Register in 1869*, Parliamentary Papers 1870, LX, p. 319, shows that by the end of the decade less than 24 per cent of vessels entering the UK Register were built of wood.

8. S. Pollard and P. Robertson, *The British Shipbuilding Industry, 1870–1914* (Cambridge, Mass., 1979) p. 14 suggests, rather optimistically, a weight saving of up to 35 per cent and a space saving of 20–50 per cent compared with wooden vessels.

9. *Statement Relating to the Advantages of Iron and Wood and the Relative Cost of these Materials in the Construction of Ships for His Majesty's Navy*, Parliamentary Papers 36, 1863, p. 301.

10. Memoir of Mr William Denny, FRSE, *Transactions of the Institution of Naval Architects* (hereafter *TINA*) 28 (1887) p. 456.

11. B. Martell, 'A Brief Review of the Progress of Mild Steel and the Results of Eight Years' Experience of its Use for Shipbuilding Purposes', *TINA*, **27** (1886) pp. 55–6.

12. A detailed description of these new vessel designs is provided in R. Craig, *Steam Tramps and Cargo Liners* (London, 1980) pp. 31–8.

13. B. Martell, 'On the Carriage of Petroleum in Bulk on Overseas Voyages', *TINA*, **28** (1887) pp. 2–3, 8.

14. R. Haack, 'The Development of German Shipbuilding', *Engineering Magazine* (August 1899) p. 909.

15. S. Terano and M. Yukawa, 'The Development of Merchant Shipbuilding in Japan', TINA, **53**, pt 2 (1911) p. 145.

16. B. R. Mitchell and P. Deane, *Abstract of British Historical Statistics* (Cambridge, 1962) p. 218.

17. Pollard and Robertson, *British Shipbuilding*, p. 38.

18. S. Pollard, 'British and World Shipbuilding, 1890–1914: a Study in Comparative Costs', *Journal of Economic History* **17**, (1957) p. 428.

19. *Report from H M Representatives*, Parliamentary Papers, 1901, Cd. 596, p. 8. Tyne and

Wear Archives Service (hereafter TWAS) 1826/3/1, Swan Hunter and Wigram Richardson and Co., Contract ledgers.

20. M. Conte-Helm, *Japan and the North East of England* (London, 1989) p. 87.
21. TWAS 1061/1369, Readheads, Letter books.
22. R. Craig, 'William Gray and Company: a West Hartlepool Shipbuilding Enterprise, 1864–1913', in P. Cottrell and D. H. Aldcroft (eds), *Shipping Trade and Commerce* (Leicester, 1981) pp. 174–81.
23. TWAS 1826/3/1, Swan Hunter and Wigram Richardson and Co., Contract ledgers.
24. P. L. Robertson, 'Shipping and Shipbuilding: the Case of William Denny and Brothers', *Business History*, **16**, (1974) pp. 37–40.
25. TWAS 31/4319-4503, 31/5086-5130, 31/7558-7618, papers of Stuart Rendel. These references deal with some of his work for the company in Canada, Brazil, Portugal, China, Russia and the Balkans.
26. Conte-Helm, *Japan*, pp. 95–6.
27. Pollard and Robertson, *British Shipbuilding*, pp. 97–8; F. C. Marshall, 'Progress and Development of the Marine Engine', *TINA*, **29** (1888) p. 29; G. Russo, 'Fifty Years' Progress of Shipbuilding in Italy', *TINA*, **53** pt 2 (1911) p. 257.
28. A. C. Buell, *The Memoirs of Charles H. Cramp* (Philadelphia, 1906) pp. 111–15.
29. J. Taylor Gause, E. Jackson and N. R. Benson, *Memoranda Concerning Foreign Shipbuilding, 1881–3* (Wilmington, DL, 1883) pp. 1–31.
30. Haack, 'German shipbuilding', p. 910; E. H. Lorenz, 'Two Patterns of Development: the Labour Process in the British and French Shipbuilding Industries, 1880–1930', *Journal of European Economic History*, **13** (1984) p. 609.
31. J. Scott Russell, 'On the Education of Naval Architects in England and France, *TINA*, **4** (1863) p. 164.
32. C. F. Laiesz, 'Shipbuilding in Germany', *TINA*, **39** (1898) p. 15.
33. D. B. Tyler, *Steam Conquers the Atlantic* (New York, 1939) p. 334; Lorenz, 'British and French Shipbuilding', p. 613.
34. D. B. Tyler, *The American Clyde. A History of Iron and Steel Shipbuilding on the Delaware from 1840 to World War I* (Newark, DL, 1958) pp. 34–5.
35. Conte-Helm, *Japan*, p. 97.
36. A. Gomez-Mendoza, 'Government and the Development of Modern Shipbuilding in Spain, 1850–1935', *Journal of Transport History*, 3rd ser., **9**, 1 (1988) p. 29.
37. Ibid., pp. 30–3; C. Trebilcock, 'British Armaments and European Industrialisation, 1890–1914', *Economic History Review*, 2nd ser., **26** (1973) pp. 260–2.
38. D. J. Jeremy, *Transatlantic Industrial Revolution: the Diffusion of Textile Technologies Between Britain and America, 1790–1830s* (Cambridge, Mass. 1981) pp. 74, 254, argued that the emigrant British artisan was the best carrier of new textile technology across the Atlantic in the early nineteenth century.
39. *Royal Commission on the Depression in Trade, Fourth Report*, Parliamentary Papers 1886, XXIII pp. 18–23; Terano and Yukawa, 'Merchant shipbuilding', p. 136.
40. TWAS 1061/1373, Readheads, Letter books. Engineers were supplied with the *SS Maria*, sold to Messrs Fratelli Cosulich in 1901.
41. C. H. Cramp, 'Sixty Years of Shipbuilding on the Delaware', *Proceedings of the Numismatic and Antiquarian Society of Philadelphia* (1904–6) pp. 179–80.
42. Terano and Yukawa, 'Merchant shipbuilding', p. 136; M. Kondo, 'Progress of Naval Construction in Japan', *TINA*, **53**, pt 2 (1911) p. 50; Russo, 'Shipbuilding in Italy', p. 270; Tyler, *Steam Conquers*, pp. 117–22; Tyler, *American Clyde*, pp. 5–6.
43. H. W. Nordvik, 'The Norwegian Shipbuilding Industry: the Transition from Wood to Steel, 1880–1980', in F. M. Walker and A. Slaven (eds), *European Shipbuilding: One Hundred Years of Change* (London, 1984) p. 195.
44. *R. C. on the Depression in Trade, Fourth Report*, pp. 18–23.
45. J. Jenkins, 'On the Course of Instruction in Naval Architecture at Glasgow University', *TINA*, **30** (1889) p. 66; J. F. C. Conn, 'The Glasgow University Department of Naval Architecture, 1883–1983', in Walker and Slaven, *European Shipbuilding*, p. 39.
46. *R. C. on the Depression in Trade, Third Report*, p. 152.

47. The Shipbuilding Employers Federation, which superseded the Federation of Shipbuilders and Engineers in 1899, represented local shipbuilders associations around Britain and also played an important role in disseminating technological information. See the minute books housed by the National Maritime Museum, SRNA/7, SEF/1/1–5.
48. TWAS 1376/1, General minute books of the North East Coast Institution of Engineers and Shipbuilders, Books 2,3.
49. Conn, 'Glasgow University', p. 33–4.
50. Tyler, *American Clyde*, pp. 71–2.
51. *R. C. on the Depression in Trade, Third Report*, p. 167.
52. *Report of the Departmental Committee on Shipping and Shipbuilding*, Parliamentary Papers, 13, 1918, p. 35.
53. Tyler, *American Clyde* pp. 62–3, 112–13.
54. Haack, 'German Shipbuilding', pp. 912–19.
55. Terano and Yukawa, 'Merchant Shipbuilding', pp. 143–4.
56. Gomez-Mendoza, 'Shipbuilding in Spain', p. 31.
57 Pollard and Robertson, *British Shipbuilding*, p. 25
58. S. Palmer, 'The British Coal Export Trade, 1850–1913,', in D. Alexander and R. Ommer (eds), *Volumes not Values* (Newfoundland, 1979) p. 334.
59. Pollard and Robertson, *British Shipbuilding*, pp. 91–2, 97–8.
60. The small fleets of China and Belgium were already dominated by steam in 1880.
61. M. Fritz, 'Shipping in Sweden, 1850–1913', *Scandinavian Economic History Review*, **28** (1980) p. 155; H. W. Nordvik, 'The Shipping Industries of the Scandinavian Countries, 1850–1914', in L. R. Fischer and G. Panting (eds), *Change and Adaptation in Maritime History: the North Atlantic Fleets in the Nineteenth Century* (Newfoundland, 1984) p. 123–5; Y. Kaukiainen, 'The Transition from Sail to Steam in Finnish shipping, 1850–1914', *Scandinavian Economic History Review*, **28** (1980) pp. 177–9.
62. E. Mansfield, 'Technical Change and the Rate of Imitation', *Econometrica*, **29** (1961) pp. 762–3.
63. O. Gjolberg, 'The Substitution of Steam for Sail in Norwegian Ocean Shipping, 1866–1914. A Study in the Economics of Diffusion', *Scandinavian Economic History Review*, **28** (1980) p. 140.
64. Kaukiainen, 'Finnish shipping', p. 184.
65. Fletcher, 'Suez Canal', p. 559; J. A. Samuda, 'On the influence of the Suez Canal on Ocean Navigation', *TINA*, **11** (1870) p. 1.
66. J. G. B. Hutchins, *The American Maritime Industries and Public Policy, 1789–1914*, (Cambridge, Mass., 1941) pp. 371–2, 375.
67. Kaukiainen, 'Finnish shipping', pp. 165–74.
68. Ibid, pp. 176–7; O. Hornby and C. A. Nilsson, 'The Transition from Sail to Steam in the Danish Merchant Fleet, 1865–1910', *Scandinavian Economic History Review*, **28** (1980) p. 128.
69. Fritz, 'Shipping in Sweden', pp. 149–50; Nordvik, 'Scandinavian shipping', p. 139.
70. W. Kresse, 'The Shipping Industry in Germany', in Fischer and Panting (eds), *Change and Adaptation*, p. 158.
71. Nordvik, 'Scandinavian shipping', pp. 135–7.
72. Kaukiainen, 'Finnish shipping', pp. 177–9.
73. J. J. Safford, 'The Decline of the American Merchant Marine, 1850–1914: an historiographical appraisal', in Fischer and Panting (eds), *Change and Adaptation*, pp. 172–3; E. W. Sager and G. Panting, 'Staple Economies and the Rise and Decline of the Shipping Industry in Atlantic Canada, 1820–1914', in Fischer and Panting (eds), *Change and Adaptation*, pp. 28–37.
74. D. Alexander, 'The port of Yarmouth, Nova Scotia, 1840–89', in Matthews and Panting (eds), *Ships and Shipbuilding*, p. 102; L. R. Fischer, 'The Port of Prince Edward Island, 1840–89: a preliminary analysis' in Matthews and Panting (eds) *Ships and Shipbuilding* pp. 67–8.
75. Kaukiainen, 'Finnish shipping', p. 178.
76. Sager and Panting, 'Staple economies', p. 11.

77.   G. Lehmann-Felkowski (ed.), *The Shipbuilding Industry of Germany* (London, 1904) p. 98; *R. C. on the Depression in Trade, Third Report*, evidence of John Scott, p. 191.

78.   Transport basing point systems define the point of commencement of a journey for the purposes of calculating the tariff or freight rate. On the assumption that long haul tariffs are normally cheaper per mile than short hauls the insertion of basing points increases the total freight charge by dividing up a long haul into several short hauls. The reasons for the establishment of basing points are manifold and can, for example, result from the actions of discriminating monopolies or the aims of state policy.

79.   Hutchins, *American Maritime Industries*, pp. 292–4.

80.   Ibid, pp. 299–302.

81.   W. Kresse, 'The Shipping Industry in Germany, 1850–1914', in Fischer and Panting (eds), *Change and Adaptation*, pp. 162–3.

82.   Kaukiainen, 'Finnish Shipping', pp. 180–2.

83.   D. H. Aldcroft, 'British Shipping and Foreign Competition: the Anglo-German Rivalry, 1870–1914', in D. H. Aldcroft, *Studies in British Transport History, 1870–1970* (London, 1974) p. 64.

84.   Gomez-Mendoza, 'Shipbuilding in Spain', pp. 25–6.

85.   Jeremy, *Transatlantic Industrial Revolution*, pp. 65, 81.

86.   Tyler, *American Clyde*, p. 5.

87.   Hutchins, *American Maritime Industries*, p. 297.

88.   Robertson, 'Shipping and Shipbuilding', p. 39.

89.   Craig, *Steam Tramps*, pp. 28–9.

6. The Transfer of Telegraph Technologies in the Nineteenth Century

Paul B. Israel and Keith Nier

Because telegraphy has been supplanted by telephone, radio, and television in the twentieth century, it is little thought of in the modern world. Yet in the nineteenth century electric telegraphs played a crucial role in the industrializing countries of Western Europe and North America by permitting for the first time instantaneous communication. Telegraphy seemed to annihilate time and space as it reshaped people's experience of the world; for the first time one could learn of distant events in time to interact with them as they unfolded. The telegraph provided the first sense of a global village as it created a paradigm for subsequent telecommunications systems that replaced it.[1]

Although a few studies have recently appeared, our knowledge of this crucial nineteenth-century technology remains woefully inadequate. In this chapter we can only sketch the history of the transfer of telegraph technology among North Atlantic nations during the nineteenth century and raise issues for further inquiry.

Telegraphy proves to be a challenge for general conceptions of technology transfer, and we believe that it can enrich the framework in which technology transfer is analysed. Studies of nineteenth-century transfers have focused on transportation or production technologies rather than communications.[2] Unlike many nineteenth-century technologies, telegraphy was not dominated by a single country of origin and its technology was transferred easily among the European and North American states, in some cases even physically stretching between countries. Furthermore, this transfer was often promoted on both sides. The economic dimensions of initial telegraph technology transfers are also less clear. Often the decision to introduce telegraph technology was based less on immediate and direct economic returns than on long-term national development or for reasons of governmental efficiency.

Telegraphy was one of the first technologies in which science played a crucial formative role. At the same time, it was a product of the dominant mechanical framework of nineteenth-century technology. It has become almost a commonplace that the successful transfer of most technologies requires the establishment of technical communities possessing sufficient know-how to use and modify the technology. In each of the countries examined in this chapter such communities already existed.

The diversity and multiplicity of telegraph technologies makes it difficult to bring order to a discussion of their transfer. While telegraph technology fell within a few broad categories no two countries used the same technology in exactly the same way. From the start there was no single electric telegraph; several systems emerged essentially simultaneously. Nonetheless there were common characteristics. Each required a power source, a transmitting device, a transmission channel, a receiving device and a means of translating ordinary language into electric signals (often in the form of a code). We will order our discussion by briefly describing the major systems (using a common technique of nineteenth-century telegraph literature which classified systems in sweeping and imprecise categories based on transmitting and receiving apparatus), and then proceed to a review of transfers in several countries.

The dearth of recent historical scholarship on the telegraph has forced us to rely on dated, technically-oriented works for such information as there is about the transfer of telegraph technologies from country to country around the North Atlantic. We lack the space to be comprehensive. We cannot cover all kinds of telegraphs and have therefore limited our discussion to those used on long-distance land lines, including only passing references to submarine cables or local urban telegraphs.[3] Nor will we discuss the transfer of individual components such as batteries, magnet and relay designs, or insulators, focusing instead only on the major systems.

Even so, we will analyse the context of their use and transfer only in the major countries that contributed most to their development – Great Britain, France, Germany and the USA. We survey the institutions, both private and governmental, which operated the new technology, the kinds of users and the messages they sent with it, and the nature of the technical communities responsible for the development and transfer of telegraph technology from one place to another. Then we attempt to point out common patterns in regard to such transfers. In doing so our concern is with how technical adaptations were influenced by national differences arising from the organization of governments, economies, educational institutions and other aspects of these industrializing societies.

AN INTERNATIONAL INVENTION

In 1877 the chief electrician of the Western Union Telegraph Co. wrote:

...no single individual can justly claim the distinction of having been the inventor of the electric telegraph. Indeed, it cannot properly be said to have had an inventor. It was, in fact, a growth rather than an invention – the work of many brains and of many hands.[4]

This highlights an important starting-point for a discussion of the transfer of telegraph technology. While much of the history of technology transfer during the nineteenth century revolves around the introduction of a new technology from a dominant originating country, telegraphy instead involves contemporaneous development in a number of countries, particularly Britain, the USA and several German states.

We commonly associate new electrical technology with the fruits of research in the scientific laboratory. While this was not often directly true of nineteenth-century electrical inventions, the development of electric telegraphs was made possible by the work of a European and American scientific community investigating electrical phenomena in the first half of the nineteenth century. A number of scientific investigators not only suggested the possibility of electric telegraphs, but demonstrated systems they had created by altering 'the delicate devices used to demonstrate electrical phenomena in the laboratory and classroom'.[5]

The earliest attempts to develop an electrical communication system grew directly out of research in electrostatics in the eighteenth century. But an electric telegraph did not become technically feasible until the early nineteenth century, with the development of electric batteries and electromagnets in scientific laboratories. In 1809, Samuel Soemmerring, a German doctor and member of the Royal Academy of Sciences in Munich used the recently-discovered effect of electrolytic decomposition to devise an electric telegraph. Soemmerring's telegraph was only a laboratory model, but it was shown in Paris, Vienna, Geneva and St Petersburg and stimulated further attempts at electrical communication.[6]

The international character of early electrical science and technology that gave rise to telegraphy can be seen in the early development of electromagnetic theory. French scientist André Marie Ampère relied on Danish scientist Hans Oersted's discovery of the relationship between electricity and magnetism to suggest the possibility of electrical communication by means of a needle moved by the opening and closing a circuit. Neither Ampère's nor Oersted's experiments in electromagnetism led directly to an electric telegraph. Instead further researches initially suggested serious drawbacks to the practicality of such a form of communication. Nonetheless continued investigations provided fresh insights as well as new apparatus that helped create a practical basis for electric telegraphs by the mid-1830s. A number of researchers soon drew on this new knowledge as they began building electromagnetic telegraphs and putting them to actual use.[7]

The first successful experimental demonstrations of electromagnetic telegraph systems occurred in the 1830s in some of the German states. One of Soemmerring's former assistants, Russian Baron Schilling, began using demonstration apparatus of his own design some time in the 1830s to impress various parties with the possibilities of electric telegraphy. Schilling's design, using the deflection of a needle, was particularly influential and stimulating. Although the Germans led in the early development of experimental telegraphs, these were designed primarily for scientific purposes and lacked the sophisticated mechanical design necessary for daily commercial purposes.[8] Only as mechanically oriented as well as scientifically knowledgeable inventors turned their attentions to the new technology did it emerge in more practical form. Although Germany led the early experimental phase of development, Great Britain and the USA took the lead in practical application.

British and American telegraph inventors experimented with several designs. The first commercial system, established in Britain (1837), was based on the needle designs of German experimenters. Soon afterwards Samuel F. B. Morse developed his system in the USA (1837–1845) and rivals in both countries began developing other alternatives. In the USA printing telegraphs were introduced by rivals to Morse, while in Britain dial and automatic systems were developed. These five types constituted the basic telegraph designs used on land lines during the nineteenth century.

Needle Telegraphs

The needle system was the only type simultaneously developed in more than one country; it was also the only system whose initial development took place partially outside the Anglo-American context. Physicist Karl Steinheil demonstrated a two-needle telegraph on lines in Bavaria as early as 1836. However it was not until 1838, the same year that a two-needle system was introduced in Great Britain, that Steinheil put his telegraph into service around Bavaria.[9]

One of the two co-inventors of the British needle telegraph system, anatomy student William Cooke, was directly influenced by earlier German work. After seeing Schilling's needle telegraph demonstrated at the University of Heidelberg, Cooke became imbued with enthusiasm for the electric telegraph, but his attempts to develop a commercially viable system of his own proved unsuccessful until he joined Charles Wheatstone. Wheatstone, a professor of experimental philosophy at King's College London, who had already undertaken a series of experiments to determine the velocity of electricity, was an experienced musical instrument maker; his combined scientific knowledge and mechanical aptitude resulted in rapid progress in improving Cooke's design.[10] Together they patented (in 1837) a system employing five sets of transmitting keys, transmission wires and receiving needles and soon put it into operation along a railway. In this and subsequent double- and single-needle designs, the transmitting apparatus sent an electric current over the line, causing a magnetic needle similar to a compass needle to deflect in one direction or the other.[11]

Morse Telegraphy

American artist Samuel Morse was attempting to introduce his telegraph system in the USA at the same time that needle telegraphs were being introduced in Britain and Germany. Morse, who was attracted by the possibilities of the telegraph after learning in 1832 of Ampère's work, spent years attempting to develop a telegraph system before joining chemistry professor Leonard Gale and mechanic Alfred Vail in 1837. Thereafter they made rapid progress on the basic system, which became known as the Morse. The first public demonstrations occurred early in 1838.[12] The basic features of this system were use of a transmitting key to open and close a circuit for varying lengths of time, which made the dots and dashes of the Morse code. The original receiving apparatus, the Morse register, recorded messages by pulling a lever instead of twisting a needle, embossing signals on a paper tape.[13]

Dial Telegraphs

Charles Wheatstone was also responsible for the initial development of dial telegraphs. He began developing one in 1839 out of a Cooke design in which the electromagnetism of a telegraph circuit controlled the movement of a clockwork.[14] In this and subsequent dial telegraphs, a moving indicator pointing to various letters and symbols on the transmitter dial sent a series of pulses over the line that corresponded to the number of characters passed over. These pulses caused a weight-driven escapement to move an indicator on the receiving instrument, which moved to the desired letter.[15]

Automatic Telegraphy

Another system developed in Britain was the automatic telegraph system designed by Scottish clockmaker Alexander Bain. Bain's system used automatic machinery operated by clockwork to transmit and record messages. Operators used specially designed perforating machines to punch holes representing Morse or other telegraph codes onto a strip of paper. They then fed this strip into a transmitter which passed an electrical contact over the perforations, causing the circuit to close intermittently and transmit signals. In the original Bain system the receiving instrument recorded the signal on chemically-treated paper by electrical decomposition. In later years chemical recorders were often replaced by more reliable, but slower, ink recorders.[16]

Printing Telegraphy

Besides the Morse, one other system was initiated in the USA. Between 1839 and 1844, Royal House devised a telegraph that printed messages in alphabetic characters that did not require translation.[17] House's system incorporated features that became standard in printing systems. A transmitting keyboard, with individual keys for each letter, sent electrical impulses to a receiving instrument, where the impulses activated a typewheel to print messages on paper strips.[18] A later design provided another key feature for long-distance printing telegraphs. Welsh-born music teacher David Hughes synchronized sending and receiving instruments through acoustical principles in the new design he introduced in the USA about 1855. The Hughes printer achieved higher speeds by pressing an inked typewheel against paper as it turned, rather than stopping to print, as did the House; the Hughes also required less battery power and was a less complex mechanism.[19]

Multiple Telegraphy

One other major class of telegraphs used extensively on land lines deserves discussion. Multiple telegraphs used a single wire to carry at least two messages at the same time. These circuit designs were largely dependent on the particular type of receiver or transmitter used, although they were most successfully employed with Morse, printing and some cable systems. Sending one message each way ('duplex') with a 'Morse' system was the first kind of multiple telegraph to achieve any practical success. Although such systems were developed experimentally in Germany and Austria in the 1850s, their use was limited.[20] The next significant development took place in the USA. Joseph Stearns introduced a modified German duplex arrangement in 1868 and by 1872 significantly increased the practicability of duplexing in general.[21] Stearns's success spurred other successful designs, including the quadruplex developed by Thomas Edison in 1874, which sent two messages in each direction. By the end of the decade French telegraph inventors developed the synchronous multiplex, which used a kind of time-sharing of the line among many messages and was applied to printing telegraphy.[22]

THE CONTEXT OF TELEGRAPH USE AND TRANSFER

Having laid out the basic telegraph systems used on land lines in Europe and America we will now explore the context in which they were transferred during the course of the century. We focus only on countries that made significant contributions to telegraph technology. This focus is very much a product of our sources; information is most readily available for these countries. Future scholars need to turn their attention not only to further examination of the countries discussed here, but also to other European and non-European cases.

The already existing network of visual semaphore telegraphs in much of Europe and, to a more limited extent, in the USA largely influenced the early introduction of electric telegraphs. Soemmerring, for example, worked in the hope of producing a communication system that might rival the French mechanical semaphore telegraph which had been used to inform Napoleon of the invasion of Bavaria by Austria. By the time electric telegraphs became practical in the late 1830s, semaphore telegraphs were already in extensive use, with government bureaucracies established to operate them. These systems were less extensively employed in the USA and Great Britain than on the Continent. In the Anglo-American setting they were used primarily in port cities for communicating shipping information for both commercial and military purposes.[23]

The pattern of government control of semaphore telegraphy on the Continent and of private enterprise development in Great Britain and the USA largely continued for the electric telegraph, although government played a role everywhere. On the Continent governments introduced and managed the new systems. Great Britain developed its electric telegraph system under private enterprise but later nationalized it. In contrast, the first electric telegraph line in the USA was erected and operated by the government but was quickly turned over to private enterprise development.[24]

There were other good reasons for promoters to turn to governments for support in developing and introducing electric telegraphy. In the nineteenth century most new inventions consisted of individual machines which their developers generally used for manufacturing, or which they sought either to manufacture and sell themselves or to license others to do so. But the manufacture of telegraph instruments would return little profit until an extensive system came into common use. In the 1830s and 1840s few institutions possessed the resources necessary to erect transmission lines, equip offices and train employees in the use of the new telegraph technology. Promoters of such improvements therefore turned to national governments, including nationalized railways, as the only institutions with sufficient capital and power for such projects. Telegraphs were initially promoted as a form of internal improvement like canals and railroads or equated with national postal systems. Only in Britain, with its extensive networks of privately-funded railways, was there an alternative source of funding at the start.[25]

The institutional and organizational structure of telegraph administration established in each country played an important role in setting parameters for the technology. These structures are thus an important point of analysis, particularly as they also provided the framework for other factors that affected telegraph transfer. The technical personnel responsible for deciding on the systems were organized within this framework. And the various kinds of users that predominated in different contexts – business, the military, the press, private individuals, railways – each sent types of messages which influenced the decisions made regarding the kind of telegraph technology employed.[26]

Germany

Unlike the other countries examined in this chapter, little recent historical work is available about the German telegraphs.[27] German political arrangements – as a loosely related group of independent states and principalities became a nation state – also make an analysis of telegraph transfer more complex. Nonetheless Germany played a crucial role in the evolution of telegraph systems throughout Continental Europe. We have therefore chosen to ferret out what information we can.

The first telegraph used in Germany was Steinheil's needle system, but this was soon replaced by other systems. In Prussia Werner Siemens' dial telegraph, a modified version of Wheatstone's, was introduced. More significantly American William Robinson and his associates successfully introduced a Morse system to several German states, including Hanover, Prussia and Bavaria, as well as in Austria.[28] Steinheil himself was instrumental in these developments as he strongly advocated the adoption of the Morse system and supervised its installation in Austria and Switzerland, where he acted as director of the new telegraph services. He also served as an adviser in Bavaria.[29]

The widespread adoption of the Morse in Germany and Austria laid the basis for a major change in the conditions affecting further transfers of telegraph technology in Europe. Prussia had not only adopted the telegraph but was seeking to extend its use across neighbouring borders. Initially this occurred for military and police reasons, but the telegraph's other administrative uses also proved significant. In 1848, Prussia reached an agreement setting up a Berlin–Frankfurt telegraph, passing through several other German states. More significantly, in 1849, Prussia and Austria agreed to build a line between Berlin and Vienna, using the recently adopted Morse system. This treaty was followed by similar agreements with both Saxony and Bavaria. In 1850 these four states created the Austro-German Telegraph Union, which was subsequently joined by several other German states and the Netherlands. By 1851 the Union decided that international traffic would be transmitted over specially designated lines and would use the Morse apparatus and the modified International Morse code. The German–Austrian example was imitated by France, Belgium, Switzerland, Sardinia and Spain, which by 1855 had formed the West European Telegraph Union. In 1865 most European states agreed to sign the first International Telegraph Convention and formed the International Telegraph Union.[30]

After its founding the ITU became an important factor in the transfer and adoption of telegraph technology. Government messages, which remained a priority in both France and Germany, took precedence on international lines controlled by ITU treaties as well. European systems strongly emphasized, in contrast with the Americans, a permanent, machine-made record of the messages. This was probably a result of their management by civil service bureaucracies concerned with assigning responsibility for transmission errors. For this reason the Morse system in Europe evolved in very different fashion from that in the USA, where sounders generally replaced the embossing register of the Morse system. In Europe the register was replaced by ink recorders. Later the ITU sanctioned the adoption of the Hughes printer, used initially for high-density traffic in France.[31]

Apart from the priority given government messages, the history of telegraph use in Germany remains unclear. Some information is readily available concerning the instruments used in Prussia about 1867. The Hughes had gained prominence on international lines and the Morse was used on most other lines, with Werner Siemens's automatic system, consisting of a three-key puncher, transmitter and modified Morse embossing register, used on lines between major cities within the state.[32] All of these systems were transferred to Germany, except the Siemens, which was itself a modification combining elements of the Morse and the Bain automatic systems.

While the history of the technical development of German telegraphy also remains unclear, certainly German electrical engineer Werner Siemens, in association with his manufacturing partner J. G. Halske, was a major figure in the development not only of German but also of European telegraph technology. Siemens, who received a science-based education at the Berlin Artillery and Engineering School, was a central figure in transferring and modifying telegraph technology introduced on German lines, and he and Halske manufactured many of the early instruments. Among his contributions were a dial telegraph, designed as an improvement of the Wheatstone, which was used on some of the earliest lines in Prussia and was popular on railway lines. He also made significant contributions to the evolution of the Morse system, including developing the polarized relay and double-current system of polarity reversals to make the signals, which allowed the ink recorder to be used on cable lines.[33]

Siemens exerted direct influence on telegraph systems employed in other countries as well. For example, his automatic, which was used in Germany, was initially developed for Russian telegraph lines in the 1850s. It also appears that the puncher employed in Siemens's system was adapted by Charles Wheatstone to his later automatic which attained wide use in Britain.[34]

Scientific and technical training in telegraphy generally followed patterns in Germany similar to those in France, with an emphasis on academic training. Although the details are unclear in the case of telegraphy, state educational systems provided training for government technical services. For engineers in state service formal technical education was required. In many of the German states courses and examinations covering electrical telegraphy were established.[35]

France

As the country with the oldest and most extensive system of semaphore telegraphs, it is not surprising that in France the earlier telegraph and its institutional framework were most influential in the adoption of new electric designs and their subsequent development. The success of the electric telegraph in Britain encouraged the French government to adopt the new technology. Alphonse Foy, head of the government's semaphore telegraph service, hoped to avoid retraining employees to use the electric telegraph and chose not to transfer directly the systems developed in Britain or America. The first French instruments, based on Foy's conception and built by Louis Bréguet, imitated the signalling system used for the semaphore. Foy hoped in this way to obviate new training or the hiring of a different class of employees, but this hope was not met.[36]

The electric telegraph eventually replaced the semaphore as an agent of government communication and control. French scholars Jacques Attali and Yves Stourdze have emphasized the importance of administrative control in the centralized French state as a dominant characteristic of telegraph communication, which they describe as a monologue dominated by the government.[37] After the telegraph system was opened to the public, the government retained first priority of use and the authority to control access and censor messages. Nevertheless, by the 1860s, official dispatches made up only about 20 per cent of all domestic messages, while business and commercial use grew to nearly 50 per cent and social and personal messages to about 30 per cent.[38]

The opening up of the telegraphs to non-government use spurred a tremendous growth in the French telegraph network. In the attempt to retain centralized control, the state created a system of lines with important technical implications that are particularly important from the standpoint of technology transfer. Beginning in the mid-1850s, the government created a hierarchy of telegraph centres – 'stations of deposit' – with which all other stations communicated. Thus the most important lines were direct wires linking Paris and major foreign and domestic urban centres, while branches communicated only with secondary deposit stations. These in turn communicated directly with principal deposit stations. Previously the most expert operators worked at the smaller station, where they were responsible for retransmitting messages sent between major cities, while the least experienced worked at large stations. This system was reversed under the new hierarchical structure as lines became separated into those of high- and low-density traffic. At the same time instruments thought best suited to each particular kind of traffic replaced the Foy–Bréguet needle telegraph.[39]

Beginning in the mid-1850s, the French began to use dial telegraphs for lightly-trafficked lines and Morse instruments for those with heavier business. Both systems were transferred to France. The dial telegraph was brought from Britain by the state railways in 1845, when they began using Charles Wheatstone's system. The dial telegraph proved well adapted to railway lines as it required little experience to operate. At the request of the railroads, Louis Bréguet soon redesigned the dial instruments in order to overcome certain perceived 'inconveniences' in the British system.[40] Although the percentage of traffic handled by the dials remained small, the number of instruments increased from 118 to 2 153 between 1857 and 1870. Even though it was much slower than other systems, the dial telegraph's simplicity of operation worked well on the lowest-density lines.[41]

The growing use of the Morse system during the 1850s and 1860s was a direct product of the increasing importance of international traffic on French telegraph lines. Although Morse had first brought a version of his telegraph system to France in 1838, its adoption was spurred in the early 1850s by treaties that established the use of Morse ink-recording instruments and the International Morse code on international lines. The adoption was also promoted by the desire for a permanent record of transmissions, particularly as growing public use led to increased complaints. A 'printed' record was considered the best means of holding individual employees accountable for, and thus reducing, errors. By 1870, Morse instruments numbered 3 255, about 56 per cent of all instruments in France. By the early 1880s there were 7 700 Morse instruments, as the number of dial instruments fell to just 663. The shift from dial to Morse instruments was facilitated as well by the transfer of the telegraph service to the Post Office. Although dial telegraphs would have been easier for the postal workers to learn to use, preference was given to the ability of the Morse to record messages and to its faster speed.[42]

Telegraph traffic in France grew dramatically during these years. Between 1856 and 1866 the number of messages on the French system increased from 360 299 to 2.8 million. Ten years later there were over eight million. The amount of international traffic escalated as well, constituting one-fourth of all messages and 40 per cent of revenues by the early 1870s. Though faster than the dial, the hand-operated Morse telegraph increasingly proved inadequate on high-density direct lines. The ink-recording Morse system used in France could obtain speeds of 20–25 words per minute, and under experimental conditions over 45 words per minute. However such speeds could not be maintained for any length of time and on most lines the system worked at 12–15 words per minute.[43]

The search for faster instruments again led the French government to investigate a system developed on foreign shores – the Hughes printing telegraph. David Hughes arrived with his printing telegraph in Paris in 1860. The system had two important advantages for the French high-density lines. First, it was fast – in 1867 the head of the French telegraphs claimed that 50 20-word messages per hour could be sent by the Hughes, in comparison to 20 for the Morse and only 15 for the dial.[44] Contributing to this speed was the second advantage: like the Morse, the Hughes was a recording telegraph, but unlike the older system it recorded by printing alphabetic characters, thus obviating the need for translation. As traffic warranted, the Hughes began to replace the Morse on major lines and by 1872 there were over 3 300 printing instruments in use.[45]

The adoption of the Hughes had important consequences for the technical development of telegraphy in France. French telegraph engineers focused on a key element of the Hughes – synchronism between sending and receiving instruments – as they sought to increase transmission speeds. This contributed to the early development of synchronous multiplexing in France because it was the key to time-sharing techniques that allowed several instruments to transmit simultaneously on one wire. Also contributing to this technical development was another imported system. The Caselli facsimile telegraph, developed by a professor of physics at Florence, allowed transmission of handwritten messages and drawings. Although used to only a very limited extent on French lines, the Caselli nonetheless was part of a technical milieu in which synchronism was the focus of attention for telegraph engineers. In the early 1870s, Frenchman Bernard Meyer developed the first important synchronous multiplex for his own facsimile system.[46]

Because of the successful adoption and subsequent development of the Hughes and other high-speed systems, including multiplex telegraphs, duplexing played a smaller role in France. Indeed, Joseph Stearns was unsuccessful in his attempts to get the government to adopt his duplex system, even though trials suggested its practical possibilities. It was initially only effective on Morse lines, which, when traffic necessitated, were switched to the Hughes. It was not until after François Ailhaud worked out duplexing techniques for French submarine cables and transferred his own knowledge to the problem of duplexing the Hughes that duplex circuits played any significant role in France.[47]

The larger technical environment of French society, combined with new electrical problems created by high speeds and the construction of submarine and subterranean telegraph lines to form a scientifically-oriented technical community concerned with electrical theory. From the beginning the French telegraph service had hired some scientifically educated engineers. The academically oriented engineering tradition of France led to the development of formal classes for operators and *inspecteurs* (those responsible for technical problems). And the scientific background required for advanced technical positions in the French telegraph service was much higher than in America or Britain.[48] The successful introduction of the Hughes printer from the USA occurred because French telegraph engineers were prepared to focus on the electrical problems of high-speed transmission. This in turn led to the development of Emile Baudot's sophisticated multiplex printing telegraph system, which combined features of Meyer's facsimile and Hughes's printer. At century's end the multiplex printing system was the basis of a line of technical development that would replace the standard systems employed in other countries.

Great Britain

Compared to the rest of Europe, the government in Great Britain moved into telegraphy relatively late (1868).[49] By the mid-nineteenth century Britain was the leading industrial nation with the most advanced market economy and its political system encouraged private enterprise and innovation. The telegraph was initially introduced there by business interests through joint stock companies. These telegraph companies found their first customers among the private railway companies, which quickly recognized the usefulness of the new technology for controlling railroad traffic, but they also began to transmit parliamentary and general news as well as government messages. Although the telegraph was only slowly adopted for general business or personal communication, commercial interests found the new technology essential to the conduct of business by 1851, especially since submarine cables then began to connect London with international markets.[50]

The private telegraph companies adopted new technology either to set their system apart from rivals or for reasons of economy. Thus the United Kingdom Telegraph Co. bought rights to David Hughes's printing telegraph and adopted Wheatstone's ABC dial telegraph, while the Electric Telegraph Co. experimented with Wheatstone's ink-recording automatic just prior to nationalization. These systems were developed internally. Nonetheless a few telegraph technologies were transferred from other nations. For example, by the mid-1850s the permanent record and speed provided by Morse recorders led to their introduction on some lines.[51]

The very importance of the telegraph for a wide range of users provided the impetus for state control, especially as criticism of high tariffs and poor service grew.[52] In 1868, Britain followed the dominant European model by transferring all land telegraph lines to the Post Office, creating a more universal telegraph system in Britain. It also produced a larger bureaucracy, including an engineering staff which became more hierarchical. The lowered news tariffs given to the press to curry favour for the nationalization act, and the costs of the larger system, encouraged the Post Office to seek technology that might increase efficiency.

The low rates for news led to a tremendous increase in press work by the Post Office and this influenced the decisions that were made concerning instruments. Whereas the private companies had sent about 6 000 words a day during the parliamentary session, by 1871 the Post Office found itself transmitting 20 000. Four years later a Treasury committee reported that the Post Office was losing money on its press work which 'heavily occupied' the lines, sometimes even at the expense of other messages. To meet the demand placed on its wires, the Post Office used the Wheatstone automatic, which also saw duty on other heavily trafficked lines. The Wheatstone achieved speeds of 60–120 words a minute, but each transmission also required time for punching the paper tape used in transmission and for translating the messages received by the ink-recorder.[53]

In 1873, the Post Office also investigated, although it did not adopt, the faster but less reliable chemical-recording automatic system developed by the American Thomas Edison. Edison's system was based on the automatic system originally developed by Bain in the 1840s and which had been used only briefly in both Britain and the USA. The engineers who investigated Edison's system believed that the faster chemical-recording system might be valuable under certain conditions. Because they objected to the battery Edison required for his system they began experimenting again with the Bain. The electrical problems created by higher speeds, as well as the problems posed by the chemical recording itself, led the Post Office to decide not to adopt such a system.[54] The Post Office did adopt another Edison invention – the quadruplex – and often used it as an adjunct to the Wheatstone automatic. The Wheatstone used half of the quadruplex circuit, the other half being left open for Morse messages.[55]

The ink-recording automatic proved well-suited to press work, where the most important problem was quickly and simultaneously transmitting long messages to several offices, but it was less suitable for many ordinary messages, where speed of delivery was more important. To meet much of its ordinary business the Post Office continued to rely for some time on needle telegraphs. This changed after a trip to the USA by Post Office engineer William Preece and controller Henry Fischer. Impressed by the Morse sounder system, Preece and Fischer recommended that the Post Office adopt it for ordinary messages. Their arguments echoed those commonly heard in the USA. They believed that the sounder system reduced errors because, when the ear has learned to read accurately by sound, the hand is sure to send accurately by sound, and this is invaluable, because where we have a good sound reader there we have a good sender, and the result is accuracy.[56]

Besides accuracy, which was also a product of its simple mechanical operation, the sounder also increased speed, 'as the clerk has not to glance his eye from one paper to the other, but simply write on as fast as he can ...' These advantages led to the widespread use of the Morse sounder system on British lines by the late 1870s.

The 1870s also saw a growing interest in multiple telegraphy in Britain. All of the systems employed in Britain were first developed in the USA. Besides the use of the quadruplex as an adjunct to the Wheatstone, duplex circuits became common. Personal visits by duplex inventor Joseph Stearns probably contributed to their introduction into Britain. They were initially more common on cable lines, which remained private in Britain.[57] Another American system that saw brief use was the synchronous multiplex telegraph system developed by Patrick Delany, which Preece saw in 1884 at the International Electrical Exhibition held in Philadelphia. Although the Delany system was only used experimentally in America, in part because it had significant problems on long lines, the British Post Office used the system at least into the 1890s.[58]

United States

Like Great Britain, from whose colonial empire it had been formed, the USA had an advanced market economy that encouraged private enterprise. As a result of its own political origins, the USA also had an even greater aversion to government interference in the economy. Nonetheless the telegraph was first introduced through government funding and initially used by the Post Office. The original Morse line demonstrated the practicality of the new technology, but not its profitability. The government refused to adopt the telegraph as a public enterprise, which is hardly surprising. By the mid-1840s, American development policy had generally turned away from direct public funding of internal improvement.[59]

As in Britain, the early development and expansion of the telegraph was achieved by competing joint stock companies, and competitive pressures and patent law encouraged the adoption of competing systems. In the USA Royal House's printing telegraph was first to challenge the Morse, with Alexander Bain bringing his automatic telegraph from Britain soon after. The Morse interests used the breadth of their original patents to stop the advance of the Bain, but the House system continued to compete. Ultimately the House had its most important role in enabling the Mississippi Valley Printing Telegraph

Co., using exclusive contracts with railways to enter new territory, to compete with and gain control of a number of Morse-licensed lines. The expanded company subsequently became the Western Union Telegraph Co., the dominant telegraph company after the American Civil War. Although its near-monopoly position led to calls for nationalization, this did not occur in the weaker regulatory atmosphere of American politics. When adopting new technology Western Union's principal concerns were increased efficiency and, most importantly, retaining the value of its existing plant and operating corps. When Western Union did develop and adopt technical improvements such as the first effective multiple telegraph systems it did so in the context of retaining the basic instruments of its Morse sounder system.[60]

Even more than in Britain, the telegraph developed in a highly commercial environment and businessmen became its principal users. Most telegraph authorities agreed that business use of the telegraph constituted about 80 per cent of total traffic and that even the bulk of press usage was for commercial and financial news. As late as 1887, Western Union president Norvin Green could claim 'that not more than two per cent of the entire population ever use the telegraph in one year, and not over five per cent of the revenues of the telegraph is derived from family and social news'. Telegraph official Marshall Lefferts had reflected upon this modest use by individuals 30 years earlier, noting that 'Citizens, as a general thing, have no conception of the amount of business daily transacted over the wires.' Both Green and Lefferts pointed to business transactions as the principal source of revenue for the industry, with newspaper copy an important but distant second.[61]

The nature of telegraph usage in the USA influenced the technology. Management's belief in the superiority of the Morse key and sounder system was sustained by a belief that it provided the most efficient means for meeting the needs of business customers. Messages could be sent almost immediately in the order in which they came to the office, without the necessity of preparing them for transmission or accumulating a backlog of messages in order to achieve economies of scale required by machine systems.[62] Furthermore the constant threat of lawsuits over transmission errors provided incentive to reduce such errors and led American telegraph officials to argue that the American Morse system reduced errors by allowing skilled operators to make corrections during the course of transmission.[63] Management's commitment to Morse technology also stemmed from a desire to preserve the investment that telegraph companies had made in the training of their operators. The only significant change in the system following the Civil War was the adoption of duplex and quadruplex forms of multiple telegraphy. These increased the number of messages that could be handled by Morse instruments on a single wire but did not radically alter the nature of the system itself.

Nonetheless attempts were made to introduce machine systems into the USA. Automatic telegraphs based on Bain's original chemical-recording system dominated American thinking about machine telegraphy. Yet proponents of automatic telegraphs made few inroads in competing with Western Union's universal system of service. If they had been willing to focus their strategy on the automatic's ability to compete for news service and other specialized businesses, such as night letters, proponents of automatic telegraphy might have carved out a market niche for this technology. Indeed Western Union adopted the relatively low-speed, ink-recording Wheatstone automatic in 1882 for press service and night messages in order to free lines for business traffic. The transfer was expedited by bringing over British operators familiar with the system. Even after its adoption in the USA the Wheatstone instruments continued to be made in London.[64]

Until the end of the century, the continuing dominance of the 'broker' or short business message in telegraph traffic reinforced the bias of American telegraphers towards the Morse system.[65] However critics believed that, by emphasizing the expeditious handling of broker messages, telegraph companies failed to attract more general business and social messages. Because other types of messages were longer, they were suitable for transmission by machine systems where high volume was more important than prompt handling. Speed was a secondary consideration for customers sending such messages, and the greater time necessary to prepare them for transmission and delivery would not obviate the advantages of higher transmission speeds.[66] By the end of the century, as competition from long-distance telephony began to change the market for long-distance communication, telegraph officials would rethink their commitment to the Morse system and respond more favourably to machine systems of rapid telegraphy, notably multiplex printing telegraphs similar to those long used in France.[67]

The commitment of American telegraph leaders to Morse technology sprang as well from their common origins within telegraph shop culture. System managers and engineers began their careers in the operating corps and were self-educated in electricity. They were immersed in the culture of the operators and committed to widely-held views that the 'knights of the key' were intellectually superior to most working men and women and to their fellow operators in Europe.[68] At the end of the century this attitude continued to inspire the expectation that the elite work-force of American operators would remain the principal source of managerial and engineering talent. But engineering rationalization combined with declining opportunities for advancement to reduce the incentive for the independent study of electrical science and technology which had been a hallmark of the many operators who became inventors, engineers and managers in the industry's first three decades. As a result, the subsequent transfer of high-speed printing telegraph technology was undertaken by those outside the American telegraph industry who were more familiar with European developments that relied on advanced electrical engineering science.[69]

CONCLUDING REMARKS

Telegraph technologies were often but not always transferred quickly, widely and with considerable ease. The problem is to identify on the one hand those conditions that made such transfers so readily possible, and on the other hand those factors that inhibited transfer in specific cases.[70]

We turn first to the general conditions which facilitated transfer. Technology's creation at the boundary of science and technology proved initially important. A scientific instrument-making tradition existed in all these countries and provided a group of mechanically skilled individuals that was already in touch with communities of electrical researchers.[71] As we have seen, the early introduction of telegraphy involved combinations of individuals with scientific knowledge and mechanical skill.

The emergence of new telegraph industries in each country contributed to the evolution of new technical communities which were crucial to the subsequent development of the technology. Because their job required literacy, it appears that from early on the operating corps contained a significant number of individuals with the education necessary to learn the basics about electricity essential to improving and extending the technology.[72] At the same time, the scientific instrument makers were supplemented by clockmakers who possessed the necessary skill in precision instrument making to contribute to the technical development of telegraph technology.[73] The literacy required of operators helped make telegraphy a technology with a strong reliance on literature as a source of knowledge that supplemented practical experience. Regardless of whether knowledge was gained through formal courses of study as in France or through self-education as in the USA, a growing literature provided the means to obtain it. By the 1850s, prominent members of the growing telegraph technical communities began to publish manuals detailing the history and operation of the various telegraph systems, and providing basic information about electricity. These books usually included details of the administration as well as the operation of European and American telegraphs; usually such information was obtained directly from foreign sources. Each country also saw the emergence of journals devoted to the new technology which contained similar material and also noted books on electricity and telegraphy to encourage further study. The technical community thus had access to a range of information on foreign as well as domestic telegraph developments. The spread of such information was actively promoted by national telegraph services and by the ITU.[74]

The nature of early telegraph technology contributed to its transfer as well. Though some of the early entrepreneurs, notably Morse, initially sought to keep knowledge about their systems secret, the necessity of hiring literate operators who either possessed or could easily learn the necessary electrical knowledge to keep the systems running made it difficult to keep knowledge of the technology proprietary. Unlike many industrial technologies that sought to replace skilled with unskilled labour, telegraphy remained largely a skilled occupation through much of the nineteenth century. The cost of building, maintaining and operating a large technical system such as the telegraph further contributed to its transfer. Entrepreneurs needed to open their system to decision makers in the government and railroad bureaucracies which financed the early lines. And government control of the new technology throughout Europe helped encourage the importation of alternative systems that provided better service; in Britain and the USA competitive pressures provided a similar incentive.[75]

These transfers took place inside a common civilization in which each country shared sufficiently similar bases of commercial and organizational experience. The telegraph could play many of the same roles in each, serving railroads, stock and commodity markets and newspapers, and often found the same firm as a customer at each end of the line. The common commercial structure of the international community was recognized by treaties explicitly declaring that the use of the telegraph was open by right to anyone. As soon as the technology was offered as a service to the public, rather than serving only as a tool for military, administrative and railroad work, extension of the network across as well as within borders was a positive development sought by all. The success of an international system in Europe encouraged standardization, at least on main lines handling international messages.[76]

Transfer was far easier under some circumstances than others. The initial introduction of any system offering the 'product' of instantaneous communications occurred fairly readily within the North Atlantic community, though resistance to possible economic dependence upon others could cause delay, as in France, where a locally designed and manufactured variation was introduced.[77] And as long as the level of investment in machinery and training in an old system or in a proposed new one remained relatively low, replacement was usually not a problem, as in the shift from needles to Morse in Germany. With the growth of nationwide telegraph lines, larger investments in personnel and material changed the context for adoption of replacement systems. Thus, even when an alternative was technically and commercially as good as an existing system, it was usually not adopted unless it offered special advantages. For an alternative system to replace one already in use the prospective advantages usually had to be very large indeed. Far more common was a pattern of displacement rather than replacement, with new technology being used for part of a system while older equipment was still retained for some uses. Thus, when the Hughes printer was adopted in France, Morse telegraphs continued to be used, often replacing older dial instruments.[78]

While transfer of telegraph technology was made possible by technical communities familiar with foreign developments and by institutions with incentive to adopt improvements regardless of their place of origin, specific systems were less easily transferred from place to place. Thus automatic telegraph systems met resistance in the USA but found widespread use in Great Britain. The Morse sounder system was adopted early in the USA and at a later date in Britain, but in Europe the ink-recording Morse was standard. In France, printing telegraphy spread quickly after its initial introduction and was transferred throughout Europe because governments were willing to form an international organization for international communication. In Britain and the USA, which required cable lines for international communication, such systems were not used on long-distance lines until the twentieth century. In each case the users of the telegraph and the kind of messages they sent were a major factor in determining the type of system adopted.

The relative importance of particular users was not only a product of economic factors, which are usually cited in discussion of technology. Political factors were also profoundly influential in determining who used the telegraph. While some attention has been paid to political factors affecting technology transfer in the nineteenth century, this has usually focused on attempts to encourage or discourage the general transfer of a technology.[79] At least in the case of telegraphy, our study suggests that investigations of the technical decisions regarding adoption of particular technical alternatives could be informed by attention to larger political contexts.

Such speculation reminds us again of the lack of a body of detailed studies regarding the decisions that were made in the adoption and retention of various telegraph systems by different states or firms. Much of what we have left out of our own brief survey is also essential for a general analysis of the movements of telegraph technologies. For example, international submarine cable telegraphy strongly influenced other telegraph technology, and also placed it in a global context. Telegraphy was the first science-based 'high technology' transferred between the industrial nations and also to developing countries.[80] In this, as in so much else, nineteenth-century telegraphy began a pattern that makes it an example of a kind of international technology transfer highly relevant to today's world.

NOTES

1. This point is made in Carolyn Marvin, *When Old Technologies Were New: Thinking About Electric Communications in the Late Nineteenth Century* (Oxford, 1988), who notes that the telegraph was 'as significant a break with the past as printing before it.' And 'all the communications inventions' since 'have simply been elaborations on the telegraph's original work'. Also see Keith Nier and Andrew J. Butrica, 'Telegraphy Becomes a World System: Paradox and Progress in Technology and Management', *Essays in Economic and Business History*, vol. 6 (1988), pp. 211–26; and Daniel J. Czitrom, *Media and the American Mind* (Chapel Hill, NC, 1982) ch. 1.
2. See, for example, David J. Jeremy, *Transatlantic Industrial Revolution: The Diffusion of Textile Technologies Between Britain and America. 1790–1830s* (Cambridge, Mass., 1981); Darwin H. Stapleton, *The Transfer of Industrial Technologies to Early America* (Philadelphia, 1986); W. O. Henderson, *Britain and Industrial Europe, 1750–1870* (Leicester, 1972); and Nathan Rosenberg, *Perspectives on Technology* (Cambridge, 1976), chs 8–11; and Nathan Rosenberg, *Inside the Black Box: Technology and Economics* (Cambridge, 1982), chs 11–12.
3. For submarine telegraphs see Vary T. Coates and Bernard S. Finn, *A Retrospective Technology Assessment: The Transatlantic Cable of 1866* (San Francisco, 1979); Charles Bright, *Submarine Telegraphs: Their History. Construction, and Working* (London, 1898); and Hugh Barty-King, *Girdle Round the Earth* (London: Heinemann, 1979), Keith Nier, 'The Paradoxical Progress of International Cable Telegraphy in the First Global Telecommunications Network', paper presented at Télécommunications, Espaces et Innovations aux XIXᵉ et XXᵉ Siècles, Les Territoires de la Communication, Paris, 1989. For urban telegraphs see Robert Rosenberg and Paul Israel, 'Intraurban Telegraphy: The Nerve of Some Cities', paper presented at the American Historical Association annual meeting, 1986.
4. George Prescott, *Electricity and the Electric Telegraph* (New York, 1877) p. 420. This quotation is itself a product of transfer. It is adapted from Robert Sabine, *The History and Progress of the Electric Telegraph* (London, 1867) pp. 36, 40.
5. Richard Schallenberg, 'Batteries Used for Power Generation during the Nineteenth Century', in *Proceedings of the Symposium on Selected Topics in the History of Electrochemistry*, edited by George Dubpernell and J. H. Westbrook (Princeton, 1978) p. 341.
6. Keith Dawson, 'Electromagnetic Telegraphy: Early Ideas, Proposals, Apparatus', *History of Technology*, vol. 1 (1976), pp. 113–22; James W. King, 'The Development of Electrical Technology in the Nineteenth Century: 2. The Telegraph and the Telephone', *United States Museum Bulletin 228* (Washington, DC, 1962) pp. 276, 279–80.
7. King, 'Telegraph and Telephone', pp. 277–81.
8. Ibid., pp. 282–8; Dawson, 'Electromagnetic Telegraphy', pp. 121–40.
9. At the University of Goettingen in 1833, C. F. Gauss, who had seen Soemmerring's apparatus in 1810, and his colleague Wilhelm Weber designed and established a needle telegraph for use between the university laboratory and observatory, but they also recognized the potential for more widespread application after officials of the Leipzig-Dresden railway attempted unsuccessfully to adapt the system to control railway traffic in 1835. It was at Gauss's request that Steinheil began working to improve their system and eventually developed his own. In his system Steinheil used the needles to provide simultaneously both an audible signal, through striking bells of different tones, and a written signal, through marking dots on a strip of paper. This was subsequently simplified by giving up the paper-marking aspect and using only bells. King, 'Telegraph and Telephone', pp. 282–4; Heinrich Schellen and Joseph Kareis, *Der Elektromagnetische Telegraph*, 6th edn (Braunschweig, 1888) pp. 380–9; Sabine, *History and Progress*, pp. 38–42; Theodor Karrass, *Geschichte der Telegraphie, erster Teil* (Braunschweig, 1909) pp. 143–4; Alvin Harlow, *Old Wires and New Waves* (New York, 1936), pp. 50–1.
10. Wheatstone 'continued to describe himself as a musical instrument maker' even after his

appointment and also appears to have remained connected with the family firm until 1848: Brian Bowers, *Sir Charles Wheatstone* (London, 1975) p. 9. On Wheatstone and Cooke also see Geoffrey Hubbard, *Cooke and Wheatstone and the Invention of the Electric Telegraph* (London, 1965); and King, 'Telegraph and Telephone', pp. 289–91.

11. Alexander Bain developed another version of a needle telegraph in Britain close upon the heels of Cooke and Wheatstone. This was not employed in Britain but was put into service, in a somewhat modified form, in Austria. Karl Edward Zetzsche, *Handbuch der Electrischen Telegraphie*, vol. 1, *Geschichte der Elektrischen Telegraphie* (Berlin, 1877) pp. 185–90. For descriptions of needle telegraph systems see Prescott, *Electric Telegraph*, ch. 32.

12. On Morse see Brook Hindle, *Emulation and Invention* (New York, 1981) ch. 4; and Paul Israel, 'From the Machine Shop to the Industrial Laboratory: Telegraphy and the Changing Context of American Invention, 1830–1920', PhD thesis, Rutgers University, 1989, ch. 2.

13. For descriptions of the Morse system see Prescott, *Electric Telegraph*, chs 30–1; and Taliaferro P. Shaffner, *The Telegraph Manual* (New York, 1859) ch. 32.

14. For Wheatstone's work see Bowers, *Wheatstone*, pp. 126–9; and King, 'Telegraph and Telephone', pp. 291.

15. There were many variations in the transmitters and receivers used with dials. For example, some employed a rotating dial moving past a stationary pointer, while others transmitted with a keyboard. In some cases printing telegraphs were used as receivers. In his *Electric Telegraph* (ch. 33) Prescott provides a considerable amount of detail about many of these variations.

16   For Bain's work see Charles K. Aked, 'Alexander Bain: The Father of Electrical Horology', *Antiquarian Horology*, vol. 9 (1974) pp. 52–60; King, 'Telegraph and Telephone', pp. 292–3. Later automatics changed the transmitter as well. For descriptions of automatic telegraphs see Prescott, *Electric Telegraph*, ch. 36.

17. On House's work see *Dictionary of American Biography*, s.v. House, Royal Earl'; George Prescott, *History, Theory, and Practice of the Electric Telegraph* (Boston, 1863) ch. 7; and James Reid, *The Telegraph in America* (New York, 1879) pp. 455–64.

18. For descriptions of printing telegraph systems see Prescott, *Electric Telegraph*, ch. 34.

19. In the USA, managers of the American Telegraph Co., which purchased rights to the new invention, discovered that the Hughes required further improvements, since the mechanism would break down under heavy use. To solve this, the company employed George M. Phelps, a Troy, New York, manufacturer, who devised an electro-motor governor that improved the synchronism and redesigned the gearing of the typewheel shaft and printing mechanism. Phelps also replaced Hughes's keyboard with one similar to that of House, thus giving the instrument its name – the 'combination printer'. For Hughes and Phelps, see Prescott, *Electric Telegraph*, pp. 139–52; and Reid, *Telegraph in America*, pp. 405–6.

20. The development of multiple telegraphy is discussed in Schellen and Kareis, *Elektromagnetische Telegraphe*, pp. 775–863; Prescott, *Electric Telegraph*, chs 38–9.

21. He introduced the use of condensers where compensation for the inductive capacity of a telegraph line was needed; this was similar to arrangements applied for other purposes in submarine cable telegraphy.

22   For Stearns see Israel, 'Machine Shop to Industrial Laboratory', pp. 193–4, 197–8. For Edison see Keith Nier, 'The Perplexing Fate of the Quadruplex', *Proceedings of the American Historical Association, 1986*, microfilm (Ann Arbor, MI, 1987); and Prescott, *Electric Telegraph*, ch. 40. For French development of synchronous multiplex systems see Andrew J. Butrica, 'From *Inspecteur* to *Ingénieur*: Telegraphy and the Genesis of Electrical Engineering in France, 1845–1881', PhD thesis, Iowa State University, 1986, ch. 3.

23. Semaphores also appear to have been used on the North Sea coast of northern Germany for communicating shipping information. Volker Aschoff, 'Frühe Anfänge der Telegrafie im norddeutschen Küstenraum', *Archiv für deutsche Postgeschichte*, no. 3 (1979) pp. 66–73; Geoffrey Wilson, *The Old Telegraphs* (London 1976); Shaffner, *Telegraph Manual*, chs 2–4.

24. See Richard John, 'The Origins of Commercial Telegraphy in the United States, 1844–47' *Technology and Culture* (forthcoming).

25. Cooke and Wheatstone tried without success to interest the Admiralty and Morse similarly tried for early support from railroads.

26. Determining who used the telegraph in each country is extremely difficult. The most commonly available statistics use aggregate figures giving the total number of messages, sometimes broken down by domestic and international messages or by messages per population or per wire. One report that does contain some statistics broken down by type of message suggests that by 1870 commercial messages were the most numerous everywhere. What varied was the percentage of such messages in relation to others, particularly government and press business: Robert Lines, 'Report on Telegraphs and Telegraphic Administration', in *Reports of the Commissioners of the United States to the Vienna International Exhibition. 1873* (Washington, DC, 1876) Table 3.

27. Information on German telegraph history can be found in a variety of sources, few of which directly address the issue of transfer. See Volker Aschoff, 'Frühe Anfänge der Telegrafie im norddeutschen Küstenraum', *Archiv für deutsche Postgeschichte*, no. 3 (1979) pp. 66–78; Johannes Bruns, *Die Telegraphie in ihrer Entwicklung und Bedeutung* (Leipzig, 1907); Julius Dub, *Die Anwendung des Elektromagnetismus mit besonder Berücksichtgung der Telegraphie* (Berlin, 1863 and later editions); Michael Geistbeck, *Der Weltverkehr. Seeschiffahrt und Eisenbahnen. Post und Telegraphie in ihrer Entwicklung dargestellt*, 2nd edn (Freiburg im Breisgau, 1895) pp. 465–525; Richard Hennig, *Die Älteste Entwicklung der Telegraphie und Telephonie* (Leipzig, 1908); Theodor Karrass, *Geschichte der Telegraphie, erster Teil*, (Braunschweig, 1909); Wolfgang Klein, 'Aus der Entwicklung der Elektromagnetischen Telegrafenapparate', *Archiv für deutsche Postgeschichte*, no. 2 (1979) pp. 147–65; Gustav Schottle, *Der Telegraph in administrativer und finanzieller Hinsicht* (Stuttgart, 1883); Rita Seidel, 'Von der electrischen Telegraphie zur Elektrotechnik. Zur Genese einer wissenschaftlichen Disziplin. Hanover als Beispiel', *Zeitschrift der Universität Hanover*, vol. 11 (1984) pp. 39–47; Heinrich Schellen, *Der Elektromagnetische Telegraph* (Braunschweig, 1850 and later editions); Horst A. Wessel, 'Der Einfluss des Militars in der staatlichen Telegrafie', *Archiv für deutsche Postgeschichte*, no. 3 (1979) pp. 86–98: and Zetzsche, *Handbuch der Electrischen Telegraphie*.

28. Morse wrote a letter to the American ambassador to Austria, the most significant German country at that time, insisting that Robinson was not an authorized representative. He did not oppose the decisions of various German states to adopt the system, but sought a reward for his inventive efforts, which he eventually received from a consortium of European countries. Klein, 'Aus der Entwicklung'; Werner Siemens, *Inventor and Entrepreneur: Recollections of Werner von Siemens*, trans. W. C. Coupland (New York, 1968) pp. 41–53, 71–83.

29. Christina Jungnickel and Russell McCormmach, *The Intellectual Mastery of Nature: Theoretical Physics from Ohm to Einstein*, vol. 1, *The Torch of Mathematics* (Chicago and London, 1986) pp. 275–82.

30. On the formation of the ITU see George Arthur Codding, Jr., *The International Telecommunication Union* (Leiden, 1952; reprinted New York, 1972) pp. 13–33, 38–76; and Anthony R. Michaelis, *From Semaphore to Satellite* (Geneva, 1965) pp. 43–9. Also see Nier and Butrica, 'Telegraphy Becomes a World System'.

31. Michaelis, *Semaphore to Satellite*, pp. 57–9, 80.

32. Samuel F. B. Morse, 'Examination of the Telegraphic Apparatus and the Processes of Telegraphy', in *Reports of the Commissioners of the United States to the Paris Universal Exhibition, 1867* (Washington, 1869) p. 125.

33. The polarized relay was a significant technical development that played an important role in telegraph designs. For example, see Reese V. Jenkins, et al., (eds), *Papers of Thomas A. Edison: Volume 1. The Making of an Inventor* (Baltimore and London, 1989).

34. Although Wheatstone never credited him, Siemens believed that Wheatstone's puncher was based on his own. Siemens, *Inventor and Entrepreneur*, p. 159.

35. Seidel, 'Telegraphie zur Elektrotechnik'; Jungnickel and McCormmach, *Intellectual Mastery*, pp. 217–18, 255.

36. Butrica, ' From *Inspecteur* to *Ingénieur*', pp. 12–21; Paul Charbon, 'Le Choix du Premier Appareil de Télégraphe Électrique Français', *L'électricité et ses consommateurs* (Paris,

1987) pp. 77–104. We have relied on Andy Butrica's recent dissertation, which provides the best history of French telegraphy. His bibliography provides a wealth of resources for the study of telegraphs in France, including older technical and historical accounts in French similar to those available in German.

37. Jacques Attali and Yves Stourdze, 'The Birth of the Telephone and Economic Crisis: The Slow Death of Monologue in French Society', in *The Social Impact of the Telephone*, edited by Ithiel de Sola Pool (Cambridge, Mass. and London, 1981) pp. 97–103.

38 Lines, 'Report on Telegraphs', Table 3; Morse, 'Telegraphic Apparatus', p 121.

39. Butrica, 'From *Inspecteur* to *Ingénieur*' pp. 51–5.

40. This information comes from Butrica, 'From *Inspecteur* to *Ingénieur*' pp. 55–6. He was unable to determine what problems the railroads experienced with the Wheatstone instruments.

41. Ibid., pp. 55–60.

42. Ibid., pp. 60–7, 78, 87, 132–3.

43. Ibid., pp. 78–9.

44. Morse, 'Telegraphic Apparatus', p. 121.

45. Ibid., pp. 77–83; *Telegraphic Journal*, vol. 3, pp. 110–11.

46. *Telegraphic Journal*, vol. 3, pp. 83–108.

47. Ibid., pp. 112–15.

48. Even manufacturers, with their practical mechanical training, received some scientifically-oriented education. Thus Bréguet audited classes at the Ecole Polytechnique and his son graduated from there. In their shop the Bréguets offered science-based technical training for their workers. Those associated with other manufacturers also attended classes at the Ecole Polytechnique, the Ecole centrale des arts et manufactures, or the Association Philotechnique. On French telegraph operators and engineers see Butrica, 'From *Inspecteur* to *Ingénieur*'; Butrica, 'Telegraphy and the Genesis of Electrical Engineering Institutions in France, 1845–1895', *History and Technology*, vol. 3 (1987) pp. 365–7; and Shaffner, *Telegraph Manual*, pp. 773–6.

49. The only substantial history of the British telegraph system is Jeffrey Kieve, *The Electric Telegraph in the U.K.: A Social and Economic History* (Newton Abbott, 1973) . As the subtitle suggests, however, technology gets short shrift in this work. Information about nineteenth-century British telegraph technology can be found in Shaffner, *Telegraph Manual*; Sabine, *History and Progress* (1867, 1872): and William Preece and J. Sivewright, *Telegraphy* (London, 1879 and later editions).

50 Kieve, *Telegraph in UK*, pp. 47–52.

51. Ibid., pp. 81–4.

52. In particular, critics faulted the telegraph companies for not providing more numerous offices and service to all towns, which they believed could be accomplished by placing telegraph service under the direction of the Post Office. The national press, dissatisfied with high tariffs and poor quality in the transmission of news, helped to lead the crusade for nationalization. See ibid., chs 6–7 on nationalization.

53. For the press subsidy see ibid., pp. 216–19; on the speed of the Wheatstone see Jenkins, *Edison Papers*, p. 150, n. 8.

54 Jenkins, *Edison Papers*, pp. 591–9.

55. Nier, 'Fate of the Quadruplex', p. 8.

56. Preece, *Recent Advances in Telegraphy* (London, 1879) p. 21.

57. Information on the adoption of duplex telegraphy and of Stearns's role probably exists in the files of the Post Office Archives and in the Cable and Wireless Archives. While Post Office engineers such as Preece played a crucial role in the transfer of telegraph technology into Britain, the use of duplex circuits on cable lines was initiated by engineers associated with the privately owned cable companies. These same engineers were important to the transfer of cable technology all over the world, including Europe and the USA. It was cable rather than land-line technology that proved the most significant British contribution to the transfer of telegraph technology in the nineteenth century. On British telegraph engineering see Bruce Hunt, '"Practice vs. Theory": The British Electrical Debate, 1888–1891; *Isis*, vol. 74 (1983) pp. 341–55; William J. Reader, *A History of the Institution of Electrical En-*

gineers. 1871–1971 (London, 1987); Rollo Appleyard, *The History of the Institution of Electrical Engineers (1871–1931)* (London, 1939); Edward C. Baker, *Sir William Preece, F.R.S.* (London, 1976); and William Preece, 'On the Advantages of Scientific Education: A Lecture Addressed to the Telegraph Staff', *Journal of the Society of Telegraph Engineers*, **1** (1871), pp. 266–76.

58.   Little is known of the Delany system in Great Britain, although there is doubtless material in the Post Office Archives. By 1906 it had disappeared from the manuals: Thomas E. Herbert, *Telegraphy: A Detailed Exposition of the Telegraph System of the British Post Office* (London, 1906). The influence of Meyer's and Baudot's work on Delany also bears investigation. Information on Delany's multiplex can be found in William Maver, *American Telegraphy: Systems, Apparatus, Operation* (New York, 1892) p. 343; William Maver and Donald McNicol, 'American Telegraph Engineering – Notes on History and Practice', *AIEE Transactions* (1910) vol. 29, p. 1312; Edwin Houston, 'Synchronism', ibid. (1884) vol. 1, paper no. 4; Edwin Houston, 'The Delany Synchronous Multi-Plex System of Telegraphy', ibid. (1884) vol. 1, paper no. 5; Thomas D. Lockwood, 'Electrical Notes of a Transatlantic Trip', ibid. (1889) vol. 6, p. 412; and Pamphlet of the Standard Multiplex Telegraph Co., c. 1884, Engineering Societies Library, New York.

59.   For the history of the American telegraph industry see Israel, 'Machine Shop to Industrial Laboratory;' Harlow, *Old Wires and New Waves*'; William Thompson, *Wiring a Continent: The History of the Telegraph Industry in the United States, 1832–1866* (Princeton, NJ, 1947); and John, 'Origins of Commercial Telegraphy'.

60   Israel, 'Machine Shop to Industrial Laboratory', chs 2, 5.

61.   Norvin Green to Postmaster General William Vilas, 17 November 1887, Green letterbook No. 8, pp . 427–33, Secretary's Office, Western Union Telegraph Co.; Marshall Lefferts, 'The Electric Telegraph; Its Influence and Geographical Distribution', *American Geographical and Statistical Society. Bulletin*, vol. 2 (1857) p. 251; Richard B. DuBoff, 'Business Demand and the Development of the Telegraph in the United States, 1844–1860', *Business History Review*, vol. 54 (1980) pp. 459–79.

62.   Although dials would have also permitted operators to correct messages during transmission, they were never used extensively in the USA on long-distance lines because they were so much slower than the Morse.

63.   William Orton, who was president of Western Union in the 1870s, even argued that the transmission of telegraph messages called for a very different kind of invention than that demanded by the normal processes of mass production. It was his belief that

>   In all probability the telegraph will never run itself. Human intervention will always be necessary to some extent. The errors which, it seems to me, dreamers upon these subjects fall into, result from the attempt to treat ideas, and the intangible processes of their transmission to a distant point, as physical things to be disposed of in bulk by the application of mechanism and power.

Orton to James D. Reid, 21 September 1869, Orton Letterbook No. 6, pp. 405–10, Secretary's Office, Western Union Telegraph Co.

64.   Western Union engineers Thomas T. Eckert and George Prescott first brought Wheatstone instruments from Britain in 1874, but the company felt little incentive to adopt them. By the 1880s, President Green, who like Orton believed that business messages were the mainstay of the company and who held similar opinions on the failure of automatic telegraphy to meet the requirements of such service, nonetheless felt automatic telegraphs could play an important role in press service (Israel, 'Machine Shop to Industrial Laboratory', p. 219). On Western Union's adoption of the Wheatstone see Reid, *Telegraph in America*, pp. 735–6 and William Finn, 'Wheatstone Automatic System', *The Telegraph Age* (1894) 14, pp. 468–71 (this article was the last of a series by Finn on the Wheatstone automatic, a typescript of which is located in the Western Union Collection, National Museum of American History, Smithsonian Institution).

65.   Estimates placed 'broker' business at 40 per cent of the total volume of telegraph traffic. Patrick Delany, 'Rapid Telegraphy', *Transactions of the International Electrical Con-*

gress St. Louis, 1904, 3, pp. 464–5; discussion of Louis M. Potts, 'The Rowland Telegraphic System', *AIEE Transactions*, **26** (1907) pp. 539–46; discussion of William B. Vansize, 'A New Page Printing Telegraph', ibid., **18** (1901) pp. 37–43.

66. Such an argument was made by Patrick Delany, a telegraph inventor at one time connected with the Automatic Telegraph Co. which promoted Edison's automatic system. Delany developed another system of automatic telegraphy in the 1890s which also failed to compete successfully with Western Union, although it was used about 1910 for a letter service known as Telepost. Israel, 'Machine Shop to Industrial Laboratory', p. 220.

67   Ibid., pp. 252–5, 272–3.

68. In his memoirs Werner Siemens, the noted German electrical engineer, noted the 'simplicity of Morse's apparatus, the relative facility of acquiring the alphabet, and the pride which fills every one who has learnt to use it, and which causes him to become an apostle of the system.' (Siemens, *Inventor and Entrepreneur*, p . 82) American operators, however, also took pride in their ability to 'read' by sound and in not relying on machines to record the message.

69. Those responsible for the new systems were electrical engineers whose profession and professional training was dominated by the newer physics-based electrical technologies of telephony and electric lighting (see Robert Rosenberg, 'Test Men, Experts, Brother Engineers, and Members of the Fraternity: Whence the Early Electrical Work Force?', *IEEE Transactions on Education*, **27** (1984) pp. 203–10. In his dissertation, 'Machine Shop to Industrial Laboratory', Paul Israel discusses the evolution of American telegraph engineering. He demonstrates that American telegraph engineers and inventors tended to focus on mechanical rather than electrical aspects of their technology. Although the latter were not ignored, they were not advanced theoretically as in Europe. To a large extent this was owing to the negligible influence of cables and high-speed telegraph systems in the USA. One product of the American preoccupation with mechanical design, in combination with the strong commercial character of the telegraph market, was the extent to which telegraphs were designed for use by non-expert operators and introduced for a variety of purposes to speed communication amongst businessmen in the large cities. Only fire and police alarm telegraphs used by municipalities saw widespread use by non-expert users in the cities of Europe (Rosenberg and Israel, 'Intraurban Telegraphy').

70. Much earlier discussion of technology transfer has little bearing on telegraphy, suggesting a need significantly to modify some assumptions. The same sort of need turns up repeatedly when sweeping claims about communications developments are considered in regard to the history of telegraphy. Some recent works with this problem are James R. Beniger, *The Control Revolution: Technological and Economic Origins of the Information Society* (Cambridge, Mass., 1986); Peter Hall and Paschal Preston, *The Carrier Wave: New Information Technology and the Geography of Innovation, 1846–2003* (London, 1988); Jennifer Daryl Slack, *Communication Technologies and Society: Conceptions of Causality and the Politics of Technological Intervention* (Norwood, NJ, 1984); and Brian Winston, *Misunderstanding Media* (Cambridge, Mass., 1986).

71. Even in the USA, which had the weakest scientific community, a regional instrument-making tradition connected to a small community of electrical experimenters played a significant role in the early development of electric telegraphy. Israel, 'Machine Shop to Industrial Laboratory', pp. 112–14; Robert Post, *Physics Patents, and Politics: A Biography of Charles Grafton Page* (New York: Science History Publications) pp. 9, 18, 29, 37, 40; Daniel Davis, *Manual of Magnetism* (Boston, 1842 and later editions).

72. This is apparent from two recent dissertations: Butrica, 'From *Inspecteur* to *Ingénieur*'; and Israel 'Machine Shop to Industrial Laboratory'.

73. Jewellers and silversmiths may also have played a significant role. See Jenkins, *Edison Papers*, p. 8.

74. Even Western Union directly promoted the diffusion of such knowledge through its *Journal of the Telegraph*.

75. The manufacture of telegraph equipment was in many ways a different story, which we cannot go into here, but even in this case the play of economic nationalism was remarkably limited.

76. This may apply to non-communications technology such as containerized shipping as well.
77. Outside the common culture, where independence was preserved, rejection of such dependence could be more total, as in China. See Zhong Zhang, 'The Transfer of Networks Technology to China: The Destruction of Woosung Railway and Foochow Telegraph', Society for the History of Technology annual meeting, 1986.
78. It appears that national telegraph services were also more willing to operate with several telegraph systems on various parts of an overall system than were American corporations concerned with competitive pressures. As we have seen, Western Union was characterized by its use of Morse sounders and keys on the vast majority of its lines, while many European nations used Hughes printers on some lines, Morse on others, dials on others, and so on. This may be related to the willingness of national systems to undertake large capital outlays for new systems for social or political reasons even if the economic 'pay-off' was not immediate.
79. See, for example, the case of textiles. Jeremy, *Transatlantic Industrial Revolution*; Carroll Pursell, Jr., 'Thomas Digges and William Pearce: An Example of the Transit of Technology', *William and Mary Quarterly*, vol. 21 (1964) pp. 551–60.
80. Imperialism, formal or merely economic, has been seen as retarding some manufacturing technology transfer but it tends to encourage transfer of telegraphy. See Daniel Headrick, *The Tools of Empire: Technology and European Imperialism in the 19th Century* (New York and Oxford, 1981); and David Headrick, *Tentacles of Progress: Technology Transfer in the Age of Imperialism. 1850–1940* (New York and Oxford, 1988).

7. International Technology Transfer in Telephony, 1876–1914*

James Foreman-Peck

The telephone provided a completely new service; conversation at a distance. Previously, rapid long-distance communication was reliant upon the electric telegraph, primarily suitable for conveying information or messages rather than conducting interchanges. Technical progress in telephony before 1914 increased the number of potential conversationalists, extended the distance over which discussions could take place, improved the quality of the sound transmitted and reduced the time necessary to set up a call.

Equipment embodying substantial and commercial technical improvements tended to be manufactured in the USA where telephony was more popular than anywhere else in the world. Similar ideas were patented and tested elsewhere but typically they were not developed to the same extent. It was from the USA, then, that most telephone technology was transferred to the rest of the world in the years 1876–1914, despite the considerable technological base in the related telegraph industry in Western Europe.

The diffusion process was a continuous one because a large market for telephone services and rapid expansion in the USA encouraged continuous improvement in telephone equipment and therefore in the quality and the cost of service. The transfer was not accomplished merely by the export of telephone apparatus and by visits to the USA to see how the telephone system there incorporated the latest advances. By the 1890s there was overwhelming political pressure in the major importing nations of Europe to manufacture their equipment domestically. A foreign company therefore had to establish a subsidiary if it wished to sell in Europe and even then a domestic company supplying less advanced equipment might be preferred. Politics not only dominated the source of telephone equipment but also the volume. The extent to which new technology was incorporated in the telephone network, and the size of the network itself, were constrained by governments, either directly through the control of procurement, investment and pricing, or indirectly by regulation.

As their telephone networks developed, other nations, in particular Britain, Sweden and Germany, began to catch up as sources of technology, by

122

importing foreign enterprise (especially Western Electric's British subsidiary), by a belated response of indigenous companies (in particular Mix & Genest, Siemens & Halske, and Stock in Germany) or by the rapid growth of multinational enterprise, in the case of Sweden's L. M. Ericsson. Patents were a barrier to industry entry during the early years. They do not, however, seem to have greatly slowed the international spread of the technology itself, although in at least some instances they did restrict national diffusion of the technology as embodied in the telephone service. Both because the primary concern is with the transfer, rather than with the generation of technology, and because US telephone history is a relatively well-ploughed field, American developments are largely ignored in this chapter, except insofar as they impinge upon the rest of the world.[1]

The first section outlines telephone technology before the First World War, describing the principal innovations: the carbon microphone, the multiple switchboard, dry core cables, the central battery system and automatic switchboards. This series of process innovations enhanced the service so much as to amount to product innovations; as the service improved more people (primarily business people) wanted it. The quantitative record of the international spread of telephony, discussed in the second section, is therefore a measure of the progress in and adoption of telephone technology. To a lesser extent, the volume and direction of trade in telephone equipment is an indication of the extent and direction of technology transfer.

The third section describes how the early US telephone patents were worked abroad, including the role of the Bell Antwerp factory in spreading US technology. The remaining four sections deal with telephone technology export, import and absorption respectively by the United Kingdom, Germany, France and Russia and Austria–Hungary, from the 1890s until the First World War.

TELEPHONE TECHNOLOGY[2]

From the beginning, telephony was the sending and receiving of verbal messages by electrical impulses simulating speech patterns through wires. Very quickly the potential of the invention began to be realized with the introduction of the telephone exchange, which switched calls between subscriber lines. The basic components of the technology then were:

1. transmitting and receiving apparatus on the customers' premises (the telephone instruments);
2. switching equipment (the exchange);

3. the line and power sources which transmitted the electrical signals (the transmission equipment).

The principal innovation was based upon Alexander Graham Bell's 1876 US patent. All subsequent widely adopted improvements in the technology before 1914 (Table 7.1) originated in the USA, although sometimes parallel developments occurred in Europe. Bell was born in Edinburgh in 1847, emigrating first to Canada in 1870 and then to the USA, where he was appointed Professor of Vocal Physiology in Boston University in 1872. Bell's interest in both electricity and speech combined in the telephone, for which he was granted a patent (that ultimately gave rise to several hundred court actions) in 1876.

Table 7.1   Development of telephone technology, 1877–1914

Date	Instruments (CPE)	Exchanges (Switching)	Transmission
1877	Bell receiver		
1879	Carbon microphone Blake, Hunnings		
1880s		Multiples	Metallic (two-wire) circuits
1890			Dry core cable
1891	Solid-back microphone		
1893		Step by step automatic	
1895	Dry battery		
1899			Inductance coil loading
1905		Common or central battery	
1911		Rotary automatic	

Note: In the nature of technology, as the text will show, these dates are rather arbitrary. Equally this is true of the classification of the common or central battery system as an exchange, rather than an instrument, innovation.

Telephone Instruments

Sound waves from speech were transmitted to a thin iron disc which, vibrating close to an electromagnet, produced a fluctuating electric current in two coils. The currents flowed along a line and round the coils of the second instrument or receiver. They produced magnetic effects on the receiver magnet, increasing or decreasing its attraction of the disc. The vibrations of the second disc therefore mirrored those of the first, generating a similar, though weaker, sound. The 1877 Bell receivers were satisfactory enough, as witnessed by the 570 000 of this model that were made.

Because the line inevitably introduced losses, the already weak signals could only be transmitted over short distances. The next fundamental innovation was therefore the carbon microphone, which used a stronger electric current from a battery. Vibration of the carbon in response to sound waves altered the resistance of a contact, passing a fluctuating current to a receiver which reproduced the original sound. Thomas Edison quickly filed a US patent for a carbon transmitter in 1877, tested in England the following year in a call between the Norwich and London offices of J. & J. Colman.[3] Edison also invented a chalk receiver (loud speaker) in an attempt to avoid Bell's patent. His nephew reached England with this device in March 1879. David Hughes, a Londoner who was teaching in America (Kentucky), in a paper of May 1878 described a microphone, which he did not patent. This microphone formed the basis of many subsequent transmitters and avoided endless patent litigation.[4] At the end of the 1870s a curate at Bolton Percy near York, the Reverend Henry Hunnings, constructed a granular carbon transmitter. The American Bell Co. paid Hunnings £1 000 for the transmitter, first used by the Globe Telephone Co., and which eventually displaced all others. Hunnings was aided and advised by a telegraph engineer, Cox. Messrs Harrison, Cox, Walker & Co. lost an action by the Bell patentees in 1882 to prevent them making and selling telephone receivers constructed with a horseshoe magnet and the Hunnings granular carbon transmitter, until the expiry of the patents in 1890 and 1891.

The Bell view was that the Hunnings carbon principle was not very successful because 'packing' of the carbon granules reduced the quality of the transmission with the passage of time. White's solid back microphone resolved this difficulty for Bell and 930 000 of the 1891 model were made for local battery use (see below). This improvement extended the scope of telephony, but not sufficiently for the US Bell system to adopt handsets.

The US Bell system held out against the European demand for these combined receiver and microphone sets until after the First World War, on the grounds that they offered too low efficiency and unstable performance for the 3 000 mile conversations of which the Bell system was capable. Long-distance communication required powerful transmitters since there was little that could be done to improve the signal attenuation with distance of the line. The handset forced the microphone into a number of positions, to which wall and desk sets were not subject, in which efficiency was reduced by carbon noise and acoustic feedback through the handle.

It is apparent that no sophisticated technological base was necessary for the early telephone, certainly nothing more than was already available in every country with a telegraph system. On reading Bell's account of his telephone in *The Scientific American* of September 1876, the Bedford brothers in Leeds replicated his results over 30 yards in October.[5] The technology became more complex as its usefulness was extended, but the initial innovation spread extremely rapidly, so that had domestic conditions been right, and patent laws permitted (as they did in Germany), any industrial country could have quickly caught up and overtaken the USA in telephony.

Exchanges

In January 1878 the first public telephone exchange was opened in New Haven, Connecticut. The following year, the first British telephone exchange opened. Not until 1881 did France and Germany acquire theirs. The early telephone connected only a small number of subscribers who could be dealt with by one operator. Each subscriber's wire passed through an indicator which signalled when a subscriber rang up the exchange, and terminated at a small jack or spring on the switchboard. Any pair of subscribers could then speak to each other if their jacks were connected with a flexible wire by the operator. As networks increased, the size of a switchboard could not increase commensurately because the length of the operator's arms did not. The standard position of 1880 took only 50 lines. Some accommodation could be achieved by communications between operators but in a large exchange matters could quickly become chaotic.

The solution of the 'multiple', developed between 1878 and 1885, was to provide several duplicate switchboards, each containing termination points for every customer in the exchange. Each line therefore had a number of jacks. Smaller jacks increased the number of connections an individual operator could make, eventually up to 10 000. These 'multiple' boards divided subscribers into groups of about 200 each served by one operator. Each operator's panel contained the indicators only for their 200, but jacks for all the subscribers in the network. Every subscriber's wire passed from panel to panel. Trunk wires for connecting different districts also came to jacks on each panel.

The first (horizontal) multiple switchboards used in Great Britain were invented by FBO Hawes, an official of the United Telephone Co. Two switchboards were manufactured in the United's workshops, one being fitted towards the end of 1883 and the other at the beginning of 1884.[6] Also in 1884 the American Bell subsidiary, Western Electric, installed a 1 000 subscriber vertical board at the Liverpool Cotton Exchange.

Since more than one connection could be made to the same subscriber at any time, 'multiples' needed a 'busy' test. The first solution was a target board that all operators could see and on which each would signify connections they had current. In 1883 Scribner, an employee of the American Bell system, patented his busy 'click' test, whereby the operator cord touching the subscriber's jack sleeve would click if the line was engaged.

Until the late 1890s, telephone systems generally operated with wet local batteries for speech and 'holding' currents. High-voltage low-frequency current was suitable to provide ringing current over lines with high resistance. The disadvantages of wet batteries attached to the subscribers' phone were their bulk, costly replacement and maintenance and the damage their fluids caused if spilled. Dry cell batteries removed this last disadvantage but were still bulky and had uncertain effective lives. Hand-cranked magnetos were, in the 1890s, typically part of the telephone subscribers' apparatus to signal the operator to set up and to terminate the conversation. (This last operation was often forgotten, so that lines remained apparently engaged for long periods, to the annoyance of other would-be callers.) A similar generator was employed at the switchboard to call subscribers. Reliability was increased and maintenance costs were reduced by the central battery (CB) system. This eliminated the need for magnetos or the necessity to maintain batteries on each subscriber's premises. In 1893 the Hayes central battery system was introduced in Lexington, Massachusetts and a larger-scale CB system was in use at Worcester, Massachusetts three years later. Bristol gained the first European CB exchange in 1900. Exchanges in Brussels and Mannheim followed in 1902. From around 1905 central battery systems could be installed widely because of more efficient line construction.

Moreover a willingness, at least in the USA, to construct a larger number of smaller exchanges reduced the length of wire connecting the average local caller to their exchange, further reducing the resistance in the line and enhancing the viability of low-current central battery exchanges. Even so the Western Electric view in 1911 was that local battery exchanges were more suitable for exchanges with under 100 subscribers. Central battery systems permitted the introduction of automatic signalling to the exchange by a caller, the use of lamps at the exchange to identify the call instead of drops, and the use of lamps as an engaged test.

Large manual switch boards required a substantial amount of organization and discipline of the work-force to operate them. These organizational skills had to be learned or imported in the same way as the manufacturing technology.

The next generation of switching equipment was the automatic exchange, based on Strowger's 1889 US patent, but not in use until 1893. The Strowger system was expensive because of the need for a switch to hunt over all subscribers' line termination points in the exchange in order to make a connection. Keith's line switch of 1906 markedly reduced these costs. According to the official National Telephone Co. history, Dane Sinclair invented the first automatic switchboard used in Britain.[7] Norway had experimented with very small-scale automatics earlier in the 1890s but judged them unsatisfactory.[8] In Germany, domestically developed equipment began operating in 1908 at Hildsheim.

Conventionally the first European automatic exchange was that installed in Amsterdam by the (Chicago-based) Erikson brothers in 1898 (when there were 22 in operation in the USA) and not until 1912 did Britain receive an automatic. There are a number of possible explanations for this lag in the adoption of the new type of exchange, but early experiments do not indicate simple inertia. Most probably the limitations of the first products used in Europe built up a resistance that was slow to change when improvements were made. In addition political uncertainties constrained the British telephone company from investing in new technology between 1905 and 1911.

The automatic switch was pioneered in the USA, but outside the Bell system, most probably because it was among the independents which served the small rural communities that such switches were most appropriate. Wanting to catch up the Automatic Electric Co., with its step-by-step Strowger exchange, Western had been working on rotary and panel systems. European administrations were also interested in automatics and so Bell decided to sell the rotary model in Europe, although the system was judged inappropriate for Bell's own use. Manufacture began in the London plant, with the first 800-line exchange being installed in Darlington in October 1914. After the war, production was moved to Antwerp, since the British Post Office abandoned that type of design.

Transmission

Earth returns in telephone transmission systems generated too much cross-talk and the increase in electric trams during the 1890s caused interference. Two-wire circuits therefore replaced the old (single-wire) system by the end of the nineteenth century in the more advanced networks. Granular transmitters, more powerful than the Blake, could not be introduced until transmission had been converted to metallic circuits because the greater inductive effect created a babble of background noise. Although overhead wires showed little tendency for the current to weaken with distance, underground wires were often required by municipal authorities. Adjacent underground wires insulated with gutta percha,[9] or oil-impregnated cotton, and their lead sheaths, attenuated the higher-frequency components of message currents, causing a loss of clarity in the reproduced speech, until suitable insulating materials were employed.

Paper proved remarkably effective, as long as the interior of the cable remained dry. By 1884, J. H. Wortendyke, a Virginian paper manufacturer, together with an employee, E. D. McCracken, had insulated telegraph cables with helical paper strips. Two years later McCracken and associates founded the Norwich Wire Co. to make both telegraph and electric lighting cable, using McCracken's own patented paper-lapping technique.[10] Lead-covered air/space (dry core) cables with the copper wires loosely wrapped in paper, proposed by W. R. Patterson of the American firm Western Electric in 1890, greatly facilitated the use of underground lines. Transmission efficiency was improved fourfold. Lead sheathing, together with plumbed joints, ensured the paper remained dry enough to function as an insulator. Loading cables with inductance coils further increased the distance over which messages could be sent in 1899, thus expanding the scope for trunk telephone conversations.

THE INTERNATIONAL SPREAD OF TELEPHONY

America's continuing ability to generate the telecommunications innovations that it transferred was based upon the strongest telephone demand in the world. Comparing the 7–8 000 calls a day made in Chicago of 1879 with the slower take-up in London, W. H. Preece from the British Post Office suggested the shortage of domestic servants to run messages in America, relative to Britain, was a large part of the explanation. Others focused on the great distances between American major population centres and the desire by business to save time, or the absence of a state telegraph monopoly anxious to prevent the emergence of competition.[11]

Table 7.2 shows that at the end of 1880 the USA was employing more than 26 times as many telephones as the next most intensive telephone-using nations, the UK and Canada. A spin-off was substantial export sales. In the year ending February 1881, almost one-quarter of the 66 763 Bell telephones produced were exported and the following year the proportion had risen to one-third, of an output of 109 349.[12] How important state monopoly could be in constraining telephone development may be judged by the fact that Italy had more phones than Germany at the end of 1881, and also more than France the following year, despite a lower level of economic development. The German bureaucracy, however, soon conceded the merits of the telephone and allowed the Post Office to push ahead with modernizing Germany's telecommunications. Von Stephan, the German Postmaster, installed telephones on rural telegraph circuits as early as 1877 and planned the opening of an exchange in Berlin the same year, but the proposal was delayed by the Police Authority until

1881. Well before the end of the decade, Germany was more fully equipped with telephones than Britain.

Early demand was primarily for business use. A London directory of 1895 shows considerable numbers of stockbrokers, manufacturers, agents, whole-sale dealers, solicitors, hotels and theatres, but few social, political and artistic names; Sir Arthur Sullivan was unusual in his milieu in having access to a telephone.[13]

According to Brock, the slowing pace of expansion of telephony in America between 1884 and 1894 indicates the contribution of patents to the spread of telephony in the USA.[14] In 1885 the USA had nearly three times as many telephones as Europe, yet by 1890 Europe had almost drawn level (Table 7.2). An alternative or additional explanation is technological. The solid-back microphone, dry core cable and the multiple switchboard transformed best-practice telephony in the 1890s, in terms of the quality of sound, the distance over which messages could be sent and the size of networks that could be efficiently handled. European expansion in the later 1880s was catching up with the rapid adoption of the first generation of telephone technology on the other side of the Atlantic. A synthesis of the two positions is that the onset of competition in the USA encouraged technological developments. After the expiration of the Bell patents in 1893, independent US telephone companies entered the scene and American expansion proceeded much faster than in Europe. The founding of at least two major US suppliers of automatic exchanges, Strowger Automatic Telephone Exchange (1892) later Automatic Electric Co., and Stromberg-Carlson (1894), date from this period. By the outbreak of the First World War the USA accounted for more than three-fifths

Table 7.2   *The international spread of telephones, 1880–1913 (000s)*

	1880	1885	1890	1895	1900	1905	1910	1913
World	59	225	475	845	2 490	6 200	11 270	14 600
USA	54.3	156	233.6	310	1 356	4 127	7 956	9 542
Canada	2	9	20*	38	52	107	284.3	499.7
GB	2	14	46	100	200.2	427	648.8	780.5
Germany	–	15.6	59.3	131.7	286.7	593.5	1 068.8	1 420
France	–	7.3	23†	34*	69.5	137.7	232.7	330
Sweden	–	5.7	16.9	45	80	124	187.4	233
Europe	–	60*	210*	460	890	1 726	2 966	4 012

Notes
*=estimate, †=1892.
Source: W. H. Gunston, 'Comparative Telephone Statistics', *The Telegraph and Telephone Journal* (November 1931) pp. 25–27.

of the world's telephones. No country approached the level of telephone penetration achieved by the USA.

What determined the optimum rate of introduction of the telephone and spread of associated technological improvements? Could the inter-country differences identified in this chapter all be the best adjustment to national circumstances? Or could European economies reasonably have aspired to the American achievement?

Rapidly rising incomes will encourage a faster rate of introduction of telephony, other things being equal, and new plant is likely to embody the latest advances. These effects could be somewhat attenuated by the system nature of the technology which created substantial technological interdependences between components of the telephone network. But they were not greatly apparent in the USA when New York was converted to common battery working in three years at the turn of the century.[15] This entailed changing all the instruments as well as the exchanges. If business did not so strongly demand telephones in Europe as in the USA because of conservatism, adequate postal and telegraph services, a lower value of time, or more abundant labour, national telephone administrations and regulatory regimes cannot be condemned for inertia. On the other hand business complaints in parts of Europe do suggest some failure somewhere.

Profit-maximizing introduction of new process technology in a steady state depends upon the rate of depreciation of existing equipment and whether the new technology reduces total costs of operation below the variable costs of the old. If European administrations insisted on more durable equipment than in the USA, that would slow their relative rate of introduction of advances. But most innovations enhanced the quality of the service and therefore raised additional considerations. What mattered was the willingness of customers to pay for improvements and their preparedness to tolerate inconveniences entailed by the introduction of the improved service. In turn these issues presuppose some method of assessing customer preferences, whether through the market, by survey or consultative groups. Conceivably the pace of intro-duction of the telephone could have been too fast and capital invested in telegraphy may have been wasted. Equally conceivable is that inappropriate technology could have been transferred between countries, given their differ-ing population dispersals, income levels and business habits, if US technology was imported unmodified. Without estimating a formal model, judgements about the optimality of the American path must be very limited. Even charting the transfers of technology is not without problems.

Table 7.3 offers some evidence on the magnitude of the transfer. Germany, the USA, Great Britain, Sweden and Japan all had positive balances of trade in telephone and telegraph equipment by 1913. Tariff protection was fairly low in all countries. Though the USA, Spain and Japan maintained moderately high levels of protection, in each case tariffs were insufficient to exercise much influence over the general direction of trade.

Table 7.3   *Imports, exports and tariffs: telephone and telegraph equipment,*
1913 (000s Reichsmark)

	Imports	Exports	Tariff (%) Telephone	Telegraph
Germany	614	11 246	5.2	4.0
France	8 100	2 953	10.6–7.4	6.5–3.8
Great Britain	3 093	5 922	0	0
Italy	2 020	46	2.1	1.6
Spain	3 002	–	21.1–14.1	16.2–10.8
Switzerland	706	122	8.4	6.5
Austria-Hungary	748	396	13.8–9.6	6.8
Sweden	–	7 149	11.2	11.3
USA	–	6 665	20	20
Japan	–	99	20	20

Source: League of Nations, *Electrical Industry*, Economic and Financial Section (Geneva, 1927).

If technology transfer were measured merely by trade in the products, Table 7.3 would imply that, by 1913, Germany was the principal source of telecom technology, and that France, followed by Spain, were the foremost recipients. More surprising is that Sweden exported a greater value of equipment than either the USA or the UK. This observation may be partly explained by the size of the Russian market Ericsson supplied and by the inability of Ericsson's Russian factory to satisfy local demand. Nonetheless the strength of Swedish comparative advantage in telephony compared with Britain's is remarkable in view of their relative stages of development and long-established British pre-eminence in telegraph cable technology. This is especially so given that these figures do not include sales of Ericsson's British subsidiary in the UK. Greater still is the distortion of the impression of true technology transfer conferred by trade data in the case of the USA. American multinationals were displacing trade in many advanced sectors. In telecommunications, where economic nationalism was given teeth by state purchasing for state telephone networks rather than by protective tariffs, the process was particularly marked. In short, the trade figures fail to reflect the very substantial technology transfer through US subsidiaries, of which Bell's were by far the most important.

THE EARLY METHODS OF US TELEPHONE TECHNOLOGY TRANSFER

In the early days of the telephone, complementarity between network operation and telecommunications manufacture was reinforced by the necessity for both functions to be licensed by the Bell patent holders. In 1881 all the separate companies manufacturing telephone apparatus under licence from the American Bell Telephone Co. (ABTC) were consolidated as the Western Electric Co. ABTC retained control, and when ABTC merged into American Telephone & Telegraph in 1899, Western Electric remained virtually the sole supplier to the Bell system. In the early 1880s Western also supplied much of the rest of the world with the equipment necessary to construct and operate their telephone networks.[16]

The sheer size and rapid expansion of the US market gave those manufacturing for it certain advantages from learning by using. Western Electric's domination of world telecommunications manufacture was, however, increasingly limited by state ownership of networks in Europe and by economic nationalism. These provided opportunities for local companies and, in the case of Ericsson, for multinational companies originating elsewhere than the USA. Economic nationalism required the state to buy from locally based companies. Even though Western Electric and Ericsson preferred to supply foreign markets from domestic factories, if they were to win contracts they were obliged to establish overseas branch plants. Some European companies had in any case acquired related technological skills in the telegraph industry and were well placed to enter the industry as competitors. Ericsson himself had begun in 1876 as a manufacturer of telegraph and electrical equipment. In addition the Bell concessionary companies abroad assumed much more independence from each other, at least as far as International Bell and Western Electric's overseas operations were concerned.

Control of the key telephone patents gave the Bell organization monopoly power over the spread of telephony on the supply side through much of the world before 1890. A number of vehicles for selling telephony were established. The early Bell technique of removing the capital constraint upon the diffusion of the telephone by licensing companies in different geographical areas, rather than by unitary expansion, was applied outside as well as inside the USA. The sole right to sell, use or lease Bell telephones outside the USA was at first granted to the Continental Telephone Co., which received its charter in Massachusetts on 7 January 1880 and was dissolved on 18 April 1894.[17] The first state to benefit from Continental's attentions was Brazil, where, on 13 October 1880, the Telephone Co. of Brazil was formed. By 1883 the company operated five exchanges with about 1 000 subscribers. Three telephone concessions were registered in Argentina in 1881; Gower-Bell, Bell and Pan

Telefono. These last two merged as the Compana Union Telefonica in 1883. Three years later they were taken over and reorganized by British interests as the United River Plate Telephone Co., the largest telephone Company in Argentina, with 7 000 of the 7 626 subscribers in 1896.[18] By 1914, Argentina's private system provided more telephones per head than did France's state enterprise, even though French living standards, and therefore telephone demand, were higher.

Founded, like Continental, in 1880, the International Bell Co. soon acquired the Bell patents for the smaller economies of Western Europe.[19] In 1882 or 1883 the Bell patents for Spain and Russia which the Continental Bell Telephone Co. had obtained were assigned to International in exchange for $200 000 of its stock. The patents turned out to be worthless and after constructing several exchanges, International Bell found itself in financial difficulties. These problems did not persist as International Bell obtained franchises in seven cities in Belgium, six in Russia, four in Holland, three in Italy, two each in Norway and Sweden and one each in Denmark and Switzerland. From 1885, International Bell began paying dividends, which from 1892 were substantial. Profits were so high that capital was repaid in order to avoid the political opprobium of the high dividends that could be distributed.[20] The other side of the coin was a restricted spread of the telephone that prevented the renewal of concessions, for example in Russia at the end of the century. The Bell concessionaire in the Netherlands similarly discredited private enterprise by retarded development, high prices and poor service, so that municipal enterprise took over when the concession expired. In Sweden, Bell's high prices were met by competition from Cedergren's Allamanna Telefon from 1883, and later from a state organization.[21]

American telephone technology came to France in three five-year concessions granted in 1879, to Gower, Blake-Bell and Edison systems. Before operations began in 1880 all concessions were obtained by the Société Générale des Téléphones. One way in which this company imported technological knowledge was in the person of R. G. Brown, former head telephone operator of the Gold and Stock Exchange in New York. In 1878, Brown had designed a handset with an Edison transmitter and a handle which served as a permanent magnet for the receiver. This design was later widely used in Europe, where L. M. Ericsson also claimed to have originated the device.

Telephone rates in France were higher than in the state-run German and Swiss systems and service was only extended to about 10 of the largest cities. In 1882 the telegraph authorities therefore decided they should extend telephony to medium-sized cities, beginning with exchanges in Rheims, Roubaix and Tourcoing in 1883. By 1889 the profitability of the telephone had persuaded the French government to assume a monopoly service.[22]

Neither Western Electric nor International Bell Telephone were able to penetrate the British market in the early years because of patent restrictions. James Brand registered the Bell Telephone Co. in the UK in 1878. The first telephone instruments were sold at £70 a pair and were made by the (British) Silvertown India Rubber & Gutta Percha Co. In 1879, with the introduction of the exchange system, the company ceased to sell instruments and instead leased them. The Silvertown company made the second exchange to open for the Bell interests, incorporating an automatic clearing signal transmitted to the exchange when a subscriber replaced the receiver. The Edison company was formed the same year to work the Edison patents. The two companies combined in 1880 under the name of the United Telephone Co. Bell had 400 subscribers at their London exchange and Edison 200. After 1890 the regional telephone companies were absorbed by the parent company under the title of the National Telephone Co. In seven years the United Telephone Co. proved very profitable on a small turnover; gross revenue exceeded £100 000 and profits were over £62 000.

Why it was so profitable may be seen from the experience of the competitor London & Globe Co. Receiving a licence in January 1883, the company was judged to be infringing the United Telephone Co's patent. At the end of 1884, United bought out Globe. No further entry occurred until 1891, with the expiry of the Bell patent. Then the Mutual Telephone Co., registered in January 1890, opened its first exchange in Manchester on 28 February 1891, using magneto telephones.[23] In contrast to the experience in Britain, Bell was unable to obtain a German patent. Siemens, already well established in telegraphy, and other companies, could therefore begin production and improvement of telephone equipment.[24]

As the first major telephone factory in Europe, established to supply the whole continent, Bell Telephone Manufacturing Co. (BTM)'s Antwerp factory played a special role in the diffusion of telephone technology. In 1881, Western Electric and Gardner Hubbard, on behalf of International Bell Telephone (IBT), agreed to establish a telephone factory either in Paris or Antwerp, in which IBT was to take 45 per cent of the shares and Western Electric, 55 per cent. The factory was not to supply competitors of either company, patents were to be pooled, and prices were to be fixed at American levels.[25]

Business in Antwerp was extremely profitable, like that of the monopoly European Bell operating companies of the 1890s. Customers of the Bell Telephone Manufacturing Co. were spread throughout the world (although the largest was Western Electric in London). Shipments in 1889 went also to Norway, Sweden, Denmark. Belgium, Netherlands, Switzerland, Germany, Hungary, Italy, the Netherlands, East Indies, Argentina and a small amount of equipment was even sent to the USA. The largest single item by value was

magnetos, accounting for more than one-third, followed by multiple switchboards (about one-sixth).

Germany and Britain were the principal overseas markets for Western
Electric. Until the telephone patent expired in 1890, Antwerp was a good
location from which to supply London. After 1890 some Antwerp work could
profitably be undertaken in London and therefore a large investment in
expanding Antwerp seemed inappropriate.[26] IBT and Western Electric agreed
on 17 July 1890 that IBT would sell all its interest in BTM Antwerp. BTM
would still supply IBT at competitive prices and IBT would buy all its
equipment from BTM or associated companies. A measure of the independence of the two organizations after the agreement is that in 1895 Western
Electric's Antwerp factory ignored a proposal from IBT to form a secret
combination in bidding for a Belgian contract.[27] The rise of economic nationalism meant that Antwerp's pre-eminence as a supplier of telephone technology
and equipment to Europe could not last. By 1914, Western Electric was the
most multinational of American companies, with nine plants in industrial or
industrializing countries.[28]

THE UNITED KINGDOM AS A SOURCE OF, AND DESTINATION FOR, TELEPHONE TECHNOLOGY

The UK was in a peculiar position in relation to telephone technology.
Although a world leader in telegraph cables, she lagged in telephone technology, primarily because of a demand that was severely constrained by domestic
political conflicts and subsidized telegraphy. Even so, Britain's central place
in world trade, and the influence which that and the Empire conferred, soon
enabled her to export technology to countries outside the Empire, as well as to
be a major importer.

Western Electric's UK subsidiary, although not manufacturing until 1898,
bid successfully for contracts within the British sphere of influence, including
some with Latin American telephone companies owned by British capitalists.
The Chile Co. bought their Valparaiso switchboards from Western in 1895. On
behalf of Western Electric, J. E. Kingsbury opened an office in Sydney in 1895,
branches were established in Johannesburg and Buenos Aires, and agents
appointed in India, Egypt, Portugal, the Straits Settlements and other countries
within London's territory. Export contracts went to supply the West Indies and
Rumania. The bulk of the London orders, though, were for the National
Telephone Co., and much of Western Electric's Antwerp factory output in the
mid-1890s was for London.[29]

Economic nationalism was rising even in the home of free trade by the end
of the century. Western Electric decided that they could not hope to continue
to win British Post Office telephone orders without manufacturing in the UK.

One of Western Electric's best pieces of business, by their London office in 1896, was the supply of a major contract for trunk line switch boards for the Post Office. The following year Parliament began an investigation into why such a large order was given to a foreign manufacturer. The Post Office decision to lay a 75-wire telegraph cable from London to Birmingham was only the first of the big contracts which Western hoped to obtain by a more visible British presence. They therefore planned to construct on the banks of the Thames a large building for manufacture and offices, that could be seen from the Houses of Parliament. In so doing Western were proposing a downgrading of their Antwerp factory to generate more business in Britain.[30]

Western Electric subsequently decided against acquiring a property in central London in 1897 because of the expense and unacceptable conditions attached to the lease. But Fowler-Waring Cables' offer to sell their North Woolwich plant supplied a satisfactory alternative.[31] The pay-offs proved slower than expected. Western experienced difficulty coming to terms with British labour productivity and delivery times.[32] Pumps ordered from Glasgow were unlikely to be ready within a year of the date of placing the order. In consequence costs were much higher than projected and losses were made. But the US management was inclined to accept the losses as an investment in entering a profitable market, especially as alterations to buildings were charged to current account. Although in July 1897 matters were set back by a fire, Western Electric's position in the British market was boosted by the National Telephone Co's contract for the purchase of Western Electric's common battery switchboard.[33]

The second multinational company source of technology for the UK was the Swedish L. M. Ericsson. L. M. Ericsson opened a sales office in London in 1898 to serve a market which was already taking about half of their telephone equipment output.[34] A new company to purchase the Beeston factory was formed jointly by Ericsson and the National Telephone Co. in 1903. British Ericsson was to limit its field of operations to the British Isles and those parts of the British Empire in which the company did not already have a significant presence; Australia, New Zealand, South Africa and Egypt were excluded. At the end of 1911, when Ericsson acquired the whole business, they decided to allow a British equity stake in the firm, but the parent company maintained a majority interest.

Ericsson were not solely importers of innovations into Britain; they were also employed for their manufacturing know-how. Ericsson accepted an order for 100 000 telephones from Dane Sinclair on behalf of the National Telephone Co. in 1898. But when Sinclair left in 1903, to be succeeded by Frank Gill, Gill opted for Western Electric's central battery system and redirected the order to Western Electric. Gill maintained that the Western Electric exchange system was unsuitable for use with L. M. Ericsson handsets. All Ericsson phones therefore had to be changed for American models, with separate receivers and microphone, at the same time as the adoption of the central battery system. The Ericsson Beeston factory was allowed to make phones for the National Telephone Co. but these were required to be fitted with solid-back microphones manufactured by Western Electric.[35] Ericsson's exports to the UK, which had reached about £120 000 by 1900, were gradually eliminated as Beeston's capacity expanded, until by the second decade of the century only about 10 per cent of the company's sales came from Stockholm. Later still th. UK imported some German technology through Siemens. Siemens only decided to enter telephone manufacture in 1910, although they had made telegraph cable since the founding of the British subsidiary in 1858.[36] In 1912 their new factory was complete. Siemens & Halske had acquired the German Strowger patent rights and developments in the technology began to reach the British company, who quickly made their own advances. The most important was the Siemens 10-point pre-selector. The company's first British patent on automatic switching was taken out in 1913.

Indigenous telephony innovation capacity was also enhanced at about the same time by GEC (though it is worth noting that GEC's principal founder, Hugo Hirst, was a Bavarian Jew).[37] GEC had made telephone instruments and small switchboards, but with the impending Post Office take-over of the network, agreed in 1905, they saw their big opportunity. 'The GEC represented to the Post Office that the prospect of patriotic buying would lead to the establishment of a new branch of the British electrical manufacturing industry. After a phase of natural hesitation, the Post Office agreed to use British material, and the result was the development of telephone works in Great Britain not only by the GEC but by other interests.'[38] GEC imported technological expertise. An American was hired as managing director of a new subsidiary, the Peel Conner Telephone Works in Salford, to take over existing telephone work of GEC. An engineer from Western Electric's Antwerp factory was appointed Chief Engineer for his knowledge of central battery exchanges. The first Post Office contract was received in 1907 for the Glasgow central battery exchange.[39]

Individuals as well as companies imported and exported technological ideas and expertise. A flow of telephonic pilgrims from Britain visited the USA throughout the period. G. H. Robertson, a Liverpool cotton broker, who in conjunction with J. B. Morgan had established Liverpool's first telephone exchange, visited the USA in 1884 to examine telephonic progress there. On Robertson's return, he set up the Western Counties and South Western Telephone Co.[40] After a short trip to the USA in 1888 the manager of the Northern District Co. adopted the American eight-wire arm as standard practice.[41] In 1888 the (American) Norwich Wire Co. made a telephone cable designed by J. A. Barrett of the American Telephone and Telegraph Co. J. B.

Atherton of Liverpool visited their Harrison, New Jersey factory and acquired the British rights, forming the British Insulated Wire Co. in 1890. Between 1899 and 1906 the General Manager of the National Telephone Co. visited the USA on four occasions, each time bringing back with him large quantities of equipment.[42]

The earlier British expertise in telegraphy provided a basis for technological export to Japan during this period, and those involved frequently moved later into telephony. Formerly employed by the Indian telegraph service, William Ayrton became Professor of Physics and Telegraphy at the College of Engineering in Tokyo between 1873 and 1878. On his return to England he held chairs in Applied Physics and Electrical Engineering in London, where he taught many future telephone engineers before his death in 1908.[43] Similarly Dane Sinclair went from the Telegraph Department of the North British Railway Co. to Japan between 1875 and 1880, for which work many years later he was awarded the Order of the Rising Sun Third Class (the highest Japanese order that could be given to foreigners). Sinclair became Engineer in Chief to the National Telephone Co. in 1882 and General Manager of British Insulated Cables in 1902.[44] Rudimentary British expertise was exported to Italy as early as 1881–5. With the formation of the Anglo-Continental Telephone Co., the 21-year-old Richard Shepherd was sent to establish telephone services in Turin and Florence. He was obliged to improvise almost every item of equipment, since virtually nothing suitable was available locally, nor was it sent from the UK.[45] In 1888, the Sultan of Zanzibar was the beneficiary of British telephone expertise.[46] Later technological knowledge was usually exported by Western Electric, once their UK manufacturing base had been established. The head of Western Electric's London telephone department visited Portugal in 1901 and was responsible for the early operation in Lisbon and Oporto of common battery exchanges.[47]

Skills in operating telephone systems as well as in providing the equipment were needed. Lilian Dakers transferred from being the National Telephone Co.'s Clerk in Charge at Bolton, Lancs, to the same position at the Alexandria exchange in Egypt.[48] Other British personnel controlled the operation of the Istanbul exchange during the early years of the First World War.

An indication of the technological level of the British telephone system towards the end of the period can be gleaned from the National Telephone Co.'s 1911 inventory (Table 7.4). The 167 local battery exchanges of over 300 lines were obsolete by US standards. The British government's decision, in 1905, to acquire the NTC's assets in 1912 offered a disincentive to investment in best-practice technology since there was some doubt about compensation levels. Even before 1905, uncertainty about the future may have been created by the 1896 nationalization of the trunk lines. Less than half the company's lines were worked by central battery systems. Transmission capital was of greater value than instruments and switchboards and a large proportion of transmission line was still bare wire. Investment in up-to-date equipment had then been less than ideal because of the political environment in which the private company had operated. In turn that created a weaker demand for plant which did not encourage domestic manufacturing.

Table 7.4   National Telephone Co.'s telephone plant and operations, 1911

	Number	Replacement cost (£)
Central battery exchanges	67	1 589 527.6
Local battery exchanges		
(over 300 lines)	167	792 980
(under 300 lines)	1273	259 811
Total	1507	2 642 364
Subscribers' apparatus		3 759 393.968
Underground plant conduits		2 840 755
cables		3 276 666.617
Overhead plant poles and standards		2 614 444
bare wire		3 348 650
aerial cable		1 017 055.378

NTC operating statistics, one day in July 1911	
Direct lines	260 171
No. of operator positions	2 509
No. of lines per position	104
No. of calls per direct line	9.5
Central battery switch	
direct lines	117 000
Hand restoring indicators	98 238

Sources: British Post Office Archives, Post 84/101, Post 84/123.

GERMANY

Germany was a world leader in electrical equipment in this period but was at first hampered by the conservatism of the state bureaucracy. Once the German authorities had approved state telephone exchanges, the Post Office was, to begin with, determined to have the best technology, tested by experience and made to last. They were prepared to pay what that cost. Despite an early advantage in the field, Siemens & Halske failed to keep up with progress in telephone technology. In 1888, later than the first installations in the UK,

Western Electric won the order for equipping Berlin and Hamburg with multiple boards. Within Western Electric, the President emphasized the necessity for the German subsidiary to be run by German speakers so the Post Office would not be conscious that the equipment was made in America. Subsequently a factory for mounting the switchboards was established with the help of a Post Office official. Since pressure also to manufacture switchboard cable in Berlin was applied, a few pieces of machinery were sent over from the USA.[49] By mid-January 1890, the Hamburg office, with 550 subscribers, was operational and the Berlin office was ready to open.

Western Electric's technological expertise continued to generate business in Germany throughout 1890. At least $200 000 of switchboard work was on hand and 150 were employed in the Telephon Apparat Fabrik. Expansion across the road was planned to eliminate night work, to allow in cable machinery and to reduce overcrowding.[50] The German competitor products were less advanced. Siemens's board, for instance, had no provision for a busy test and one could not easily be provided.[51]

Siemens & Halske's deficiencies in the telephone technology created an opportunity for other German enterprises. Stock, a former toolmaker employee of Siemens & Halske, mass-produced components for telephone exchanges, drawing upon L. M. Ericsson's expertise. In 1893, Stock (later Deutsche Telephonwerke) won contracts for three large telephone exchanges. Founded in 1879, Mix & Genest at first specialized in private branch exchanges. Then they too drew upon Swedish engineering knowledge and were awarded German Post Office contracts. Felten & Guillaume were long-established, internationally competitive cable manufacturers.[52] Western Electric began permanently manufacturing in Germany as the only means of continuing to receive orders. Once indigenous manufacturers were established, Western Electric were regarded as foreigners whom officials wanted to freeze out, although occasionally they were thrown a sop. By 1895 the German Post Office preferred to pay higher prices for poorer-quality products made in Germany.[53] Nonetheless the prospect of a complete rebuilding of the Berlin system to cope with the increasing number of subscribers and the impact of the projected electric railway on grounded telephone lines tempted Western Electric to form a genuine German company to get local people to use local influence.

Local German telephone apparatus production boomed in the 1890s, rising by 386 per cent from 1.75 million marks in 1890–1 to 8.5 million marks in 1898, overtaking lamp output. Within Germany, Siemens & Halske had begun supplying the Brazilian market in 1890, having defeated the American competition, but their new 10 000-line exchange, displayed in 1896, failed to win German or Austrian Post Office orders. By the turn of the century an innovative call indicator and expanding demand contributed to a restoration of their market position, but Mix & Genest were still the largest German telephone employers. Export prospects for German telephone equipment were as rosy as the production figures by 1897, when a report on the Amsterdam telephone service indicated a good reputation for the products; future equipment purchases were likely to be made in Germany since that country had made more progress in electric and telephone construction than England, the report stated.[54]

Less favourable judgements were made of the German telephone network, however. According to Lawes Webb, the chief characteristics of the German system were cheapness, conservatism and an unwillingness to disclose information. Single-wire overhead lines were maintained long after two-wire and underground systems were adopted in the USA and the UK. When underground cables were introduced in large cities they consisted of masses of single wires in one large iron pipe, instead of each cable being laid in a single duct. Technical mistakes were also made in switchboard practice and subscribers were allowed to install extension cables of all kinds and connect them to exchange lines. As magneto switchboards were gradually replaced by common battery boards, subscribers' heterogeneous installations had to be replaced. A great variety of equipment therefore existed side by side, by contrast with the US situation, and with a consequent loss of efficiency in the service.[55] The network tended to employ the products of German manufacturers, but did not do so invariably. In Munich most switchboards were supplied by Ericsson of Stockholm, microphones for subscribers and receivers by Friedrich Reiner of Munich and multiplex receivers by Frank Welles of Berlin (Western Electric). Most subscriber stations were still connected by single wires. All materials for Munich apparatus were made in Germany in 1897. Berlin instruments were based on dry cells and accumulators, all made in Germany, chiefly by a considerable number of Berlin firms.[56] On the other hand, despite Webb's criticisms, Munich had as many telephones per head as New York, and Stuttgart as many as Chicago, in 1902. This may not have been entirely owing to the efforts of the German telephone administration, though. Preece thought the effectiveness of the telephone service in Berlin compared with that of London was at least half due to the training and discipline of German subscribers. Magneto calling was introduced into 30 of the larger exchanges between 1892 and 1895. All new exchanges thereafter were fitted with those systems until the advent of the common battery. The German telephone administration limited the rate of modernization of the system with common battery operation by the growth of the system or depreciation of existing equipment, on the grounds that businessmen disliked the accompanying disturbance. Adoption of the automatic exchange, according to German officials, was constrained by the unsuitability of the form available in the first decade of the twentieth century to long distance traffic and systems with many private branch exchanges, but at least as important a contributor was the inexperience of the supplier. Ludwig Loewe & Co., a manufacturer of cartridges, acquired the European Strowger patent rights, excluding France and the UK, in 1901. After difficulties with the experimental automatic exchange at Hildesheim the Post Office asked Siemens & Halske to take over the development of automatic telephony for the German network. The company bought the Loewe patents and rapidly adapted and innovated on their basis.[57]

FRANCE

The French telephone system remained backwards and expensive throughout the period, primarily as a result of government policy. With a weak and erratic demand for equipment, the domestic manufacturing industry was uncompetitive, and therefore French innovation potential was poor. In consequence France was very much an importer of telephone technology. Nonetheless, although weaker than in Germany, there was a desire for national technological independence which militated against permanent reliance on foreign telecommunications subsidiaries. At the same time, foreign supply was a means of breaking domestic cartels.

In the longer term, the state system, established as a monopoly in 1889 because of poor private performance, proved unresponsive to public pressure. From 1900, French public opinion began to refer to a telephone 'crisis'. Germany spent more on expanding its telephone system in 1902 than the French proposed for three years after 1906. Yet by this last date the Parisian telephone system was clearly served by too few staff, with too few lines between exchanges and inadequate plant for the volume of traffic. An official reported to the French Parliament:

> Our telephone administration displays a sort of oriental fatalism. The Administration delights in reiterating that the French character, frivolous and effervescent, does not lend itself to a good telephone service! When the Administration is bombarded with questions and well-justified complaints, the only reply is that 'this is France and the telephone service will always be inferior here'.[58]

The 1907 commission on the budget listed improvements needed by the French network. Not only did the Parisian system need reorganizing and more long-distance lines required constructing, but metallic circuits were still needed to replace single wires, more modern telephones were required, as were more common battery exchanges, more multiple switchboards, longer night service and more public call offices. Lack of capital ensured that such improvements would not be made, but so did poor administration. The acquisition in 1904 of electrical instruments to detect line breaks, widely used in the USA, failed to reduce the average interruption of service due to accidental breaks in the line.

A failure to place fuses in telephone cables at the point where they entered the exchange, universal practice in the USA during the 1890s, was responsible for bringing to a standstill the telephone service of the principal business district of Paris when a surge of current almost completely destroyed the Gutenberg exchange in 1908. Broder blames the policy of the French Postal and Telegraph administration for the subsequent weakness of the Société Industrielle des Téléphones, the principal French telephone manufacturer.[59] Certainly official procurement was slow and uncertain, as Western Electric discovered. The French placed a sample order for Patterson (dry core) cables with Western Electric in 1890, but under extraordinarily optimistic terms. Western Electric was required to ship machinery to Paris and to find a factory site. Matters moved slowly because every order had to be signed by the Minister, a process which at best took a month or two.[60] Western Electric's Paris contracts were held up on the same economic nationalism of all the large European states. M Baron, the Vice President of the Congrès Télégraphique, and the principal Post and Telegraph official, told Aboilard (Western Electric's partner in Paris) that the Postes et Télégraphes was divided into two camps. The first wanted a system revised by one of their agents, M Mandroux, not on technical grounds, but because, if they adopted Western Electric's multiple system, they would be 'throttled' by the American company. The second group consisted of the technical men and the young ingénieurs who wanted the Western Electric system because it was the best.[61] Although Baron had indicated that a decision would be reached in 15 days, it was not. Western Electric's representative revised the estimate to 'within ten years'. 'The sensible officials deplore the exasperating slowness of their administration. But they can't help themselves', he wrote. But some orders were coming through, for cables and for 100 wire switchboards which were enough to pay the expenses of a Paris office, and perhaps an assembly shop.[62] M Baron announced, just before the summer vacation of 1890, that the lack of a Western Electric works in France meant that on political grounds he could not give the order for 50 kilometres of cable. He promised that, if Western Electric did establish a factory as soon as possible, he would keep them working on Patterson cables (5 kilometres at a time, for which he required no special credit). In addition Western Electric would get the contract for the Paris multiple (in November) and even for the Mandroux model, if the French tried it ('There is every reason to think that we want to spend our money so foolishly', remarked Baron). The Postes et Télégraphes had been 'regularly swindled' by the Société Industrielle des Téléphones and therefore would welcome Western Electric as an alternative supplier.[63]

Western Electric leased 3 150 square metres on the Avenue Bretouil behind Les Invalides to serve as offices and for small-scale mounting of switchboards. An additional building was necessary for cable manufacture. The site was a short walk from the headquarters of the telegraph administration and very close to the telegraph storehouse. Western Electric would have preferred a smaller financial commitment but were unable to find suitable premises to rent.[64]

There was some speculation that Western Electric would have to manufacture entirely in France to win the multiple contract. Western Electric told Baron that that would nearly double the price for a 6 000-subscriber board. Baron assured him that if there were competition the matter might arise but, since there was none, Western Electric might import what components they chose. Western Electric then planned the split on a 50–50 basis, the woodwork, mounting, cables and connections being undertaken in France.[65]

Pressure to manufacture in France continued to be tempered by the administration's desire to buy at low prices.[66] Diversification of telephone equipment sources was motivated by a belief that existing suppliers operated a price ring. The French Post and Telegraph administration suspected that, in the bidding for the replacement telephone exchange in the Rue Gutenberg in Paris, burnt down in 1908, the established manufacturers had formed a cartel.[67] They therefore invited foreign tenders. Siemens & Halske bid but were unacceptable because they were German. L. M. Ericsson were approached and given the contract for the 6 300-line exchange. Ericsson delayed delivery to other customers in order to fulfil the French order rapidly, and thereby greatly enhanced their standing with the French Postes, Télégraphes, Téléphones (PTT). It was made clear to Ericsson, as it had been to Western Electric, that they would be unable to sell in France permanently unless they established a French factory. The Société des Téléphones Ericsson was formed in May 1911. A Paris businessman with strong Swedish business connections, A. van Minden, was elected chairman of the board. The Colombes (Paris) factory was completed in 1912.

RUSSIA AND AUSTRIA-HUNGARY

These vast but less developed empires were a large potential market for telephone technology imports, yet they were also high risk areas, for political reasons. Because of the political risk, the American company, Western Electric, was at first loath to go beyond exporting, as the host governments required, leaving the field open to L. M. Ericsson. Siemens & Halske operated considerable branches in both empires, that in Vienna employing 700–1 000 in the 1890s, and had been responsible for establishing much of the early Russian telegraph network in the decade after 1855. However, with diversification into electrical light and power equipment in the 1880s, the company had lost its position on the technological frontier of telecommunications. By 1913 they had recovered, but most of the 4 500 in Siemens & Halske's St Petersburg factories at that date were supplying light and power equipment. There were

indigenous Austro-Hungarian firms in telecommunications and Russia possessed some enterprises engaging in technologically related work. In both
cases, as in much of the rest of Europe, small, slowly growing national markets
proved an inadequate base for such firms to compete with established multinationals.

Within Western Electric there was a conflict of opinions over the desirabil-
ity of establishing plants in these empires. Their man on the spot, Welles,
maintained that marginal returns to Western Electric were higher in overseas
projects than in developing the US market. The new building projected in 1895
for New York would cost at least half a million dollars, whereas one-tenth of
that sum would be adequate to start another European branch. According to
Welles, money had to be invested in buildings in Europe for the 'moral effect',
as in the Paris project of 1890, but business prospects warranted the outlay.
Welles favoured a plant in St Petersburg, in part because it would deal a blow
to Western's principal competitor, Ericsson, in one of his major markets (and
also to a competitor in Antwerp). The International Bell concession would
expire in 1899 and would not be renewed, Welles (rightly) maintained.[68]

Russia possessed at least one company with the technological background
suitable for a joint telephone manufacturing venture with Western Electric.
Welles proposed collaboration with Heisler, a manufacturer of a French system
of rangefinders for the Russian Navy. Welles was impressed with the quality
of the Heisler plant's work: better than was possible in Western Electric's
Antwerp factory, he noted. Heisler was already projecting a telephone factory
of his own.[69] Kingsbury in London supported the project.[70] Enos M. Barton, the
telegraphist founder of Enos & Barton who became president of Western
Electric, was warier because of the medium-term political risks of economic
nationalism in Europe: 'The Company is not in a position to seek permanent
investments in distant foreign countries except under the prospects of prompt
and liberal returns and under circumstances that will promise a benefit to its
factories that are already established ...'[71] Barton preferred strengthening
Welles's potential partner in Russia, Heisler, to weaken Ericsson, and avoiding
permanent investment.[72] Russia was even further away than Austria–Hungary
(where Welles also favoured a subsidiary) and the administration was 'venal'.
Ultimately, despite Barton's misgivings, Western Electric took the plunge in
both markets.

Viewed from Sweden, Russia was quite close. The early Bell concessionaires
in Moscow, St Petersburg and Warsaw proved more concerned with profits
than spreading the telephone. The St Petersburg concession in 1901 was not
allowed to return to International Bell but was won by the municipality and
those for Moscow and Warsaw were obtained by the Swedish company SAT.
Each city was given a common battery system over the following four to five
years, which quintupled subscribers. An unusual difficulty faced by the

Russian long-distance service was the frequent interruptions between Moscow and St Petersburg caused by copper wire thieves.

From the 1890s, Russia was a major export market for Ericsson. Unlike Western Electric, Ericsson lacked a secure home market from 1896, when the network operators, Telegrafveket and SAT, decided to establish their own factories. Like Western Electric, Ericsson was under pressure from local post and telegraph administrations to manufacture locally. A Russian factory therefore looked increasingly attractive. In 1897, Ericsson began assembly in rented premises in St Petersburg and three years later the business was moved to a purpose-built property.[73] A Russian engineer was made responsible for technical management and for contacts with the Russian authorities. Negotiations for Russian orders were also facilitated by the appointment as chairman of the board in 1908 of the Swedish Consul-General in St Petersburg.

Not until 1904 did the Russian factory show a profit. Operations were disrupted by the civil disorders in 1906, but steady expansion resumed from 1907. Russian-based production could not satisfy demand and the proportion of Russian sales accounted for by imports from Sweden rose to 22 per cent by 1913. Russian Ericsson supplied apparatus to SAT's Moscow and Warsaw networks and to those of many other Russian towns. Between 1905 and 1914, Russian Ericsson sold goods of a value almost half that of the parent company's total.

Western Electric had been tempted by Welles's enthusiasm to enter the Austro-Hungarian market in 1895 when the government, having taken over the telephones, identified a need for big multiple exchanges, for which there was no properly equipped local factory. Welles began negotiating with a local firm, Czeija & Nissl (Nissl, in 1877, had experimented with the telephonic transmission of music in Vienna). Barton preferred the Vienna proposal to the St Petersburg, but only on condition that capital was not tied up until the order was definitely obtained.[74]

Austrian officials invited bids from Viennese firms, from the German firm of Stock, for whom German diplomatic pressure was being exerted, and from Western Electric, for samples. Whatever the outcome, the likelihood was that the samples would be used as copies for domestic manufacture. Western Electric entered their bid through Czeija & Nissl, who put in a request for all foreigners to be excluded, as a means of ousting Stock. After the Americans had supplied some exchanges, Siemens & Halske received a trial order in 1897. The equipment was withdrawn after six months and Western Electric again triumphed.[75] The Budapest telephone system was reconstructed in 1903 with a common battery plant of the best American type. Like the Germans, the Austrian administration began experiments with automatic exchanges in the first decade of the twentieth century, before the acceptance of the automatic in the UK but long after that in the USA.

Supported by valuable bank connections, Ericsson formed a Hungarian company in November 1911 and an Austrian company in January 1912. The companies took over the factories of telegraph and telephone manufacturers Deckert and Homolka, with whom a collaboration agreement for exchange equipment for central battery systems had been signed in 1908.[76]

With Western Electric, Siemens & Halske and LM Ericsson manufacturing subsidiaries, both the Russian and Austro-Hungarian empires almost entirely relied on foreign sources for the technology embodied in their telephone networks by 1913. Having achieved one telephone to every 200 persons by 1913, Austria–Hungary's wholly state-owned network scored higher than Russia's mixed system, where 60 per cent of the telephones were privately owned, with one for every 500 people. Average income per head, however, was perhaps as much as 40 per cent lower in the Russian empire than in Austria–Hungary.[77] That Russian telephone penetration was at a level comparable with that of Italy and Spain, both of which were rather more developed countries, suggests that the regime implemented at the turn of the century had improved Russia's absorption of telephone technology.

CONCLUSION

The pace of diffusion of telephone technology was limited only by the effective demand of the recipient economy. Profit-seeking multinational enterprise was willing to introduce best-practice technology, sometimes in conjunction with local manufacturers, as in Austria–Hungary, wherever a market could be found, patents permitting. The American Bell system was prepared to provide equipment that it did not use itself, such as the handset combining receiver and transmitter, and the rotary automatic exchange, when there was a demand in Europe. If insufficient host country skilled labour was available to operate the technology, source country personnel were readily available.

On the demand side there was some question as to how suitable automatic exchanges were in lower-wage economies or for small rural offices, but with this and the other major telephone innovations, the main motive for their introduction tended to be an improved quality of service rather than a reduction in costs. Such improvements extended the demand for service. Initially that demand was less when the telegraph, an efficient postal service and/or cheap messengers were readily available. But the principal constraint upon the spread of the telephone was the attitude of the state as embodied in the economy's legal framework.

Untrammelled way leaves facilitated the spread of telephones under either private or public ownership. Limitations on investment imposed upon state enterprise restricted the pace of diffusion in some economies, especially in

France, as did sheer inefficiency. A desire to protect an established state telegraph monopoly was not helpful, in Britain among other countries, once the telephone was seen as a competitor rather than a complementary device. Similarly an interest in encouraging national manufacturers, as in Germany, or in developing domestic employment and technology could have raised prices of equipment, or reduced the quality, and so retarded telephone development. It is in some combination of these influences on the demand side, rather than in supply-side factors, that an explanation for differing absorptions of telephone technology, and therefore also for variations in telecommunications penetrations, between states at similar levels of development before 1914 must be found.

NOTES

*An earlier draft benefited from comments of H. D. Bickley, Paul Israel, David Jeremy, Geoff Jones and Alan Smith, none of whom is responsible for remaining errors and omissions.

1. Three recent books have addressed various aspects of the early American telephone industry using Bell archive material: G. D. Smith, *The Anatomy of a Business Strategy: Bell, Western Electric and the Origins of the American Telephone Industry* (Baltimore, 1985); N. Wasserman, *From Invention to Innovation: Long-Distance Telephone Transmission at the Turn of the Century* (Baltimore, 1985); R. W. Garnet, *The Telephone Enterprise: The Evolution of Bell System's Horizontal Structure, 1876–1909* (Baltimore, 1985).

2. The following section is based upon the standard sources for technological history: J. Kingsbury, *The Telephone and Telephone Exchange* (London, 1915); F. C. C. Baldwin, *A History of the Telephone in the United Kingdom* (London, 1938); M. D. Fagen (ed.), *A History of Science and Engineering in the Bell System: Vol 1. The Early Years, 1875–1925* (New York, 1975); and R. J. Chapuis, *A Hundred Years of Telephone Switching, 1878–1978* (Amsterdam, 1982).

3. R. H. Robertson, *The Story of the Telephone: History of the Telecommunications Industry in Britain* (London, 1948) p. 15.

4. *The Telegraph and Telephone Journal*, (November 1927).

5. Ibid, April 1933.

6. *National Telephone Journal*, (November 1911).

7. Ibid, December 1911.

8. W. H. Preece and H. C. Fischer, 'Report on the German and Scandinavian Telephone Systems' (1896) British Post Office Archives, Post 3/21, pp. 3–4.

9. Gutta percha, resembling india rubber, was obtained from gutta percha trees, mainly in the Malay peninsula, Borneo, Sumatra and Ceylon. It is a leathery solid which, unlike rubber, is not flexible or resilient. In addition to the demand from electricity-using industries, deriving from its remarkable insulation properties, its resistance to acids gave gutta percha employment in chemical and glassworks.

10. P. V. Hunter and J. Temple Hazel, *Development of Power Cables* (London, 1956) p. 78.

11. Kingsbury, *Telephone*, p. 209. Preece's reference to his own preferences implies he is thinking primarily of communication within a building. S. W. Stratton, *Telephone Service of the United States* (Washington, 1921) p. 204.

12. Calculated from Smith, *Anatomy*, p. 161.

13. W. H. Gunston, 'Comparative Telephone Statistics', *The Telegraph and Telephone Journal*, (November 1931).

14. G. W. Brock, *The Telecommunications Industry: The Dynamics of Market Structure* (Cambridge, Mass., 1982).

15. H. Lawes Webb, *The Development of the Telephone in Europe* (London, 1911) p. 52.

16. Standard Telephone and Cable, *The Story of STC 1883–1958* (London, 1958) p. 4.
17. V. A. Berthold, *A History of the Telephone and Telegraph in Brazil 1851–1921* (New York, 1921) pp. 52–8.
18. V. A. Berthold, *A History of the Telephone and Telegraph in Argentine Republic, 1857–1921* (New York, 1921) pp. 25–7.
19. Lewis to Waterbury 27 October 1903, International Bell Telephone Co., Reorganisation 1903, AT&T Archives, Box 1260. Mira Wilkins, *The Emergence of Multinational Enterprise: American Business Abroad from the Colonial Era to 1914* (Cambridge, Mass., 1970) pp. 49–51.
20. Welles to Barton 27 November 1903, Box 1260, AT&T Archives New York.
21. H. Lawes Webb, *Development*, pp. 60–2, 70–2, 74–6; Preece and Fischer, 'Report' (1896).
22. A. N. Holcombe, *Public Ownership of Telephones in Continental Europe* (Cambridge, Mass, 1911) pp. 269–75.
23. Robertson, *Story* pp. 15–34; C. R. Perry, 'The British Experience 1876–1912: The Impact of the Telephone during the Years of Delay', in I. de Sola Pool (ed.), *The Social Impact of the Telephone* (Cambridge, Mass, 1977); *The Post Office: An Historical Summary* (HMSO, London, 1911).
24. G. Siemens, *History of the House of Siemens* (Freiburg/Munich, 1957) I, p. 130.
25. V. A. Berthold, *A History of the Telegraph and Telephone in Chile* (New York, 1924) pp. 27, 30.
26. P. Young, *The Power of Speech: A History of Standard Telephones and Cables, 1883–1983* (London, 1983) p. 9.
27. Welles to Barton, 8 February 1897, AT&T Archives Box 1311.
28. Wilkins, *Emergence*, pp. 212–3.
29. Barton to Hudson, 13 August 1888, AT&T Archives.
30. Barton to Hudson, 1 April 1895, ibid.
31. WE Co. London Cable Factory, (Directors' Minutes 24 November 1897), Ibid Box 1311. The price was £87 000; £20 000 cash and 4 per cent bonds for the balance. Fowler-Waring Co. was established by John Fowler of Leeds to manufacture concentric-conductor cables (which were relatively immune from interference from mains electricity), developed by R. S. Waring of Pittsburgh.
32. Barton to Hudson, 16 March 1899, AT&T Archives Box 1311.
33. Young, *Power*, p. 16.
34. A. Attman, J. Kuuse and U. Olsson, *L. M. Ericsson: 100 years* (Stockholm 1978) I, p. 197.
35. Ibid., p. 201.
36. J. D. Scott, *Siemens Brothers, 1858–1958* (London, 1958) p. 68.
37. R. Jones and O. Marriot, *Anatomy of a Merger: A History of GEC, AEI and English Electric* (London, 1970) p. 68.
38. A. G. Whyte, *Forty Years of Electrical Progress: The Story of GEC* (London, 1930) p. 64.
39. Robertson, *Story*, p. 95. An example of an already established British telephone manufacturer was the Helsby company, which originated from a woollen-manufacturing business, founded in 1825 by John Taylor. In 1881 one of Taylor's grandsons visited the Paris Electrical Exhibition and, impressed by the potential of electricity, determined to reorientate the family business. The two brothers, together with Professor John Hopkinson, built the Deeside Electrical Works at Neston in Cheshire. In 1886 they moved to Helsby in Cheshire as the Telegraph Manufacturing Co., manufacturing gutta percha and rubber cables and covered wires, galvanometers, line equipment, Morse railway telegraph instruments, telephone cords, Wheatstone Bridges and paraffin condensers for use on submarine cables. In 1889, helped by Dane Sinclair, the company manufactured their first 200-lines vertical switchboard for Paisley in Scotland. Shortage of labour in the village of Helsby prompted the opening of a new factory devoted to making telephone instruments and switchboards in Liverpool, in 1893. In 1902 the company merged with the British Insulated Wire Co., becoming British Insulated & Helsby Cables Ltd. The Liverpool factory gained an independent identity in 1911 as the Automatic Telephone Manufacturing Co.
40. *National Telephone Journal* (NTJ) January 1909.
41. Ibid., November 1906.

42. Ibid., June 1906.
43. Ibid., December 1908.
44. Ibid., September 1906.
45. Ibid., February 1909.
46. Ibid., 1907.
47. Ibid., August 1908.
48. Ibid., November 1908.
49. Barton to Hudson, 29 November 1888, AT&T Archives.
50. Barton to Hudson, 15 January 1890, ibid.
51. Zwietusch to Antwerp, 6 June 1890, ibid.
52. Siemens, *History*, I, pp. 133–4. Felten & Guilleaume began life as steel-wire rope manufacturers in Germany in 1826, diversified into telegraph cables in 1853 and into power cables in 1888.
53. Welles to Barton, 4 March 1895, AT&T Archives Box 1142.
54. 'Report on European Telephone Administration' (1898) p. 39, British Post Office Archives.
55. Webb, *Development*, pp. 64–5. Siemens, *History*, I, p. 131, 161, supports this assessment, implying that von Stephan had stayed too long. Matters began to improve with the appointment as Postmaster General of von Podbielski at the turn of the century.
56. 'Report on European Telephone Administrations' (1898) p. 27, British Post Office Archives.
57. Holcombe, *Public Ownership*, pp. 430–3; Siemens, *History*, I, pp. 261–4; Preece and Fischer, 'Report' (1896) p. 90; 'Telephony in Europe 1895', vol. 2, AT&T Archives. In 1906 the number of long-distance calls in the German network was more than one-fifth of the number of local calls. Comparison with the USA is vitiated by different definitions of long distance. For every 100 direct lines in Germany in 1905 there were 60.6 indirect connections through private branch exchanges. In the USA the party line did much of the work performed by the private branch exchange in Germany.
58. *Journal Officiel*, 17 Mai 1906, Documents Parlementaires – Chambre Annexe no 3121, pp. 313–24; Holcomb, *Public Ownership*, pp. 294–309; Webb, *Development* pp. 63–4, H. L. Webb, 'Preliminary Report on Europe 1907–8', British Post Office Archives.
59. A. Broder, 'The Multinationalisation of the French Electrical Industry, 1880–1914: Dependence and its Causes', in P. Hertner and G. Jones (eds), *Multinationals: Theory and History* (Aldershot, 1986) p. 182.
60. Welles to Brown, 24 May 1890, AT&T Archives.
61. Aboilard to Welles, 2 June 1890, ibid.
62. Welles to Brown, 17 June 1890, ibid.
63. Aboilard to Welles, 28 July 1890, ibid.
64. 'Some of the electrical works are in places that would be deemed poor accommodations for pigs by an Illinois farmer': Barton to Hudson, 18 September 1890, ibid.
65. Welles to Barton, 23 September 1890, ibid.
66. Welles to Barton, 24 April 1895, ibid. From 1900 the Aboilard partnership became a licensee of Western Electric, ultimately under the name of Le Matériel Téléphonique.
67. Attman, Kuuse and Olsson, *Ericcson*, I, p. 207.
68. Welles to Jackson, 20 September 1895, AT&T Archives.
69. Welles to Barton, 8 August 1895, ibid.
70. Kingsbury to Barton, 29 February 1896, ibid.
71. Barton to Welles, 17 October 1895, ibid.
72. Barton to Welles, 11 October 1895, ibid.
73. Attman, Kuuse and Olsson, *Ericcson*, I, p. 191.
74. Barton to Welles, 7 October 1895, Welles to Barton, 8 August 1895, AT&T Archives.
75. Welles to Barton, 11 November 1895, ibid: Siemens, *History*, I, p. 136.
76. Attman, Kuuse and Olsson, *Ericcson*, I, p. 209. Deckert, an Austrian, had patented in 1889 a granular carbon telephone transmitter with a carbon diaphragm screened with gauze, and Deckert telephones were used in the Austrian system in the 1890s.

77. J. S. Foreman-Peck, 'Competition and Performance of the UK Telecommunications Industry', *Telecommunications Policy* (1985) pp. 215–28, Table 1.

8. Technology Transfer in the Origins of the Heavy Chemicals Industry in the United States and the Russian Empire

Kenneth Warren*

Technology transfer involves the creation of a new operational environment which may make the transplanted activity very different from that of the areas from which it was derived. There may be changes in the types or proportions of raw materials used, differences in market structures and in the composition of various joint products or in scales of production. The attitudes and skills of workers, and the qualities of management will not be the same as in the old country. In short, different challenges and fresh opportunities together shape what is effectively a new industry. Not infrequently the later milieu, though initially difficult, has eventually proved much more favourable for the realization of the full potentials of the new technology than the original homeland of either the invention or its initial industrial application. As with Bessemer's process, the continuous rolling of steel, and automobile engineering, this applied also to heavy chemicals. Both Leblanc's process at the beginning and Solvay's in the last half of the nineteenth century produced their most spectacular results only when transferred from their countries of origin to other, bigger, more dynamic, less tradition-bound operational environments.

Chemical manufacture was not an industrial leader in the Victorian age. Agriculture, mining, iron and steel, textiles and engineering were the giant sectors; the chemical trades were handmaids supplying fertilizers, explosives, acids and fluxes, soaps, dyes, lubricants and coatings to these various dominant trades. However, from the 1880s, transition into the new era of the second industrial revolution, an age of steel, electricity and chemicals, marked the start of a much more important role for the industry. At this time it became one of the pioneer research and development (R & D) industries, these functions of fundamental importance to its future growth being heavily concentrated in Europe and to a quite disproportionate degree in Germany. To newly industrialized or industrializing countries overseas it had earlier diffused more slowly than such other basic activities as mining, the metallurgical industries or textile manufacture. This was the case in both the burgeoning, free-enterprise industrial structure of the USA and in the Russian Empire, making a belated economic spurt under a loosely planned development programme. In both countries an essential precondition for the successful transfer of the chemical industry proved to be the establishment of high protective tariffs; in each there was help from the leading European pioneer of the new technology.

By the 1880s the USA was already the world's largest economy. In some individual manufacturing sectors its primacy was then or soon after firmly established. America's steel production passed that of Britain in 1890; before the end of the decade it was making almost 40 per cent of the world total. It was ahead of Britain in coal by 1900, and rapidly extending its lead. The Russian Empire lagged sadly behind in both industries, but, spurred by Count Sergei Witte's forward planning – which a British commentator supposed had '... committed Russia irrevocably to the capitalist system'[1] – steel production surged in the 1890s, so that the output of 1900 was more than five times that of 10 years before. After decades of slow and often uncertain progress both countries were also at last making headway in chemicals. As they did so, their situations became distinct from those of the older established European producers. At the same time, the two new producers had national operating environments providing marked contrasts with each other.

The Russian Empire was well over 150 per cent bigger in area than the USA and at the turn of the century had 145 million inhabitants, as compared with the latter's 80 million, but economically and in terms of conditions favourable for development it ranked far behind. Its national wealth was computed by Mulhall to be 40 per cent as great; in per capita terms it was at only 26 per cent the US level. Provision of infrastructure lagged badly. In 1880 the USA already had 87 800 miles of railway, the Russian Empire 15 000 miles; by 1907 the ratio had slightly worsened against Russia, despite years of the most heroic constructional endeavours, the respective lengths then being 236 949 and 39 088 miles. Those implanting a new industry in the USA also benefited from a much more mature general manufacturing structure acting as both supplier and buyer. The wider context of social and cultural conditions and general ethos favoured American development even more. At all levels the US education system was more fully developed and higher in quality; free enterprise was in one of its most confident expansion phases and, as yet, little trammelled by the bureaucracies of the state.

When the new chemical industries were successfully established in the USA they grew rapidly. Within a decade or so levels of output, productivity and profitability grew to rival or to exceed those of the longer-established European producers. Calls on transatlantic sources for the factors of production declined, and American chemical engineers began to make their own contributions to the advance of technology. Within 40 years of beginning large-scale chemical manufacture, the USA was pioneering the first, tentative steps to a major new stage, that of petrochemicals. Here too the industry remained responsive to changing economic circumstances and, for such a large-scale industry, surprisingly flexible as to location. In the Russian Empire central initiatives could encourage and protect industries but could not inculcate either the same competitive edge or a capacity to offer ready response to changing circumstances. After the Revolution, through the New Economic Policy and into the Stalinist planning era, chemicals was something of a cinderella industry, and for many years there was little incentive to pioneer further improvements or to build up new locations.

In heavy chemicals, both the USA and Russia made a slow start, but afterwards the former proved more expansive and adaptive than the latter. Transfer of the technologies not only highlighted contrasts between the precocious but now essentially too small and, sometimes at least, slow-growth and conservative economies of Europe and their new subcontinental-sized rivals, but also brought out the essential differences between East and West. In what follows these themes are illustrated by an examination of the alkali industries.

INITIAL BACKWARDNESS

Alkali production in the twentieth century has been dwarfed by that of the end-products of many other sectors of the heavy chemical industries. Ammonia and fertilizers, ethylene and plastics – these have become the great growth lines. Within some national industries the alkali trades have become a by word for staid technology or even inertia. Even so, in many respects the Victorian alkali industry was the parent stock for the gigantic and ever-widening chemical trades of today. This was so in the emergence of new lines of production out of older ones, in choice of plant locations which have often been perpetuated and in the foundation of great firms which later diversified almost out of all recognition. Naturally Britain and Western Europe illustrate this theme particularly well, but this heritage was also one of the implications of American and Russian alkali developments.

Today the USA and the USSR occupy leading positions in world alkali production. In 1986 the former made 27 per cent and the latter 19 per cent of the world's output of sodium carbonate. A year before, the USSR announced plans to increase its soda ash production by 60 per cent by the year 2000. Until the final 15 years of the nineteenth century there was effectively no large-scale heavy chemicals industry in either country. Why did they lag so much, and why and how were the technological foundations then laid for their breakthrough to world leadership?

The alkali industry for more than two-thirds of the nineteenth century depended on the Leblanc process, pioneered in France during the Revolution and, greatly improved and elaborated, applied on a much larger scale in Britain in the early decades of the next century. It involved a number of distinct stages, used a range of minerals and was energy- and labour-intensive. The ammonia soda process was both simpler and more economical, but design of plant to make it a practical proposition had to await the inventive skills of Solvay, and further development work and chemical engineering improvements made by Ludwig Mond. In the 1880s and 1890s a third way of making a limited range of the alkalies, especially caustic soda and bleaching powder, by the electrolysis of brine, was gradually elaborated and became a rapidly expanding industry. The ammonia soda and electrolytic processes at last gave an opportunity to make a mark in alkali to countries lacking the experience and established position of European firms which had easy access to a range of minerals, technical skills and able, but relatively cheap labour. (Figure 8.1)

In 1884 the UK made 430 thousand tons of soda ash. In the same year American output was one thousand tons and that of Russia only slightly more. Ten years later there had been substantial progress but, even so, US production was still only 19 per cent and Russian output 11.5 per cent of the UK level. Explanation of this slow growth is perhaps easier to provide for Russia. It was still an ill-organized giant of vaguely appreciated but undeveloped potential. Home demand was deficient. By contrast, there was a favourable market situation in the USA, but it had been inadequately protected to support home producers who were burdened by high wages costs. At a time of declining freight charges for bulk, long-distance oceanic transport, this labour cost penalty made America uncompetitive. When the Europeans adopted the new, labour-saving ammonia soda process, almost invariably under Solvay's patent, they were providing the means for others to subvert their old dominance. Now, at last, US industrial promoters could see a suitable technology for their circumstances. Even then high levels of protection were needed to justify large outlays on a process in which the learning time might be considerable. A further vital element in their success was the international development strategy of the Solvays and their willingness to encourage plants using the process overseas in return for a share of the stock and for regular and full information on their costs and technical progress. Solvay promoted a world dissemination of his process rather than, as with earlier innovations in some other industries, trying to check technical diffusion. Nevertheless there was a lag of about a decade before the Russians and the Americans took up the new method of alkali production after its commercial success had been proved in the European core economies of Belgium, France, Germany and Britain.

Effective tariff protection for chemicals came later than for iron and steel products. The latter were above all used in massive infrastructural investments,

Figure 8.1   Processes in the manufacture of alkali products

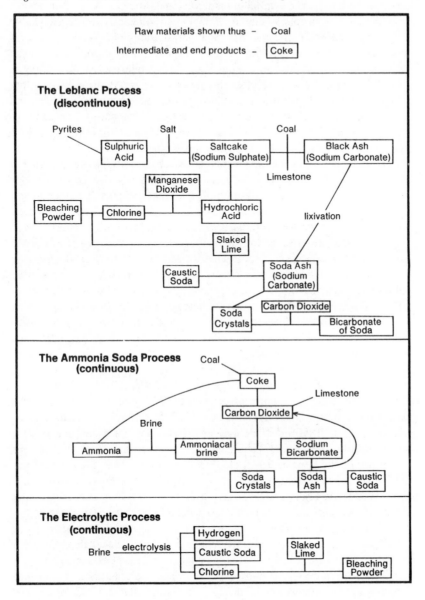

and pre-eminently in the building of the railway networks which were recognized as both basis and symbol of modernity and progress. As a result of this, independence from outside sources of steel supply was early seen as a desirable step to national economic maturity. By contrast, though important, alkali was not used in such obviously central activities, but largely in further industrial processes – in glass and soap making, in the textile industries, in oil refining as well as going in the form of bleaching powder and bicarbonate of soda, into almost all homes. To the propagandists of protection it was a less obvious, less emotive rallying point than steel: in the trade figures it occupied a much lower place. In 1869, for instance, US imports of soda products were worth \$2.5 million, but of iron and steel \$29.2 million.

For both countries action to provide effective tariff protection was an essential precondition for a large chemical industry; without such duties western Europe would continue to supply their requirements. It was their good fortune that protection coincided with a new technology which suited their circumstances better than the old. It has been said that at the time of the Crimean War economic progress 'had made no more than scratches or pockets in the surface of agrarian Russia'. From then to the early 1870s Russia followed what western commentators called a 'liberal' tariff policy. In 1876 new protective duties were introduced. There were general rises in the scales in 1881/2 and in 1890/1. The results were impressive in encouraging industrialization, which almost trebled in the 15 years to 1900, and in increased foreign investment, with an eightfold increase in the 1890s. By some criteria at least chemicals made more than average progress. Between 1887 and 1902, industrial workers increased by 71.4 per cent, but in chemicals by 184.4 per cent.[2] Effective protection for American industry began with Civil War tariff legislation. After that there was a period of uncertainty, and in 1872 a general cut of 10 per cent was made in duties: this was reversed in 1875. The 1883 tariff made various changes, but in 1890 the McKinley Tariff Act brought a decisive general increase in protection and, following cuts in 1894, these high duties were confirmed by the Dingley Tariff of 1897. For soda ash and caustic soda even the high rates of the Dingley Tariff were below those of a few years before, but they were made high enough to give protection to a new technology now rapidly getting into its stride. The different dates of protective legislation in the two countries, taken with the shrinkage of imports and the timing of surges in alkali production, suggest that the Russian industry was above all a child of the tariff, the American industry of growing demand and the effects of technological change in a setting of buoyantly confident free enterprise, but further boosted by the imposition of duties (Tables 8.1 and 8.2). Certainly the significance of technological change should not be underestimated. The switch from the Leblanc to the ammonia soda process involved transfer from salt to brine as the source of sodium chloride, large fuel economy and labour cost savings. It brought out what had until then been merely latent assets of the two large countries. By contrast, Britain and to a lesser extent other European economies had been disadvantaged in adopting the new technology by the need to write off a large capacity in an older technology. In Britain, Solvay ash production did not exceed that of Leblanc ash until 1895; output by the latter process was never significant in either of the new producers.

Russian and American advance in alkali production came at a time when a new technology had been installed and proved in Europe and could be introduced behind tariff barriers of a height so adjusted as to displace traditional foreign suppliers. The capacity of the biggest of those overseas suppliers, the UK, to meet this challenge was compromised by the persistence of an old technology and antiquated equipment, operated in too many small units, and all the other disabilities which went with these circumstances in the way of old methods, organization and ideas. The new producers had the reverse of these conditions as assets, but had to learn much that the Old World already knew. Moreover neither in Russia nor in America was there a completely clean slate. However humble their early history, the genesis of both industries can be traced

Table 8.1   British alkali exports to the Russian Empire, the United States and others, 1865–97 (£000s)

Destination	1865	1870	1875	1884	1889	1893	1897
Russian Empire	64	126	197	176	121	122	68
United States							
Atlantic ports	384	622	955	976	840	977	420
Pacific ports	6	5	27	36	22	40	20
All other countries	388	477	1 121	902	590	719	771

Source: British Parliamentary papers.

Table 8.2   US annual average imports of soda ash, 1867–9 to 1900–2 (000 long tons)

1867–1869	52.7	1879–1881	121.0	1891–1893	165.0
1870–1872	62.0	1882–1884	130.3	1894–1896	129.7
1873–1875	75.7	1885–1887	121.7	1897–1899	46.0
1876–1878	82.0	1888–1890	137.7	1900–1902	22.3

Source: Pennock (1904) p. 670.

back far beyond the period of breakthrough. It was not without significance for the form of their later development.

THE RUSSIAN EMPIRE

In the 1870s Russia's imports of British alkali ranked her third as an overseas market to the USA and the German Empire. She also imported Belgian and German material. Yet it had long been recognized that her own potential for chemicals was considerable. There had been thought about this, even imaginative schemes, but little achievement. The opening and then the gradual exploration of the Volga and Ural country since the mid-sixteenth century had proved the existence of large reserves of salt, though in the mid-1880s little short of one-fifth of the Empire's supply was being imported.[3] Expansion of mining and metallurgy in the Urals led to plans from some economic thinkers for associated cheap production of sulphuric acid and hopes that this in turn might lead on to other chemicals – of which inevitably, given the demands and the technology of the time, soda ash would be an important member. By 1850 about 30 plants produced sulphuric acid.[4] When the eminent chemist Dmitri Mendeleev visited the Paris Exposition in 1867, he took the opportunity to study the French chemical industry, with the hope of improving soda manufacture in his home country. All these plans led effectively to nothing. Russia's tariff policy was part of a more effective development programme from the end of the 1870s.

In 1882 European Russia produced chemicals of all kinds worth 6.6 million roubles, but imported them to the value of 57.89 million roubles.[5] The new duties were soon reducing her import bill. In 1885 the Empire imported over three-quarters of its alkali requirements, by 1900 only about 5 per cent. Even as early as 1890, Russia bought only £106 000 of British alkali, a mere 1.2 per cent of her total imports from that source, and 46 per cent less than the level of 15 years before. However this achievement also depended on the effects of two other measures taken by central government at the same time as it raised the duties – the abolition of the salt duty and the inducements offered by an Imperial ukase, which provided for a premium equal to £50 000 to be paid to any entrepreneur setting up a large soda plant. Russian capitalists – with outside technical assistance – responded.

In 1885, Russia had a rail mileage less than one-eighth that of the USA; consequently in its first phase the new industry was much more oriented to navigable waterways (Figure 8.2). The basin of the Kama river in the western part of the government of Perm, some 800 miles east of Moscow, was richly endowed with mineral resources. It had been a source of salt for many years. Before the abolition of serfdom in 1861, salt had been mined along the river;

Figure 8.2   The alkali industry in Russia up to the Revolution

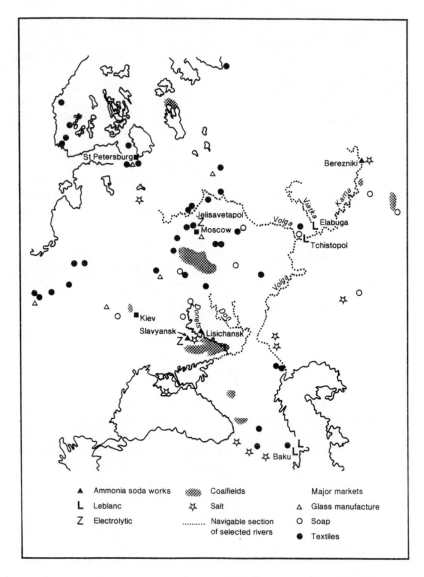

afterwards, as the labour provision for the mines became more difficult, brine extraction gradually became more important than mining. Like other cargoes, salt was then shipped out on pine-log barges, each holding from 5 000 to as much as 8 000 tons. A major destination was the great June fair at Nizhni Novgorod, not only an outlet for the cargo, but the place where the barge itself was broken up and sold for fuel. The Kama basin was well placed for access to coal and sulphur, which were also shipped throughout the great Volga trading system. This became the early focus for the new industry. Here, to the amazement of British chemical experts, accustomed to calculations of movement costs from, say, the Cheshire saltfield to St Helens or from lime kilns in the Peak to Northwich, long-distance transport was involved with products and to a lesser extent with raw materials. The difficulties may be illustrated by the logistics of one of the few Russian Leblanc soda works, built in 1890 by P. K. Oushkoff at Elabouga in Vyatka government, mainly to produce caustic soda. The description is by an English partner, R. Bowman.

> If we take the night train from Moscow and travel all night we reach Nizhni Novgorod the following morning; and by taking the steamer from there and travelling one day and night down the Volga and one day and night up the river Kama, we come to a little village perched upon the hillside, called in English 'the quiet hills'. Leaving the boat here, a drive of a quarter of an hour over the brow of the hill brings us to the only Leblanc soda works in Russia ...

For over half the year, when navigation was closed, the works sent out products by horse and sledge for distances as great as 600 miles.[6] Soon after the new tariff and promotional aids were announced, Russia's first ammonia soda plant was built in the same region.

In about 1873 a wealthy steamship owner from Perm, Ivan Lubimoff, acquired salt mines on the east bank of the Kama at Solikamsk. By the middle of the next decade he also controlled coal-mines some way to the south-east, at Lunievsky, the pits being linked by rail to the Kama. These resources and possibilities of water transport persuaded Lubimoff and his technical advisers, the Solvay Co., to build where the coal railway met the river, a place later called Berezniki. Construction, apparently begun in 1880, was slowed by climatic difficulties, but three years later the plant was completed.[7] Salt and fuel were cheap and there were nearby supplies of good-quality limestone. Early problems were shortages in supplies of ammonia and – something which must have been foreseen – the shortness of the navigation season on the Kama. However, in the mid-1880s, production rose, reaching 11 500 tons by 1887. Encouraged by this, and spurred on by another increase in protection, the company, now reorganized as Lubimoff and Solvay, decided to expand. They did so in part by building a second plant, much nearer major industrial centres.

By 1887 a site was acquired at Lisichansk on the Donets River in the Ekaterinoslav government of the Ukraine. The salt deposits of Artomovsk were 50 km to the south-west and the pits of the great southern coalfield were even closer. As it was nearer than Berezniki to major centres of alkali consumption, Lisichansk was to become the largest Russian Solvay works.[8] By the first half of the 1890s, Lubimoff and Solvay were maintaining that they were able to supply the soda needs of the Empire, and the Imperial government was reported to be revising railway tariffs to reflect this new situation. The two plants annually produced 47 000 tons of soda products in the mid-1890s.[9] Later a second southern works was built in a similar situation, but 60 km to the west, at Slavyansk, where additional supplies of brine were available from salt lakes.

In 1891, Mendeleev was employed by the government to set up a new system of duties for heavy chemicals, and it seems to have been only after this that the Elabouga Leblanc operation became profitable. It produced about 3 000 tons of soda products a year or about 6 per cent of the combined output of the two ammonia soda works. A few other alkali operations of various types were now established. Between 1890 and 1897, according to Kropotkin, the number of works making soda went up from two to 10, and by 1899 output was over 82 000 tons.[10] Well over half of this came from the two ammonia soda works. Most of the other operations were in or near the Volga basin.

A Leblanc works made sulphuric acid, caustic soda and bleaching powder at Tchistopol, near the confluence of the Kama with the Volga. Predictably, a British visitor expressed surprise at the long distances over which its raw materials were carried.[11] Down on the Caspian Sea, Baku became an important alkali centre, especially for caustic soda, used in its oil industry, which in the late 1890s was out-producing the whole of the USA. Annual Baku caustic consumption was estimated as 6 545 metric tons. It was supplied in part from plants along the Volga, and nearly one-third came from the regeneration of material already used once in the refineries. There were advantages in local production of the rest. Fuel, salt and sulphuric acid were at hand and, owing to the nearness of the outlets, the caustic could be marketed in liquid rather than in solid form. The firm of Tagijev already had a caustic works there by 1897; Nobels had plans for one.[12] By 1900 the area had the country's biggest concentration of capacity.

An interesting oddity was the small Leblanc caustic soda works at Barnaul in western Siberia. Its circumstances were revealing as to the high production costs and high prices which remoteness and difficult transport conditions made possible. Output was extremely small – about 410 tons a year. It sold the caustic at 3 roubles per pood (36 lb) at the works and at 3 roubles 80 kopecks at Tomsk, over 200 miles to the north but accessible by steamer along the Ob. (At the same time, because of the competition of British material, the price in St Petersburg was 2R 40k to 2R 50k; in Moscow, nearer to home supplies but more isolated from imports, it was 2R 70 to 2R 80.) Barnaul's position gave it effective protection against rival Russian works which had to dispatch their product by water along the Volga and then transship to the new Trans-Siberian Railway for a journey of 1 400 miles into its immediate tributary territory. Further east still, beyond Lake Baikal, British alkali, delivered through Pacific ports, commanded the market until the First World War. Brunner and Mond, rather than any Russian works, Leblanc or Solvay, supplied the Piankov Glass Works, the Portland cement works at Primorski and some five soap works, though the glass works at least claimed that they could get salt cake from around Lake Baikal for 30 per cent less than they were paying Brunners for soda ash.[13]

By the early twentieth century, electrolytic alkali works had been built in the Ukraine, in the central industrial region and in Russian Poland. Not until well after the Czarist era were such plants put up at large hydro power sites in the Volga basin or further east. Some decades before this big water power sites had been developed in North America. In many other ways too, the USA, though also a late starter, had pushed far ahead of Russia.

THE UNITED STATES

Well before the end of the Victorian age the American economy was larger, wealthier and more complex than that of Russia. Consistently from the 1860s to the early 1890s it took at least half of British alkali exports. In 1893, US purchases amounted to just over £1 million of UK overseas sales totalling £1.8 million. It was in that year that an American described his country as the 'prop and mainstay' of the old country's United Alkali Co.[14] Yet at that time home production was beginning to advance rapidly and by 1894 was already 60 per cent greater than that of Russia. Having reached a peak of £1.25 million in 1890, within 15 years British deliveries to the USA fell to £74 thousand – from 60 per cent to 5 per cent of her exports.

In the arid and semi-arid west there are important sources of natural soda, both in the beds of the 'playa' lakes of the Great Basin and in parts of the High Plains. Laramie, Wyoming had processing works for natural soda in the mid-1880s and in the whole of that state there were said to be 'several' such works a decade later.[15] But this soda was mixed with other chemicals which had to be removed, and the situation was poor for marketing. Demand was mainly in the east, especially in the manufacturing belt of the north-east, then at the peak of its pre-eminence in the nation's economy – in 1870, soda imports of US Pacific ports were only 0.8 per cent those of Atlantic ports. The north-east was the great market for alkali both for industrial use (soda ash, caustic soda, bleaching powder) and for domestic purposes (soda crystals, bicarbonate of soda and bleaching powder). High charges for movement, both at the local and the national levels, cancelled out any original production cost advantage of natural soda. In 1875 a Union Pacific Railroad geologist had noted that two soda lakes were 65 miles distant by the shortest wagon road from Rawlins station – and the Seminole Mountains lay in between. Some years later the Railroad built a small black ash plant at Laramie. At the end of the century it was reckoned that western natural soda operators could make the product for not over $7 a ton, of which a little over half was the cost of preparation for marketing. At the same time manufactured soda ash could be made for $9. As the freight rate from Wyoming to Chicago was then about $5.75, the whole of the manufacturing belt was far beyond the competitive sphere of apparently 'cheap' western producers – which had only the poor compensation that their sparsely populated regional markets were also protected by distance.[16] In the east, before the ammonia soda process was introduced, the main source of alkali was not indigenous; indeed home producers found it almost impossible to survive.

Over many years there were various not very successful attempts to set up an American alkali industry (Figure 8.3). The logic of home production seemed clear. As an 1877 editorial in the *Journal of the Franklin Institute* observed – after referring both to a report in the same issue of James Mactear's address on the chemicals industry to the British Association's Glasgow meeting and to America's huge import bill for alkalies – 'As all these products are bulky, and derived from the cheapest of raw materials, coal, salt, and limestone, the development of American chemical industry in this direction would appear to be one of the most obvious growths to be immediately anticipated.' Fifteen years later Wyatt reckoned that the cost of making salt cake in England by Leblanc's process was about $7.30 and for bleaching powder $15.00; his 'realistic' estimates for the USA were $7.70 and $16.76 respectively.[17] However, lacking both skilled and cheap labour, and facing an established trade adversary, the Americans could not find any secure place in the Leblanc industry, though they made numerous attempts to do so.

The process was tried at Wilmington and on the Hudson. In 1869, in Jackson, Michigan, a salt district where coal also was available, manufacture was begun of soda ash, washing soda, bicarbonate, caustic soda and hydrochloric acid. It failed to become an important producer.[18] Over a longer period repeated efforts were made in the Pittsburgh area. Here there was ample coal, access to salt and water transport both for materials and products. Major outlets were available in the glass works of the district, the nation's biggest concentration, and there were excellent rail connections to other consumers both east and west. As well as various projects in the city and its immediate neighbourhood, most of which had short lives, there were longer-term operations 50 miles up the Allegheny River at the small but hopefully named settlement of Natrona, where the Pennsylvania Salt Co. was incorporated in 1850. Its local salt supplies proved inadequate and from 1864 it operated a patent modification

Figure 8.3   The alkali industry in the United States up to the First World War

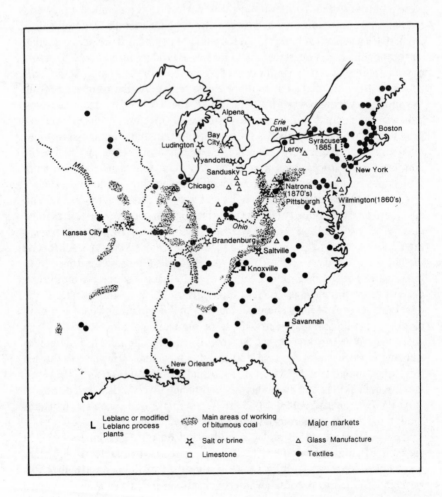

of the Leblanc process using cryolite imported from southern Greenland. Production remained small, no more than about 4 000 tons a year in the late 1890s. In the early decades at least it was not an efficient operation. A British visitor in 1876 found that Natrona employed about 350. Its lixiviating tanks were 'very small' and placed at different levels, so that the waste was thrown from one to another. The economics of the cryolite process were suspect. He estimated that at the source in Greenland, where the mines only worked between May and October, the mineral cost £4 a ton. Sea freight to Philadelphia added £2 and rail carriage from there to the works another £1. Labour and other charges of £4 brought total costs to £11, or roughly equal to the delivered price of imported Leblanc soda ash.[19] It was in new technology, not in minor modifications of the old, that the USA was to make its belated breakthrough.

The development of the American ammonia soda industry was almost coincident with that of the Russian Empire. Most of the projects were well placed for both brine and fuel (Figure 8.4). The Chance and Hunt representative, James Stark, who had reported on Natrona, also gained information on the early reactions of Americans to the Solvay process. At the Manufacturing Chemists Association dinner in June 1876 he spoke to Mr Chapell of Chicago and St Louis, Solvay's American representative. Chapell told him they were putting down ammonia soda works in both cities, but when Stark visited him in Chicago he found that nothing had been done.[20]

The first US ammonia soda plant was built by the brothers, Herman and Hans Frasch, at Bay City, Michigan in the late 1870s. It was not a success and was dismantled after two or three years. Herman Frasch tried again in 1887, this time in Cleveland. His second plant was more successful, surviving into the early twentieth century, when it was making 30 tons of soda ash daily. Eventually it too succumbed. It is interesting to consider why Frasch failed. There were some material disadvantages. The Cleveland plant was never big enough to enjoy the scale economies of some of its rivals, and its salt was at the very considerable depth of 2 200 feet. Neither of these considerations need have been decisive. Probably important was the fact that Frasch had other pressing business interests and was an inventor as well as a businessman. He was engaged in petroleum production in the northern Appalachians and in Canada and made important contributions to refining technology, taking out 21 US patents in this field between 1887 and 1894. In 1891 he introduced his process for extracting sulphur from the deep deposits of the Gulf Coast and after this was involved in operations there. He also patented his own ammonia soda process. Whatever its merits it was not as successful as the Solvay process.[21] Frasch gained the honours of the pioneer; others enjoyed more tangible rewards by applying technology innovated elsewhere.

The saltfields of Onondaga County, western New York State, had been worked for generations before they were chosen as the location for the first American Solvay plant. They were on the main line of various railroads, and on the Erie Canal; the area had nearby sources of limestone, and was not too far from Pennsylvanian coal. Between 1879 and 1881 the American William Cogswell negotiated with Solvays for an agreement. Not surprisingly, Brunner and Mond were not happy at the prospect of a large Solvay plant in their US market. Eventually the American proposals were accepted and both Solvay & Cie and Brunner Mond took a financial interest in the new Solvay Process Co.[22] Designs for the plant were drawn up by Solvay engineers in Brussels: French

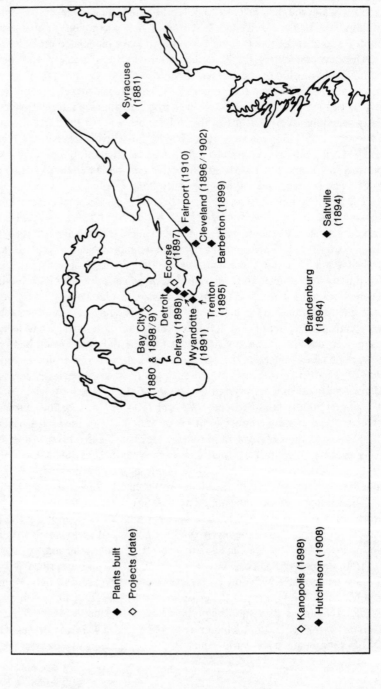

Figure 8.4 The ammonia soda industry in the United States up to the First World War

and Belgian engineers helped to build it on Lake Onondaga in a suburb of Syracuse, which eventually became the industrial community of Solvay. Production began early in 1884. In the course of that year the capacity of the plant was raised to 50 tons a day, or approximately 17–18 000 tons a year. In the same year Britain made 52 000 tons of ammonia soda and 380 000 tons by the Leblanc process.[23] After that the Solvay plant rapidly built up its output, tripling in 1887 alone. In that year an agreement was reached under which Brunner and Mond agreed to a phased withdrawal from the American market, making good their loss in part at least through the returns on their share of Solvay Process Co. capital. In the early 1890s the new company showed great resolution in pursuing cost reduction by streamlining its operations. To this end it developed new sources of brine, mechanized its limestone quarries and secured its supplies of ammonia by being the first American concern of any kind to build by product coke ovens. By 1896 it had raised its daily capacity to 500 tons.[24]

In the 1890s attention switched to the saltfields of lower Michigan: their attractions were to prove greater even than those of New York State. There were two main foci – around Saginaw Bay and along the Detroit River. Both possessed coal, limestone and salt, but the advantages of the Detroit area were particularly marked. Here the salt was at a depth of 1 400 feet, there were excellent facilities for transport by water, and plenty of waterside sites for plant. By rail there was easy access to the then booming glass industry in the natural gasfields of Indiana, whose tally of glassworks increased from four in 1880 to 21 in 1890 and 102 by 1900.[25]

In 1893 the Michigan Alkali Co., associated with the extensive glassmaking interests of the Ford family in western Pennsylvania, built ammonia soda works at Wyandotte. It also had operations on the edge of Detroit. Responding to this challenge and also to the obvious opportunities offered by the area, the Solvay Process Co. decided to build its second works there. In 1898 it chose a site at Delray on the south side of Detroit. At Trenton, Michigan, the firm of Church and Co. made ammonia soda, though nothing more about that firm has come to light and they were not to be long-term factors in the trade. In 1898, recognizing that it could do better than continue its long struggle on the Allegheny, the Pennsylvania Salt Manufacturing Co. also erected alkali works at Wyandotte.

Such projects eroded still further the position of the United Alkali Co. (UAC) in American markets, and it resolved to respond. As in Britain, its reactions were not very decisive. It formed a subsidiary, the North American Chemical Co., whose articles of association provided for manufacturing operations in Bay and Wayne counties, Michigan. The first plant was built at Bay City, but failed to go into soda ash production, as had been expected, remaining instead only a salt and potassium chloride operation. Later, however, it seems to have produced at least some soda ash.[26] In 1897, UAC's chief chemist, Ferdinand Hurter, and a few years later two of its senior directors, John Brock and J. E. Davidson, visited Michigan. They were reported as so impressed by Detroit's possibilities as to be planning a river front soda ash plant at Ecorse.[27] This too failed to materialize.

These early developments seemed to indicate that the ideal locations were along the shores of the Great Lakes; there were, however, early attempts in other areas, some of them clearly sub-optimal. Along the Ohio river weak brines were sometimes found during borings for oil. It was in response to one of these that a works was built at Brandenburg, Kentucky, 30 miles west of Louisville. The brine was concentrated for use in the process, but the plant was small, 5 tons a day being turned out in January 1895 when Syracuse was making 320 tons.[28] This plant failed to become a permanent feature of American alkali production.

More interesting in many ways was an operation still further south, in the hill country of western Virginia. It was promoted by six capitalists, only two of whom were from the district. The Mathieson Alkali works there was built in 1894 at Saltville at the head of the north branch of the Holston River, where salt had been worked at least as early as the 1830s. Good coal supplies were near at hand, but in other respects it was ill-served. The Holston was a small stream which provided inadequate water in summer, and the plant's discharges brought complaint from riverine landowners. Saltville is more than 100 miles above Knoxville, then the upper limit for all-year navigation by steamboats in the whole Tennessee drainage system. It was also the terminus of a short branch line from the Norfolk and Western Railroad. More generally, the Saltville plant was poorly located in relation to the great markets for alkali - 'somewhat away from the points of consumption', as an 1896 commentator gently put it.[29] There were also suggestions that in its earliest days it was indifferently managed, so that in 1898, when it was announced that a Solvay Process Co. man was to be brought in to a top post, one trade journalist wrote: '...we may expect a decided change in this aspect of things from this plant in the future...'.[30] Yet though disadvantaged in these ways and rather small – its share of US 1903 production was about 7 per cent – it survived.

In the first decade of the twentieth century there was more evidence of the vigorous growth as well as the sometimes wasteful duplication of facilities in an unceasingly competitive environment, a remarkable contrast with the relatively slow pace and fixed forms of development in the Russian Empire. In 1899, dissatisfied with buying large tonnages of alkali, the Pittsburgh Plate Glass Co. organized a subsidiary, the Columbia Chemical Co., which by 1901 had built a soda ash plant at Barberton, south-west of Akron, Ohio. The salt beds here were thick, though at a depth of 2 800 feet; civic leaders were eager to promote new industry. In 1910 two other Pittsburgh glass firms joined another from Washington, Pennsylvania and a large Cincinnati soap maker to organize the Diamond Alkali Co., with headquarters in Pittsburgh, but with its plant at Painesville next to the harbour of Fairport, on Lake Erie. Far to the west, in the late 1890s, a works was planned for Kanopolis on the Smoky Hill River in central Kansas; a decade later the state got its ammonia soda works, but it was located many miles to the south at Hutchinson on the Arkansas River. It was soon afterwards controlled by Solvay Process men.

Between 1900 and 1909 US production of soda ash more than doubled; by the latter date one-third of world production was American, overwhelmingly from six large plants in the north-east. By this time too it had a number of electrolytic alkali works, largely concerned with caustic soda and bleaching powder. Some of these, including operations at Saltville and Bay City, were not well located for cheap sources of power. Commentators, including – perhaps understandably – J. D. Pennock of the Solvay Process Co., which made caustic by a different process, were sceptical of their commercial success. The continuing importance of the tariff in this trade was strikingly illustrated at this time. The Dow Chemical Co's Midland, Michigan bleach plant was engaged in a price war with overseas concerns. Gradually the price of bleach, $3.50 a hundredweight when Midland began production of it in 1897, had come down to $1.68. The price war reduced it to $0.87. As a brief account of the company put it, 'Dow hung on tenaciously, but would undoubtedly have fallen before its older and wealthier foe had it not been for a tariff of 4 tenths of a cent per pound.'[31] In short, in that conflict the tariff amounted to half the price at which the rivals were struggling for business. As with ash there was a growing market for caustic soda and, continuing to expand, the industry gradually concentrated on major power sites, notably at Niagara, where it helped to degrade the environmental quality of the wider setting of that superb natural feature. Between 1899 and 1914 the proportion of American chemical output made by electrolytical processes increased from 3 per cent to 15 per cent.[32] (Figure 8.5).

In all this headlong process of economic growth to a leading place in the output and also in the technology of the alkali industry the USA owed much to imported factors as well to its own unique momentum and vigour. The Solvay Process Co. had to resort to Europe not only for the patents, but also for training of staff in Solvay's Dombasle works in Lorraine, only three of its workers having been in an ammonia soda works before. Neil Mathieson had been prominent in the Widnes alkali industry – including trying the ammonia soda process on a small scale there – before he sold out to the United Alkali Co. Mathieson alkali products were well known in the USA and the promoters of the Saltville plant decided there would be advantage in acquiring the use of that name for their operations. Neil Mathieson's son Thomas was engaged to supervise construction. Shortly after production began, in the summer of 1895, he returned to England. Most of the capital for Saltville seems to have been

Figure 8.5   Electrolytic alkali plants built in the United States up to 1902

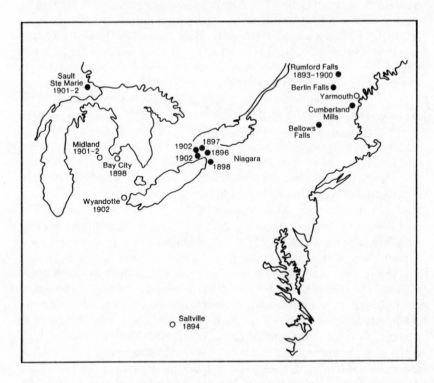

American, but technical equipment and much of the machinery came from England. It did not prove satisfactory in the new operational environment. As the company long afterwards recorded, 'Soon after operations started, the design and construction of the plant, being based on the English methods of manufacture, were found inadequate to compete successfully with other American manufacturers. All the operations were carried out by hand and the products, although satisfactory in quality, were produced at excessive cost. It was therefore necessary to convert to mechanical handling.'[33] An Anglo-American finance company had been involved in the promotion of the abortive scheme for a plant at Kanopolis, Kansas.[34] As seen above, the United Alkali Co. played a part, if not a very positive or distinguished one, in the shaping of the American industry.

Time and again individuals from European plants brought in their expertise at various levels within the hierachies of the new firms. This was noticeable in design and in the vital form of middle-rank control. When the Pennsylvania

Salt Manufacturing Co. put up an electrolytic alkali plant at Wyandotte, construction was supervised by Thomas Kirkham, late of Runcorn. Two other major parts in that electrolytic operation were played by the Englishmen George Bell and A. E. Gibbs.[35] Even earlier in the American caustic soda industry important roles were played by two foremen from St Helens, Wolff from Greenbank works and Bradley. J. B. Ford's Michigan Alkali works initially cost $100 000. It was built by two English chemists, the Wood brothers, but it was poorly designed and did not function economically. Convinced that the operation was bound to fail, Ford followed the precedent that he had followed in the plate glass industry and sent to England for technically trained men. Herbert and John Watson accepted his proposals and moved to America. Soon after this the Scot, W. T. Orr, and the English chemist, H. R. Browne, were brought into the plant. Capital was increased, by 1896 to as much as $2.5 million. Productivity was transformed. At Wyandotte the first plant after reconditioning by the Watsons made 15 tons of ash daily with the employment of 90 men; by 1895 a new plant had been built which employed 600 but turned out 250 tons a day.[36]

Another Scot played a still more distinguished part in the American alkali industry. In 1887, the 19-year-old Hugh A. Galt became a chemist with the Eglinton Chemical Co. in Ayrshire. Two years later he emigrated to the USA; his mastery of alkali technology was soon recognized. Shortly afterwards he was engaged by J. B. Ford to superintend his new Wyandotte plant, and then he had oversight of the building of the two plants owned by the successor concern, the Michigan Alkali Co. John Pitcairn chose him at the end of the 1890s to pick a site for, to construct and to supervise the operations of a plant to supply the soda ash needs of the Pittsburgh Plate Glass Co. (PPG). Galt built the Barberton Works and stayed on as Columbia Alkali's General Manager. In 1920, he was made a director of PPG and Vice-President in charge of their Columbia Alkali Division, a position which he retained until his retirement in 1940.[37]

Not without some difficulties the technologies of the alkali branch of the heavy chemical trades had been firmly planted in the USA in the course of not much more than a decade. In 1892 an American chemicals specialist could write, 'Of all the arts which we have cultivated and improved, the manufacture of chemicals has made the least progress and received the least attention.' By contrast, in the same year, the European alkali expert, George Lunge recognized one field of great American potential: 'We poor Europeans may well tremble as we think of the enormous advantages for all applications of electricity enjoyed by the U.S....'[38] Four years later, although the advance was now well under way, a review of progress still ended on an uncertain note: 'The United States stands at the front in the manufacture of iron and of mechanical appliances, and holds an eminent position in textile industries, but in the alkali trade there is ample room for growth ...'[39] However, within a few months of that assessment, a British trade journal had to recognize that the industry in the old country possessed nothing so complete as the plant which their ex-compatriot, Galt, had put up for Michigan Alkali, and a little later still it acknowledged that, both in soda ash and in caustic soda, '...all interest is concentrated in America, and poor Lancashire is nowhere.' When Columbia Alkali brought in its caustic plant the same journal admitted it was '...the finest caustic soda works in the world. There is really nothing like it anywhere else.'[40] Reviewing the year's work, the New Year 1900 number of the *Chemical Trades Journal* ruefully recorded: 'The chemical manufacturing spirit of the States has been aroused, and we are doomed to feel their activity.'[41]

There were still to be exceptional cases in which the Old World had – or thought that it had – something to teach the New. An example of this was seen when, before the First World War, the Solvay Process Co. lost ground to its US rivals, its share of national output of ash falling from 90 per cent in 1900 to 46 per cent in 1914. Early in the summer of the latter year Solvay & Cie sent out a mission to investigate; Brunner and Mond were represented. Solvays forced through technical and managerial changes.[42] Generally, however, the Americans were striding ahead, particularly of their late masters, the British chemical firms. This came out interestingly in relation to Professor F. S. Kipping's 1908 Presidential address to the Chemical Section of the British Association. His controversial criticisms of the decadence of the British industry, though especially concentrated on dyestuffs, led an American reviewer to write: 'The discussion certainly showed that the manufacturer is not taking advantage of the scientific knowledge now so liberally provided. The works chemists are not treated as they should be and there is little cooperation between manufacturer and scientist.'[43] By contrast, although its beginning had been so long delayed, the apprenticeship stage of the US alkali industry had now been completed; technology transfer from the Old World to the New had been achieved.

In the twentieth century the American industry continued to grow and to respond to changing raw materials, technology and demand by means of important, sometimes dramatic locational changes. After the 1950s the natural soda industry began to supersede the ammonia soda process. In 1986 the last Solvay works closed. In the USSR, growth was less rapid, and more of the old, pre-Revolution pattern remained.

At the Silver Jubilee celebrations of his own company, at the very time when the US alkali industry was coming into existence, Ernest Solvay had observed: 'Industries like men grow old, and in celebrating their silver wedding you are too often only celebrating their decline...'[44] It was an arresting remark, but it ignored the fact that, as the early history of the Russian and still more the American alkali plants showed, industries obtain a new lease of life or new vigour when their technologies are transferred to a new setting. Even then, as with humans, origins and early experiences leave their mark in maturity and even into old age. Individuals and societies are both very variously endowed.

The development of the alkali industries of the USA and of the Russian Empire/USSR shows that technologies may be transferred successfully and may flourish in their new settings. However, as comparison of the two instances indicates, some hosts prove more congenial than others. The critical factors are, on the one hand, the appropriateness of the new technology and, on the other, the responsiveness of the society to which it is transferred to its challenges as well as to its opportunities. Herein there lies no neat prescription for countries which today are seeking success in implanting the industrial processes of the advanced industrial economies. This historical case study suggests that capitalism is more capable than a command economy of making the necessary adjustments, but for any country the task is not an easy one. As in past instances, so too today, those who wish to reap the benefits of applying an imported technology must rise to the challenge of the occasion.

NOTES

*The author of this chapter wishes to acknowledge his indebtedness to the generous interest and friendly criticisms of Dr Peter Morris of the Open University.

1. B. Pares, 'Reaction and Revolution in Russia', in *Cambridge Modern History XII, The Latest Age* (Cambridge: 1910) p. 322.
2. M. K. Vyvyan, *New Cambridge Modern History, X The Zenith of European Power: 1830–1870* (Cambridge, 1960), chap. xiv, p. 364, and J. L. H. Kemp, in *New Cambridge Modern History,* XI *Material Progress and World-wide Problems: 1870–1898* (Cambridge), p. 368; *Encyclopaedia Britannica,* 11th ed (Cambridge, 1911), article on Russia.
3. P. Kropotkin, 'Russia', in *Encyclopaedia Britannica,* 9th edn (Edinburgh, 1886).
4. Pavel Kryukov, *Ocherk Manufackturno Promyshlennykh Sil Europeiskei Rossi,* (1855) p. 69. (I am wholly indebted to Dr A. Ryder for this reference.) P. I. Lyaschenko, *History of the National Economy of Russia to the Revolution of 1917* (New York, 1949).
5. Kropotkin, 'Russia'.
6. R. Bowman, in *Journal of the Society of Chemical Industry,* (29 April 1893) pp. 314–15.
7. *Chemical Trades Journal,* (23 July 1887) p. 65.
8. See Mendeleev's enthusiastic celebration of what he considered to be the world ranking economic potentials of this region in D. Mendeleev, *Principles of Chemistry.* 3rd English edn, (London, 1905), I, pp. 369, 370, footnote 8.
9. *Chemical Trades Journal,* 11 (30 July 1892) p. 647; 14 (31 March 1894) p. 212; 20 (29 May 1897).
10. P. Kropotkin, 'Russia', in *Encyclopaedia Britannica,* (10th edn, 1902).
11. J. C. Ridley, *Reminiscences of Russia, The Urals and Adjoining Siberian Districts* (Newcastle upon Tyne, 1897) p. 73.
12. *Chemical Trades Journal,* 20 (29 May 1897).
13. E. S. Little, *Review of Far Eastern Trade of Brunner and Mond for 1915* (privately printed, 1915/16).
14. S. Wyatt, 'The Progress of the Chemical Industry', in R. P. Rothwell, *The Mineral Industry, Its State, Technology, and Trade,* I (New York, 1893) p. 57.
15. *Journal of the Society of Chemical Industry,* 16 (31 May 1897) p. 478.
16. *Engineering and Mining Journal,* (2 October 1875) p. 532; *Journal of the Society of Chemical Industry,* 16 (31 May 1897) p. 478; (31 January 1900) p. 87.

17. *Journal of the Franklin Institute*, 3rd series, **CIII**, 1877, p. 13; Wyatt, 'Progress of the Chemical Industry'.
18. V. S. Clark, *History of Manufactures in the United States*, **III** (New York, 1929) p. 29.
19. Using limestone and cryolite, the Natrona works made alumnite of soda. This was then mixed with fluoride of calcium and saturated with carbonic acid gas to produce hydrate of alumina and sodium carbonate. See J. F. Stark, 'Report of Visit to USA', May–July 1876' pp. 39, 40, 57, in Chance and Hunt Records/23, ICI Archives, Widnes. J. D. Pennock, 'Progress of the Soda Industry in the United States since 1900', in the proceedings of the Fifth Internationaler Kongress fur Angewandt Chemie, Berichte I, (Berlin, 1904).
20. J. F. Stark, 'Report of Visit to USA'.
21. Pennock, 'Progress of the Soda Industry', p. 662; T. P. Hou, *Manufacture of Soda with Special Reference to the Ammonia Process* (New York, 1942) p. 35; *Journal of the Society of Chemical Industry*, **15** (31 December 1896) p. 877; *Chemical Trades Journal*, **30** (18 January 1902).
22. W. J. Reader, *Imperial Chemical Industries, A History. I The Forerunners 1870–1926* (Oxford, 1970) p. 64.
23. G. Martin, S. Smith and F. Milson, 'The Salt and Alkali Industry', *Manuals of Chemical Technology*, **VI** (London, 1916) p. 37.
24. W. Haynes, *The American Chemical Industry* **VI**.
25. *Chemical Trades Journal*, **27** (29 September 1900).
26. *Chemical Trades Journal*, **24** (4 February 1899) p. 93.
27. *Chemical Trades Journal*, **21** (27 November 1897) p. 343; (18 January 1902).
28. J. A. Bradburn, 'The Manufacture of Alkali by the Ammonia Process and the Alkali Trade of the United States', *Journal of the Society of Chemical Industry*, **15** (31 December 1896) p. 879.
29. *Journal of the Society of Chemical Industry*, **15** (31 December 1896) p. 885.
30. *Chemical Trade Journal*, **22** (19 March 1898) p. 202.
31. Haynes, *The American Chemical Industry*, **VI**, p. 114.
32. J. W. Richardson, 'The Electrochemical Industries of Niagara Falls', in *Electrochemical Industry*, (September, October 1902), and in *Review of American Chemical Research*, **IX**, i, pp. 51–3; Haynes, *The American Chemical Industry*, **III**, p. 283. For further details see M. M. Trescott, 'The Rise of the American Electrochemical Industry, 1880–1910'; *Studies in the American Technological Environment* (Westport, Conn, 1981).
33. Haynes, *The American Chemical Industry*, **VI**, pp. 264–8.
34. *Chemical Trades Journal*, **30** (18 January 1902) 'The Caustic Soda Trade of the States'; **24** (28 January 1899) p. 59; **22** (19 March 1898) p. 202.
35. Haynes, *The American Chemical Industry*, **VI**, p. 331.
36. Haynes, *The American Chemical Industry*, **VI**, pp. 488–90.
37. *National Cyclopaedia of American Biography*, **34** (New York) entry on H. A. Galt.
38. Quoted V. S. Clark, *History of Manufactures*, **II**, p. 524; G. Lunge, quoted Haynes, *The American Chemical Industry*, **III**, p. 275.
39. J. A. Bradburn, 'The Manufacture of Alkali', p. 885.
40. *Chemical Trades Journal*, **20** (20 March 1897) pp. 205–6; **22** (1 January 1898) pp. 1–2; **28** (26 January 1901) pp. 63–4.
41. *Chemical Trades Journal*, **26** (6 January 1900) p. 2, K. Warren, *Chemical Foundations: The Alkali Industry in Britain to 1926* (Oxford, 1980) ch. 16, especially pp. 194–6.
42. W. J. Reader, *ICI*, pp. 291, 292.
43. C. W. S. Allen, in American Chemical Society's *Chemical Abstracts*, **3** (1909) p. 360, reviewing F. S. Kipping, in *Chemical Trades Journal*, **43**, (14, 21 November 1908).
44. Quoted W. J. Reader, *ICI*, p. 95.

REFERENCES

Valuable surveys will be found in the following;
L. F. Haber, *The Chemical Industry during the Nineteenth Century* (Oxford, 1958).
L. F. Haber, *The Chemical Industry*, 1900–1930 (Oxford, 1971).
W. Haynes, *The American Chemical Industry*, 6 volumes (New York, 1945–1954).

PART 3

West to East before 1914

9. The Transfer of Cotton Manufacturing Technology from Britain to Japan

Tetsuro Nakaoka

THE EARLIEST IMPORT OF TECHNOLOGY

In the autumn of 1865, two Japanese samurai visited Platt Brothers & Co. at Oldham, Lancashire and proposed to buy a full line of equipment for a cotton spinning factory. The company suggested a spinning mill with 2 560 throstles and 2 640 mule ones. The plan seems to have been beyond their budgetary limits. It took several rounds of negotiation before they reached the final contract the following February, when they agreed to buy a plant of slightly smaller size, as shown in Table 9.1. The equipment arrived in Japan early in 1867. The mill was constructed at Kagoshima, at the southern end of Japan. Six engineers from the company directed construction and trained local workers in the operation of the mill. The mill was completed in June 1867 and began to work as the Kagoshima Spinning Mill affiliated with Satsuma-han ('han' means the clan of the Japanese feudal system). This was the first cotton spinning mill in Japan based on transferred Western technology.

It was set up at a time of radical political change, the 'Meiji Restoration', in which the Japanese feudal system under the Tokugawa shogunate was abolished and the whole country was put under the reign of the Tennou (Emperor). In November 1867, Tokugawa Yoshinobu, the last Shogun, turned his political power over to the Tennou. The new government was organized under the Tennou, but it was very weak, having no substantial control over the country. In order to consolidate its political basis the new government decided to overthrow the whole shogunate system by military action. War began in January 1868. This is not the place to describe the political change in detail. However two developments were pertinent to the context of this industrial analysis. The first was that the political upheaval drove all British engineers back to their country soon after the construction of the mill, though they were supposed to stay at Kagoshima for at least two years. Needless to say this seriously affected the effect of technology transfer. The second development

181

Table 9.1   List of machines of Kagoshima Mill

Prime mover: steam engine	1
Opener	1
Scutcher	1
Grinder	1
Carding engine	10
Drawing frame	1
Flyer frame	1
Intermediate frame	2
Roving frame	4
Throstle frame (308 spindles)	6
Mule frame (600 spindles)	3
Power loom:	
48-inch width 6 shuttles	10
45-inch width 4 shuttles	50
45-inch width 2 shuttles	20
45-inch width 1 shuttles	20

Source: Taichi Kinukawa, *Honpo Menshiboseki Shi (A History of Cotton Spinning in Japan)*,
          vol. 1 (1937), p. 25.

related to the political situation of the Satsuma clan. They were the most influential and strongest of the forces which supported the new government. But over the course of political reform they became more and more critical of the new government, eventually taking up arms against it. After the defeat of the Satsuma rebellion in 1877, Kagoshima became a periphery in Japan, both politically and industrially. This also seriously affected transfer of technology from this first mill.

What was the aim of the hasty import action of a Western cotton mill by the Satsuma-han in the midst of political disturbances? Since the 1840s (that is just after the Opium War) Japanese samurai had been keenly discussing how to cope with the threat of Western fleets approaching Japan. Satsuma-han was the most militant and urged fighting against them. It launched a great expansion in armaments in the 1850s but had to stop half-way because of lack of both engineering competency and financial resources. Its chief port, Kagoshima, had been devastated by a British naval squadron in 1863, in retaliation for actions against Western personnel and ships. Through these experiences Satsuma-han gradually realized that the power of Western countries was supported not only by their modern armaments but also by the wealth of their nations, and that industrialization would be a key to the wealth of a nation.

Tomoatsu Godai, one of the two samurai who made the contract with Platt Brothers & Co. summarized this idea by saying that, if Japan wished to become strong militarily, she must become rich first. He went to Britain with plans for industrialization: modernization of sugar refining, cotton spinning, gold mining and so on and mechanization of the irrigation system were the main targets[1]. However all he could buy with his small financial resources were one cotton spinning mill and guns for the battle against the Tokugawa government.

Why did he choose a cotton mill? Perhaps because of the influence of Kakutaro Ishikawa. Since the 1840s, many hans had become increasingly eager to recruit samurai who were well-informed about Western science and technology. Ishikawa was one such samurai recruited to Satsuma-han. In the 1850s he was engaged on a steamship building project, part of the armaments expansion plan mentioned above, but which was unsuccessful. In the 1860s his concern shifted to the cotton-spinning industry. In 1863 he submitted to the lord of the Satsuma-han a report which recommended the importation of Western cotton-spinning frames, promotion of weaving cotton stripes, and their sale on the Osaka market[2]. While he stressed that the cotton industry would be one of the most profitable industries in a future Japan, he pointed out that industrial growth would meet a bottleneck in the low efficiency of traditional spinning. Further development would require imports of superior Western spinning frames. The report seems to have been adopted by the lord. After the establishment of the Kagoshima Mill, Satsuma-han imported another mill equipped with 2 000 mule spindles and constructed it at Sakai in south Osaka. Ishikawa worked with British engineers throughout the construction process of the Kagoshima Mill and was trained by them in construction techniques as well as in setting and adjusting spinning frames. In the construction of the Sakai Mill he directed all construction, setting and adjusting machinery without any help of foreign engineers.

In 1873 there were three cotton-spinning mills, all imported from Britain, working in Japan: Kagoshima, Sakai and Kashima Mill in Tokyo. This last was owned by a cotton merchant, Manpei Kashima, and was a small water-powered mill. The type of its spinning frames is uncertain. It is said to have been throstle or an early form of ring. Its total number of spindles was only 576. However such a small size and the use of water power might have been most appropriate to contemporary Japan. Only this mill achieved good business results. As we can see from Table 9.1 Kagoshima Mill was too large and sophisticated to be maintained with the primitive mechanical skills of the Japanese of the time. In addition, Satsuma-han had a political burden, as explained above. It sold the Sakai Mill to the Ministry of Finance in 1872. Though Kagoshima Mill survived until 1897, it did not realize any profits, except in two or three good years. Ishikawa's foresight was too far ahead of the time.

THE TRADITIONAL COTTON INDUSTRY BEFORE THE IMPACT OF THE WEST

The impact of Western technology reached the Japanese cotton industry just when the abolition of the feudal system was opening up new opportunities and possibilities. We therefore need a brief account of the industry's development in the Edo period to understand the economic effect of this impact.

Silk and hemp were known to ancient Japan. Of course silk clothing and fabrics were confined to the upper class; common people wore hemp. Cotton clothes began to be reported in written documents around the fourteenth century, all referring to clothes imported from Korea and China.[3] The beginning of cotton cultivation came perhaps between the end of the fifteenth and the mid-sixteenth century. All techniques for cultivation, spinning and weaving were of Chinese origin. In the Edo period under the Tokugawa Shogunate (1603–1867), cotton diffused gradually in people's daily lives and took the place of hemp. Eventually it became the most popular clothing. Correspondingly cotton cultivation spread all over Japan. In the late Edo period we can notice three important cotton manufacturing regions: Kinki region surrounding Osaka, the nationwide distribution centre of cotton goods of the time; Kanto region north of Edo; and the region corresponding to the present-day Aichi prefecture.

Techniques were not very advanced. Cotton yarn was spun from 'shino' using a primitive spinning wheel. 'Shino' is drawn cotton comparable to the sliver in the West. Raw cotton was ginned, beaten with a cotton bow, and drawn into 'shino'. In some advanced regions a special trade had developed for each division of this work, but generally production depended largely on peasants' side-work or by-occupation undertaken when agricultural work was slack. Spinning and weaving especially were jobs of peasants' wives and daughters. The loom shown in Figure 9.1 which was called 'jibata', was commonly used for weaving cotton. Usually a wholesale dealer traded in all sorts of cotton goods. He organized the spinning and weaving process largely on the putting out system, and distributed not only clothes to urban clothing shops but also beaten cotton, 'shino', and hanks to remote local manufacturers.

Though cotton cultivation was concentrated in three regions. cotton weaving diffused more evenly all over the country. Daimyos (territorial magnates heading the ruling class under the shogun) were usually eager to promote local industry and put a special emphasis on the cotton textile industry. In some hans even samurai of a lower class were encouraged to take up cotton weaving as a by-occupation. Thus many local cotton industries developed successfully around the end of the Edo period. Their products were branded with the name of the region and sold in the national market with a good reputation. They constituted an important basis for development after the Restoration.

Figure 9.1   Jibata

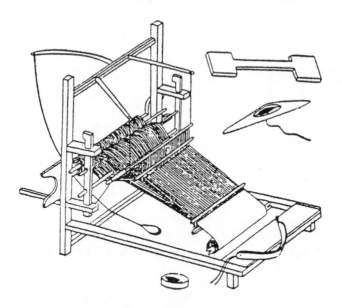

Source: Ozeki, Masunari, *Kishoku Ihen* (1830).

The first Western impact on the traditional cotton industry came with the opening of ports after 1854 (Treaty of Kanagawa). The importing of Western cloths such as calico, muslin and camlet increased rapidly. They were welcomed as new materials for traditional kimono and haori (overcoat), especially for the lining cloths. Some local cotton industries were reported to have been damaged by competition from imported cloths. But the influence was restricted because the imports were accepted mainly as curious new materials and not as substitute goods for traditional cloths[4]. In addition, most consumers of imported cloths were Daimyos and other rich classes so the popular market was not much affected. The development was important, however, because imports stimulated a new fashion in kimonos and prepared for later developments.

The second impact came with Civil War in the USA. The dislocation of the American South created a world shortage of raw cotton. Japanese raw cotton exports therefore commenced. This resulted in a shortage of cotton yarn in the domestic market and caused serious problems for local weavers. In turn, this forced weavers to use imported cotton yarn and so acquainted them with the properties of cotton yarn spun on spinning frames. They noticed that imported yarns were much stronger in tension than domestic yarn spun by hand. Also they were astonished by the thinness of high-count yarn because they used relatively thick yarn of around No 10 count spun from short stapled raw cotton of Chinese origin. They found that this fine yarn could be used as a completely new raw material.

THE DEVELOPMENT OF THE WEAVING SECTOR AFTER THE RESTORATION

The social disturbance of the Meiji Restoration necessarily resulted in a sharp decline in textile production, but with the recovery of social stability the weaving sector (both cotton and silk) began to develop vigorously. The abolition of many feudal restrictions and the principle of the free market liberated the weavers' latent energy on the supply side. The abandonment of laws which designated costume according to social classes and the establishment of freedom of costume liberated people's interest in fashion on the demand side. In such an activated business environment, the Western impact after the opening of ports was strongly felt in the weaving industry and caused remarkable changes.

Firstly weavers invented various new types of textiles, using imported cotton yarn. One example was silk-cotton mixed cloth that used high-count cotton yarn as weft and local silk as warp. At first this cloth was often sold as pure silk, which caused many problems. But around the mid-Meiji period it established its status in the mass market as a cheap substitute for silk. Another important new cloth was Han-to (half-foreign) cloth with imported thick yarn as warp and local hand-spun yarn as weft. This cloth enabled improved productivity of the weaving process. In the traditional weaving process using 'jibata' and hand-spun yarn, weak warps often snapped when the weaver beat up. This was the most important cause of lowered productivity of weaving. Therefore substitution of strong imported yarn for weak local yarn as warp greatly improved productivity. Local hand-spun yarn remained in use as weft in order to give the final cloth a hint of the appearance of a traditional cotton cloth. Consumers did not like excessively radical changes.[5]

Adoption of imported yarns as warp made way for a change of cotton loom. Since the late Edo period many efforts had been directed towards using silk looms (which were far more efficient than 'jibata') for cotton weaving. As a result, the 'takabata' loom, shown in Figure 9.2, was used for cotton weaving. Nevertheless it failed to overcome fully the warp snapping problem and did not diffuse widely. The use of strong warp eliminated this difficulty and the 'takabata' began to diffuse rapidly in the weaving sector. It was followed by the introduction of the flying shuttle. In 1872, the Kyoto prefecture dispatched three silk weavers to Lyon to learn techniques related to the Jacquard loom.

They came back the following year with various textile machines, including the flying shuttle. Though diffusion of Jacquard machines was rather slow, the flying shuttle was modified by local carpenters to fit the 'takabata' (Figure 9.3) and began to spread very rapidly through the weaving sector. In the late 1870s the use of 'takabata' and the flying shuttle was common in the three advanced regions: Kinki region surrounding Osaka, the Aichi prefecture, and Kanto region to the north of Tokyo.

Figure 9.2   Takabata

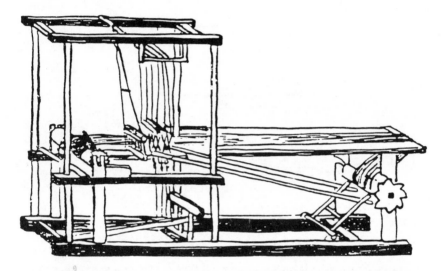

Source: Nihon Kogakukai (ed.), *Meiji Kogyo-shi (A History of Industry in Meiji Japan)* (1930).

This type of loom constituted the standard loom of the weaving sector in the Meiji period. Though imported power looms were far more efficient, the skills necessary to operate them were extremely rare in Japan at that time. Mr T. Ishii, a historian of Japanese looms, estimates the productivity of this loom as about three to four times that of 'jibata'[6]. A combination of cheap labour and such a productivity increase was enough to sustain the rapid growth of the weaving sector. All the more important was the fact that local loom carpenters could easily construct the loom. They proceeded to invent a further advanced loom which could simultaneously perform shedding, picking and beating up by a single motion of a foot pedal. Using this loom they successfully developed wooden power looms of various types in the late Meiji period. Many mechanisms

Figure 9.3   The flying shuttle modified to adapt to takabata

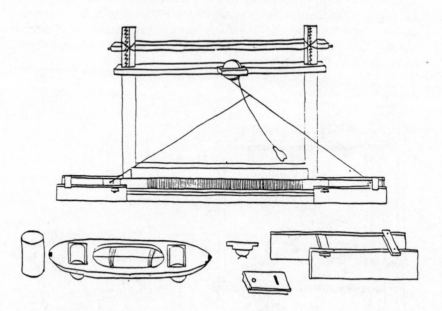

Source: *Meiji Kogyo-shi* (1930).

incorporated in them were borrowed from Western looms and modified to suit the wooden construction.

However borrowing from Western techniques did not always produce positive effects on local industries. Until the early 1880s local textile industries had suffered from the wrong use of imported artificial dye stuffs. Dyers used imported chemical dyes without the slightest scientific knowledge necessary for applying them properly. The dyes did not fix in the textiles and this resulted in innumerable claims from the consumers. The government, as well as some advanced prefectures, dispatched students abroad to learn chemistry. It was not until they returned and collaborated with local governments in the training of dyers that the textile industry could overcome the problem.

In spite of such troubles the weaving sector continued to grow throughout the late nineteenth century (see Table 9.2). Table 9.3 shows a further striking fact – that there were over a million textile workers and 660 000 weaving houses in Japan in the late 1890s. The average figure of 1.58 workers per house tells us that the development had been achieved by means of an extremely small-scale mode of production. Most Japanese historians agree in regarding this as a sign of contemporary Japan's industrial backwardness.

From the viewpoint of technology transfer, however, we have to point out some peculiar aspects of this development. The first is the hybrid nature of technical change. Clearly changes arose from the influence of imported Western materials and techniques, but they appeared in local looms and weaving or dyeing techniques. As a result, this industrial growth was not accompanied by any large increase in the import of machinery, in particular of looms.

Table 9.2   The trend of output from the cotton industry (thousand Kins)*

	Cotton textiles	Cotton yarn	
		Handspun	Mechanically spun
1861	28 100	27 800	–
1867	16 700	14 200	200
1874	25 600	13 400	700
1880	59 700	27 100	1 100
1883	45 100	14 100	3 900
1888	89 900	27 100	10 600
1891	91 700	19 800	52 800
1897	156 900	16 700	161 600
1900	153 800	–	156 700
1904	141 900	–	145 200

*Kin is a Japanese traditional unit of weight: 1 Kin = 0.6 kg. Output is expressed by weight of ginned cotton used.
Source: Satoru Nakamura, *Meiji Ishin no Kisokozo (The Infra-Structure of Meiji Restoration)* (1968), p 221.

The second is the enormous amount of employment created by this development. As we can see from Table 9.3, employment was created evenly in almost all prefectures. Production processes were organized mainly by cotton dealers, just as in the late Edo period. Some cotton merchants were able thereby to accumulate a large amount of capital which they could invest in the modernized spinning sector in the 1890s.

The third, and perhaps the most important, aspect for the next development was that the weaving sector had prepared a domestic cotton yarn market which was favourable to an infant spinning industry. We explain this in the next section.

Table 9.3   Numbers of weaving houses and workers in 1895

Prefecture	Weaving houses (A)	Workers (B)	Workers per house (B/A)
Aichi	42 032	86 054	2.0
Kyoto	13 208	59 754	4.5
Osaka	22 333	59 310	2.7
Kumamoto	40 353	46 196	1.1
Saitama	36 289	45 696	1.3
Ehime	34 470	45 270	1.3
Yamaguchi	29 801	41 130	1.4
Shimane	34 253	39 367	1.1
Kagoshima	35 323	35 561	1.0
Niigata	22 407	35 029	1.6
Nagano	24 101	32 792	1.4
Tottori	22 267	32 259	1.4
Gunma	13 862	30 603	2.2
Shiga	20 998	28 226	1.3
Ooita	27 530	26 959	1.0
Japan total	660 408	1 042 866	1.58

Source: Noshomu Tokeihyo (12-ji) (12th Statistical Book of the Ministry of Agriculture and
          Commerce) (1897).

IMPORT-SUBSTITUTION POLICY OF COTTON YARN

Japan's trade balance had been in deficit since the Restoration. This was partly
the result of the stagnation of silk exports, which had constituted about 70 per
cent of Japan's export trade since the opening of ports, but largely it was a
natural result of the rapid growth of the textile industry. As imported cotton
yarn was the prime mover of the industry on the supply side, yarn imports rose
as domestic demand for textiles increased. In the 1880s imports of cotton yarn
surpassed those of cotton textiles and accounted for the largest proportion of
total imports (about 20 per cent) (Table 9.4).

About this time Japan faced a serious economic crisis resulting from three
combined causes: an enormous war expenditure due to the Satsuma rebellion,
a large decrease in the international price of silver, which was Japan's standard
coin, and the accumulated trade deficit. To overcome this crisis, the government implemented many policies, including the import-substitution of cotton
yarn.

Table 9.4   The import of cotton textiles and yarn (000 yen)

	Total imports (A)	Import of cotton textiles (B)	(B/A)	Import of cotton yarn (C)	(C/A)
1868	10 693	2 542	0.24	1 239	0.12
1870	33 741	2 982	0.09	4 522	0.13
1872	26 174	4 888	0.19	5 335	0.20
1874	23 461	5 404	0.23	3 573	0.15
1876	23 964	4 908	0.21	4 151	0.17
1878	32 874	5 007	0.15	7 205	0.22
1880	36 626	5 523	0.15	7 700	0.21
1882	29 446	4 219	0.14	6 562	0.22
1884	29 672	2 488	0.08	5 153	0.17
1886	32 168	2 316	0.07	5 905	0.18
1888	65 455	4 691	0.07	13 611	0.21
1890	81 728	4 129	0.05	9 928	0.12
1892	71 326	4 668	0.07	7 131	0.10
1894	117 481	6 958	0.06	7 977	0.07
1896	171 674	11 610	0.07	11 371	0.07
1898	277 502	10 878	0.04	8 547	0.03
1900	287 261	18 438	0.06	7 043	0.02

Source: Toyo Keizai-shinpo (ed), *Nippon Boeki Seiran (Statistical Survey of Japan's Foreign Trade)* (1935).

The main lines of the policy were as follows. The government imported equipment for ten cotton-spinning mills of equal size (2 000 mule spindles). They were sold to competent entrepreneurs in cotton-cultivating regions who paid for them over 10 years with no interest. In addition, various measures were prepared for supporting financially entrepreneurs who were willing to enter the spinning industry.

As the result of this policy, 17 cotton spinning mills, all utilizing equipment imported from Britain and mostly on a scale of 2 000 spindles, started up in the first half of the 1880s. One of them was established in the Aichi prefecture as the government-affiliated Aichi Mill, where Kakutaro Ishikawa and some skilled workers, transferred from Sakai Mill, trained workers for the newly established mills in the operation and construction of spinning machinery.

The results of their business were miserable. The worst among them, Ichikawa Mill, was bankrupted three years after the start and was transferred to a different owner. Most mills could not produce yarn of good quality and consequently could not sell their products well. They met with great difficulties in the operation and maintenance of their mills and consequently production costs were relatively high, in spite of extremely cheap labour costs.[7]

Meanwhile, Eiichi Shibusawa, a famous business leader in the early Meiji period, was preparing to start up a cotton-spinning mill. In his opinion a scale of 2 000 spindles was too small for the cotton-spinning business to be internationally competitive; that is, to be able to substitute for imports. He decided that a scale of 10 000 spindles would be appropriate in Japan at this time. A mill on this scale required a far larger amount of capital than the mills recommended by the government. Therefore he decided to organize it as a joint-stock company, counting on rich former Daimyos as stockholders. He was so far-sighted that he hired as mill manager a person who was studying in Britain – Takeo Yamanobe, a former samurai of Tsuwano-han. Yamanobe was studying business-related subjects at London University when Shibusawa asked him to become the manager of a mill which he proposed to establish. Yamanobe changed his course to mechanical engineering and after finishing that course he went to Manchester, became an apprentice in a cotton-spinning mill and mastered spinning practices. All this experience was very helpful for his managerial work in a large mill in which all the equipment and techniques were imported from Manchester and most of the work-force was unskilled in mechanical operations.

In 1883 the Osaka Spinning Co. started with 10 500 mule spindles and made a profit from its first year. It increased in size to 31 320 spindles in 1886 and continued to develop rapidly. This development provided a model of successful enterprise in the cotton spinning industry and many newcomers, pursuing economies of scale with 10 000 spindles, followed in the late 1880s. This created the rapid growth of the industry in this decade, as shown in Table 9.2.

COMPARING THE SUCCESS OF OSAKA SPINNING CO. AND THE FAILURE OF OTHER MILLS

The sharp contrast between the miserable failure of 2 000-spindle mills under heavy government protection and the brilliant success of a much larger private spinning business was so impressive that many arguments have been advanced to explain both the failure of one and the success of the other. Here I will focus on the argument of Professor Naosuke Takamura, the author of one of the most reliable studies of the economic history of the Japanese cotton spinning industry.[8]

As regards the failure of the 2 000-spindle mills, Professor Takamura points to three important causes. First of all, he stresses the shortage of capital. Though the hire-purchase of equipment over ten years and with no interest may seem very favourable to entrepreneurs, it covered only a small part of their business expenditure. Mill entrepreneurs were usually rich farmers or local manufacturers of soy sauce or wine who entered the spinning business out of a sense of patriotic duty, and with no background in production by machinery. However mill manufacture forced them into unexpectedly high expenditure. The average expense for the construction of a mill was said to be 52 400 yen, including 22 000 yen for the equipment (paid for by hire-purchase). At least 30 000 yen for the construction and an additional 10 or 20 000 yen for the working capital were required at the start of the enterprise. This amount was already at the limit of a farmer's or local manufacturer's ability. And once actual expenditure surpassed their budgets, they could not afford any additional investment or overhead expense.

Secondly, government resources were also very limited. While the imported equipment arrived at Japan in November 1880, the government decided the following year to adopt a strict retrenchment policy, forced upon it by a large financial deficit. Government expenditures were drastically cut back; for instance, entrepreneurs were requested to pay for the services of government engineers. This imposed further burdens on poor entrepreneurs who were struggling to overcome the shortage of capital.

Thirdly, Professor Takamura points to the incompetence of local engineers, as represented by Ishikawa. Their faulty mill design often resulted in the need for additional construction work requiring unnecessary expenditure. Their worst mistake, he argues, was the adoption of water power as motive force. In many mills water could not provide enough power to drive the machinery and a steam engine was additionally required. However, few could afford to buy a steam engine. The inferior performance of water turbines constructed in Japanese shipyards was also responsible for this situation.[9]

Professor Takamura's explanation for the success of Osaka Spinning Co. naturally reflects this analysis of 2 000-spindle mills. That is, Shibusawa's success depended on assembling relatively large amounts of capital – 280 000 yen, of which 38 per cent was paid by former Daimyos: the company were determined to succeed in business without reliance on government help; and Yamanobe was a more competent engineer than Ishikawa, in that he prudently adopted steam power and took care to ask for guidance from foreign engineers in setting up equipment. The equipment was imported from Platt Brothers & Co., who sent an engineer to Japan to supervise plant construction and installation of equipment. In addition to these three points, Takamura believes the appropriateness of the scale (10 000 spindles) was important.[10]

Though I appreciate that these views are generally adequate and correct from an economist's viewpoint, I would like to add some comments on them from the engineering point of view. In order to estimate the appropriateness of choice of technology we must consider the state of mechanical skills in contemporary Japan. Let us return to the fact that, among the earliest mills, only Kashima Mill achieved good business results. It had a scale of only 576 spindles and was powered by a water turbine. Kagoshima Mill was powered by a steam engine, but maintenance of its power transmission system was extremely difficult, especially that of the gears transmitting power from the main shaft to branch shafts; they very often broke, resulting in frequent shutting down of the mill.[11] The average worker's operational skills were so low that destruction of machine parts was not infrequent. Sometimes substitute parts were not available and they had to be ordered from Britain. Of course, this meant that the machine was idle until new parts arrived. It may be remembered that the Satsuma-han contained perhaps the most experienced reservoir of engineers in Japan around the time of the Restoration, but even here the early small-scale cotton mill was unprofitable. Why only Kashima Mill could achieve good business results can be explained by the appropriateness of technology to the supply of engineering skills: that is, the very small size of spinning frames, the simple construction of the power transmission system (all machines were driven by a single main shaft), water power with abundant water supply, and its location in Tokyo.

This last was the most decisive. With a shortage of skills inside the mill, easy access to engineering aids from outside was essential. The existence of a machine-shop or a foundry near the mill, however primitive their techniques, was extremely helpful to mill operation. Easy access to foreign engineering resources through agency houses in Yokohama and Kobe port was also essential. Probably there were only two places in Japan at this time where transferred spinning mills could work successfully: Tokyo and Osaka. Since the Restoration modern engineering works had been concentrated in these two cities, which were also near to the ports of Yokohama and Kobe, respectively. The fate of most of the 2 000-spindle mills was determined immediately they located far from the two cities, in rural regions. Most mills worked worse than Kagoshima Mill. I do not deny that Ishikawa was careless when he adopted water power for all mills with no regard to their location. Japanese rivers change their flow drastically with the seasons. In winter several mills located near a mountainous area could hardly operate half their spindles. However, even if they adopted steam engines, I believe the results would have been very poor.

OSAKA AND THE JAPANESE COTTON SPINNING INDUSTRY

Between 1885 and 1889 seven new cotton spinning companies – four in Osaka, two in Tokyo and one in Aichi – were established, five of them with more than

10 000 spindles each. In addition three of the 2 000-spindle mills enlarged their mill size to around this scale.

They were managed according to the model established by Osaka Spinning Co. For instance, many companies employed an engineer as their mill manager, expecting him to play the same role as Yamanobe. The higher technical education system established after the Restoration was then beginning to produce human resources competent to perform this function. Engineer–managers visited Manchester and Lancashire often, gathering information about new machines and techniques, choosing appropriate ones, and coming back to their mills with them.

A remarkable example of the contributions made by these engineer–managers was a shift in spinning technology from mule to ring. Most newly-established companies installed ring spinning frames along with the mules which had been mainly used in Japan since the Kagoshima Mill was built. Mill managers were beginning to be interested in the ring as a new technology and wanted to compare its performance with the mule's on the shop-floor, while they eagerly collected information about it in Britain. On his visit to Platt Brothers & Co. in 1887, Yamanobe was advised that the ring might be more appropriate to Japan than the mule. But he had already begun, in 1886, to test ring frames in his second mill.[12] In 1890 and 1891 another five companies started up, all with Ring frames. This showed that they had plumped for ring technology.

Professor Yukihiko Kiyokawa has made an excellent statistical study which clarifies the background of their decision.[13] As I have explained above, the domestic market for cotton yarn depended on the development of the traditional weaving sector and consequently on the nature of innovations which caused this development. That is, weavers demanded thick, strong yarn suitable for warp. In addition, the traditional technology was based on raw cotton of Chinese type. In the transition period, imported yarn spun from raw cotton of different types caused many problems, in particular at the dyeing stage. Market demand at this time thus concentrated on strong yarn of 10–20 count spun from short stapled Chinese cotton. Ring technology was ideally adapted to this range of production. Professor Kiyokawa showed that in 1890 the average output per spindle was 67 per cent higher by ring frames than by mules. In addition, the quality of yarn produced by rings met greater demand. He also demonstrated that ring technology yielded higher output per unit of capital and required smaller input of capital per unit of labour. This was very favourable to Japan at a time when capital was scarce and labour was abundant.

Thus the Japanese cotton spinning industry was consolidating its basic technology at the beginning of the 1890s. It was based on ring frames imported from Britain and designed to spin thick yarn of 10–20 counts from short stapled raw cotton of Chinese type. It may be noted that this favoured Japan in the East

Asian market because Chinese and Korean weavers also demanded thick, strong yarn spun from Chinese cotton. Based on this technology engineers proceeded in the 1890s to develop techniques for using Indian cotton in spinning fine yarns. The Japanese style of work organization was also consolidating around this time. One of its characteristics was the engineer–manager. His role was important, given the scarcity of mechanical skills. When the Osaka Spinning Co. introduced power looms in 1887, Yamanobe went to Britain, learned how to operate and maintain power looms, came back and trained weavers how to run the imported power looms. In this way, managers often combined the roles of foreman and skilled mechanic. This adequately compensated for the lack of skills among mill workers and sustained the good performance of their mill. Another important characteristic was the two-shift working system which was also pioneered by the Osaka Spinning Co. It was indispensable in decreasing the capital costs of imported equipment.

Osaka was the best location for mills with such technology and work organization. Of 11 mills with over 10 000 spindles in Japan in 1890, seven were located in Osaka, which enjoyed relatively abundant engineering resources. The Osaka mint and the Osaka arsenal had shops which could do rather sophisticated machining work. There were two shipbuilders at Kobe, which had the engineering skills to build steel steamships in 1890. There were settlements of Western merchants both in Osaka and Kobe, through which various kinds of technical help could be obtained. Most importantly, Osaka stood in a cotton-weaving region which led developments in the traditional weaving sector. By the 1890s cotton yarn spun on ring spinning frames had become indispensable to their weaving techniques and manufacturers demanded yarn spun from cotton of Chinese type, being dissatisfied with imported yarn.[14] This situation greatly assisted the infant spinning industry in Osaka. Another advantage for Osaka was the availability of cheap coal. Coal was transported by small boats through the Inland Sea from north Kyushu. Transportation costs were extremely low. Steamships were required to transport coal to Tokyo and this resulted in a 20 per cent higher price for coal in Tokyo than in Osaka.[15]

Such conditions made Osaka the centre of the Japanese cotton-spinning industry. In fact it was the best place in Japan to assimilate the latest techniques brought back from Manchester and to adapt them to Japanese conditions. As shown in Table 9.2, the production of cotton yarn on imported ring frames improved dramatically in the 1890s.[16] From this came the export of yarns to the East Asian market in the latter half of the decade: just 30 years after the two samurai visited Manchester.

NOTES

1. His report submitted to the lord of Satsuma (Tadayoshi Shimazu), Nippon Keieishi Kenkyusho (ed), *Bibliographical Source Book of Tomoatsu Godai* **4** (Tokyo, 1974) pp. 17–26.

2. This report is printed in Taichi Kinukawa, *Honpo Menshiboseki Shi (A History of Cotton Spinning in Japan)*, vol. 1 (Osaka 1937) pp. 146–8.

3. Koji Ono, 'On the Origin of the Cotton Textile Industry in Japan', in his *Nippon Sangyo Hattatsu-shi no Kenkyu (Studies on the Development of Industry in Japan)* (Tokyo, 1981) pp. 210–96; Keiji Nagahara, 'The Development of Cotton Cultivation', in K. Nagahara and K. Yamaguchi, (eds), *Nippon Gijutsu no Shakai-shi (A Social History of Japanese Technology)*, vol. 3, *Spinning and Weaving* (Tokyo, 1983) pp. 69–102.

4. T. C. Smith, *Political Change and Industrial Development in Japan: Government Enterprise, 1868–1880* (Stanford, 1955) pp. 26–9 emphasized the destruction of traditional handicraft industries at this time and pointed to the effect of 'changing consumption habits of the Japanese people' as the result of the impact of imported goods. However he seems to have overestimated restricted observations in special regions: for instance, Tokyo, as regards the changing consumption habits and, for the destruction of handicrafts, some peripheral districts, such as Toyama, Shimane and Iwate. The change in people's consumption habits actually occurred in such a way that they retained traditional habits mainly, while introducing Western influences. As a result the effect on traditional handicrafts was stimulative rather than destructive. Heita Kawakatsu, 'The Prices of Foreign and Local Cotton Cloth in the Early Meiji Period'; and 'The Quality of Foreign and Local Cotton Products in the early Meiji Period', *Waseda Seijikeizaigaku Zasshi*, nos. 244–5 (1976) pp. 508–35; and nos. 250–1 (1977) pp. 184–211, presents a different view from Professor Smith.

5. Tetsuro Nakaoka, 'The Role of Domestic Technical Innovation in Foreign Technology Transfer, *Osaka City University Economic Review*, **18** (1982) pp. 45–62; T. Nakaoka, T. Ishii and H. Uchida, *Kindai Nippon no Gijutsu to Gijutsu-seisaku (Technology and Technology Policy in Modern Japan)* (Tokyo, 1986) pp. 80–91, describe this process in detail. Satoru Nakamura, 'The Change in the Japanese Cotton Industry and World Capitalism', in his *Meiji Ishin no Kisokozo (The Infra-Structure of Meiji Restoration)* (Tokyo, 1968) pp. 209–65, is an important study on the change in the cotton industry during this period.

6. Nakaoka, Ishii and Uchida, *Kindai Nippon no Gijutsu*, p. 156.

7. Sanshi, Orimono, To-Shikki Kyoshinkai (Organizing Committee for the Exhibition of Cocoons, Yarns, Textiles, and Ceramic and Lacquer Ware) (ed.), *Menshi Shudan-kai Kiji (The Record of the Conference on Cotton Yarn)* (Tokyo, 1885) pp. 28–34.

8. Naosuke Takamura, *Nippon Bosekigyo-shi Josetsu (An Introduction to the History of the Japanese Cotton Spinning Industry)* (Tokyo 1971) pp. 1, 2.

9. Ibid., pp. 40–3, 48–57.

10. Ibid, pp. 63–5.

11. T. Kinukawa, *Honpo Menshiboseki Shi*, vol. 1, pp. 90–2.

12. O. Shoji and Y. Uno, *Yamanobe Takeo-kun Shoden (A Short Biography of Takeo Yamanobe)*, (Osaka, 1918), pp. 29–30, notes that Platt Bros. & Co. were studying the spinning frame particularly adapted to Japan and recommended the ring to Yamanobe when he visited the company in May 1887. However the Osaka Spinning Co. had already introduced ring frames totalling 4 020 spindles in its second mill which was planned in 1884 and started in 1886. This suggests that Yamanobe had been interested in ring spinning before his visit to Lancashire.

13. Yukihiko Kiyokawa, 'On the Choice of Ring Spinning Frames in the Japanese Cotton Spinning Industry', *Keizai Kenkyu*, **36** (1985) pp. 214–27.

14. Nakaoka, Ishii and Uchida, *Kindai Nippon no Gijutsu*, pp. 94–6.

15. Kenji Imazu, 'Coal Transportation in pre-war Japan', in Y. Yasuba and O. Saito (eds), *Proto-Kogyoka Ki no Keizai to Shakai (The Japanese Economy and Society in the Period of Proto-industrialization)* (Tokyo 1983) pp. 257–77.

16. I have discussed very little the developments after 1890, mainly because of limited space; also it would be necessary to utilize some important works to which I could not refer in this chapter. For example, Kajinishi Mitsuhaya, *Nippon Kindai Mengyo no Seiritsu (The Rise of the Modern Cotton Industry in Japan)* (Tokyo 1950) and Shiso Hattori and Seizaburo Shinobu, *Meiji Senshoku Keizai-shi (An Economic History of the Textile Industry in the Meiji Period)* (1937) are two important works written before the book by N. Takamura, *Nippon Bosekigyo-shi*. They are all by Marxist historians. There is no comparable book written from the neo-classical perspective. Gary Saxonhouse and Gustav Ranis, 'Determinants of Technology Choice: the Indian and Japanese Cotton Textile Industries'; idem, 'Technology Choice and the Quality Dimension in the Japanese Cotton Textile Industry'; G. Saxonhouse and Yukihiko Kiyokawa, 'Supply and Demand for Quality Workers in Cotton Spinning in Japan and India', all in K. Ohkawa and G. Ranis (eds), *Japan and the Developing Countries* (Oxford 1985) and Yukihiko Kiyokawa, 'Entrepreneurship and Innovation in Japan: an Implication of the Experience of Technological Development in the Textile Industry', *The Developing Economies*, **22** (1984) are a few works on technology transfer during this period.

Kaoru Sugihara, 'Patterns of Intra-Asian Trade, 1898–1913', *Osaka City University Economic Review*, **16** (1980) presents an important view on intra-Asian cotton technology transfer during this period.

10. The Transfer of Railway Technologies from Britain to Japan, with Special Reference to Locomotive Manufacture

Takeshi Yuzawa*

BRITISH LOCOMOTIVES IN WORLD MARKETS IN THE LATTER PART OF THE NINETEENTH CENTURY

The railway emerged during Britain's pioneering experience of industrialization, using the most developed materials, such as iron, and the technologies of mechanical engineering. In many ways the railway was a symbol of the final stage of the Industrial Revolution. After two railway booms in the 1830s and 1840s, the major network of railways in Britain was largely complete[1]; at the same time they became a sound and stable investment. Railways in Britain reached maturity when the country was in fact the 'Workshop of the World'.

However British railway investors turned their attention to overseas markets from the end of the 1840s.[2] When British power was integrating every corner of the world economy railways played an important role. D. R. Headrick described the railways as one of the tools of the empire to control undeveloped countries.[3] Railway investment in foreign countries brought three kinds of interest to Britain. Firstly, railways ensured good returns to their investors. Secondly, with increasing foreign investment, the export of capital goods such as rail, carriages and locomotives was expanded enormously. Lastly, the railways constructed by the British in underdeveloped countries could transport British manufactured goods from their ports to deep inside those countries, and raw materials might be exported to Britain in the other direction.

However, Britain's railway industries were gradually losing ground in the world market by the late nineteenth century. There were many arguments about the cause of this decline, evident even in the case of the locomotive industries, which utilized some of the most advanced technologies. Some contemporary evidence explaining the situation of the British locomotive manufacturers was provided by W. W. Evans, who collected various data relating to the comparisons between British and American locomotives.[4] Largely from the late 1870s British locomotives were losing their competitive edge in terms not only of prices but also of their technologies. Mr Breton, the engineer-in-chief of the Great India Peninsula Railway, reported in 1878 to the Agent-General in London 'on the subject of the superior working results of American locomotives as compared with English railway experience'.[5] To this comment Messrs Neilson & Co., one of the major locomotive manufacturers of Glasgow, instantly admitted that 'the ordinary American type of engine, such as is in use in America, is, we have not the slightest doubt, better adapted for [Indian] railways as now constructed than the engine used in this country', and that 'it is more flexible, and adapts itself better to the line than our excessively rigid engines'. Furthermore they explained the American locomotive's competitiveness in terms of price: 'it has also the advantage of being less costly, though, we quite believe, equally efficient in its details, by reason of these being of simpler construction and frequently of cheaper materials'.[6] Asserting that they were exporting engines to America, Neilson & Co. defended themselves: 'we undertake that our engines will give equal satisfaction, both as regards design and general excellence of workmanship, and will prove quite as economical as those made in America'.[7]

The Engineer and *The Railway Engineer* in the late 1870s and early 1880s published articles on 'American and British Locomotives', comparing the performances of locomotives in both countries.[8] By the end of the nineteenth century there were lots of articles pointing out the problems of British locomotives, not only in business journals but also in governmental publications such as *The Board of Trade Journal.*[9] At the beginning of the twentieth century British locomotive manufacturers failed to gain orders from the Egyptian government as the result of competition from American makers. The House of Commons Committee investigated the prices of locomotives manufactured in Britain and America in 1902. Though the price of British locomotives was more reasonable than American ones in the case of designs and specifications imposed by the Egyptian Railway Board, it was reported that American firms could supply engines differing from the Egyptian designs and specifications in certain particulars, yet having equal power and performance, and with prices 19 per cent lower than the British ones. More importantly, British firms completed orders in 48 and 90 weeks, on two occasions, whereas the American firm delivered comparable locomotives in 18 and 35 weeks, when following the Egyptian designs and specifications, or 12 and 30 weeks, respectively, if certain changes were allowed. It could not be doubted that 'the main reason why so many orders for railway and other plant required in Egypt had recently been given to America, is that American firms have been able to execute them with extraordinary rapidity'.[10] American firms had adopted the system of standardizing parts of engines, which brought them superiority in delivery and costs.

Turning to comparisons between British and German locomotives, the Parliamentary report also revealed aspects of the competition between those two countries' manufacturers of railway locomotives. A letter from the Under Secretary of State for India to Messrs Dubs & Co. noted that,

> as you are no doubt aware, orders for locomotives have recently been given to firms by various German railway companies, and his Lordship finally decided that he would await the result of these orders, which may be regarded in the light of an experiment, before entrusting to German manufacturers, for the first time, an important contract for locomotives for State railways.

Further he pointed out that,

> if it should be shown by experience that the German manufacturers are able and willing to turn to work which, though possibly inferior in respect of finish, is for practical purposes equal or nearly equal to that which is produced in this country, at prices materially lower, and with the further advantages of much earlier delivery, it is obvious that, in justice to the interests of India, he will be compelled to accept foreign tenders, and, possibly, to accept them on large scale.[11]

To this inquiry, Messrs Dubs & Co. replied, with a familiar argument, that 'the German firms estimated to use much cheaper materials, while their standards of workmanship and finish are much below those of their British competitors'.[12] Nasmyth, Wilson & Co., who were also asked the same question by the Under Secretary of State for India, answered that 'our contention was, and is, that until the Continental work is indisputably proved to be as good or better than the British, to cast in our teeth the lower price and quicker delivery urged in support of the Continental makers, was hardly fair to us'. They contended also that German firms were, at present, unused to English standards and requirements, and that very possibly, 'when they do become better acquainted with the tests imposed, they will decline to continue recent low prices'.[13] Still they appeared to be quite optimistic about their competitiveness against German locomotive manufacturers.

As far as the Japanese market was concerned, British locomotive manufacturers as a whole could cope with foreign competition up to the beginning of the First World War. For instance, Neilson & Co. exported 231 locomotives to the Japan Imperial Railway between 1889 and 1911 and, to other major private railway companies, 50 locomotives between 1889 and 1907. There was a great increase in the supply of locomotives from that company to Japan at the turn of the century, whereas the total number of locomotives exported to Japan was only 65 up to 1898.[14] Beyer, Peacock & Co. exported 138 locomotives to Nippon Tetsudo, the largest private railway company, from 1894 to 1904, and another 80 locomotives to other companies, including 46 locomotives to the Imperial Railway. Since Beyer, Peacock & Co. produced about 5 000 locomotives between 1854 and 1907, the proportion sold in Japan was trifling.[15] Sharp, Stewart & Co. exported 35 locomotives to the Imperial Railway from 1870 to 1897, in addition to six to Nippon Railway and two to Kyushu Railway.[16]

As Table 10.1 shows, British rolling stock, especially locomotives, could compete in Japanese markets to the end of the nineteenth century, when British supremacy gradually declined, mainly because of foreign competition, but also because of the growth of an indigenous industry in Japan, set up with the support of British resources. The following section examines the transfer of British railway technology and materials to Japan.

Table 10.1   Total number of locomotives in Japan

Built	Britain	USA	Germany	Switzerland	Japan
1872	10	–	–	–	–
1877	36	–	–	–	–
1882	47	–	–	–	–
1887	95	2	–	–	–
1892	240	26	28	–	–
1897	484	282	55	3	11
1902	684	524	70	11	30
1907	966	908	160	11	95
1912*	983	995	226	11	162

*1912 includes the number up to July of that year.
Source: Tsusho Sangyosho (MITI). *Shoko Seisakushi, (History of the MITI's Policy)*, vol. 18 (1976) p. 164.

INTRODUCTION OF BRITISH RAILWAY TECHNOLOGY INTO JAPAN

Three stages can be identified in the transfer of railway technology into Japan. The first was to import locomotives and the related machines from Britain with the engineers who could operate or maintain them. At first the government had to depend completely upon foreigners, not only in constructing the railway lines, but in managing and running the railway. The second was to learn from those engineers on the job or to study abroad directly. The government and some railway companies established training schools and young students were dispatched to Western countries to study up-to-date technology and production methods. The third stage was to construct railways and manufacture carriages, locomotives and other related machines without the help of foreigners.

Western powers dominated the Far East in the middle of the nineteenth century and competed with each other for rights to construct railways in Japan. At first a French banker, Fleury Herald, and then A. L. C. Portman, a secretary of the American legation, got permission from the Edo government in December 1867 to construct a railway from Edo (Tokyo) to Yokohama. However, after the overthrow of the Edo government in 1868, the British minister, Sir Harry (Henry) Parkes negotiated with the new Meiji government and took the initiative for introducing British engineers and railway materials. He persuaded the government not to permit the foreigners to construct lines but to construct them itself. The new government, while rejecting the former government's contract with Portman, was keen to build railways by itself, realizing that neighbouring countries were colonized or occupied by westerners using railways as tools for the purposes of domination.

Thus the new government decided to construct the railway with the advice and support of the British minister, Parkes, and also of Horatio Nelson Lay, formerly a vice-consul at Shanghai who came to Japan to undertake railway construction. Parkes introduced Lay to S. Okuma, one of the key figures in the Meiji government, who was then vice-minister of both the Home Office and the Exchequer. Lay convinced high officials of the importance of railways and recommended them to raise money by issuing government bonds in London. The Japanese government in 1869 contracted with Lay for raising money, employing engineers and purchasing the railway materials from Britain. He had to raise one million pounds by the end of May 1870 for the line from Tokyo to Yokohama and later three million pounds for the line from Tokyo to Kobe through Kyoto and Osaka, and from Kyoto to Tsuruga. Lay started to raise money in London and, with the advice of Edmund Morel, who was recommended by Parkes to be the engineer-in-chief of the Japanese Railway Bureau, purchased materials for the railway in England. Within months, however, the Japanese government cancelled the contract with Lay because they learned that the bond of the Japanese government would be issued at 12 per cent interest. They had assumed Lay would raise the money personally through his connections with wealthy men and thought that Lay's commission of 3 of the 12 per cent interest was too high. The Japanese government switched the contract to the Oriental Bank after they paid Lay and his agent the £70 000 penalty for breaking the contract. After this trouble, the Oriental Bank, in turn, took charge of providing money for the railway, introducing engineers and purchasing railway materials. In these circumstances, British railway technologies were exclusively transferred in the first stage of Japanese railway development.[17]

Even though Lay's contract was cancelled by the Japanese government, Morel remained as the first engineer-in-chief of the Railway Bureau with responsibility for constructing the line between Shimbashi (the terminal in Tokyo) and Yokohama. Morel had graduated at King's College in London, studied civil engineering in Germany and France, and became a member of the Institution of Civil Engineers at the age of 24. He came to Japan in April 1870 after completing the construction of a railway in Ceylon. He laid the foundations of the line by recruiting as his assistants other British engineers, such as John Diack, John England and Charles Shepherd. They took an important part in the technology transfer from Britain to Japan, though Morel died of tuberculosis in September 1871, at the age of 30.[18]

There were 104 foreign engineers and labourers working on Japanese railways in 1876, one of the peak years for the number of foreigners. Of these 94 came from Britain, two each from America, Germany and Denmark and one each from France, Italy, Finland and Portugal. British influence was overwhelmingly important, judging by these numbers of foreign employees in Japan. They ranged from high ranking positions, such as director, engineer-in-chief and locomotive superintendent, to the lower ranks of engine driver, mason, carpenter, blacksmith, platelayer and so on.[19]

It is often stressed that foreign employees received high salaries compared with Japanese officers of the higher rank. For instance, Morel was paid 1 000 yen a month after the second year of his employment, compared to the prime minister's monthly salary of 960 yen. This caused high labour costs which sometimes attained from 6 to 10 per cent of the total costs of the construction. The policy of the Meiji government was to employ the foreigners temporarily, until Japanese employees could master the skills and know-how, or students dispatched directly could learn those kinds of technologies at Western universities. [20] The government stopped employing foreigners around 1880, because by then Japanese engineers and managers could largely construct and run railways and manufacture railway goods, sometimes by importing essential machine parts. Locomotives were the last thing which were manufactured by Japanese factories because of their complicated structure and the high standards of materials, manufacture and engineering.

In the early stage of Japanese railway history, the introduction of the technology was not discussed thoughtfully or studied carefully by Japanese leaders. The reason why the government chose the gauge of 1 067mm (3 feet 6 inches) was not clear. According to the recollections of S. Okuma, E. Morel asked him the size of gauge, but he did not recognize the importance of the meaning of the gauge. Presumably Morel recommended a 3 feet 6 inches gauge from his experience in Ceylon, and Okuma agreed with his choice, considering the restricted land space for railways in Japan, as well as the lower construction costs. [21] When Masaru Inoue later addressed the question of the Japanese gauge, he also supported the existing one, even though he well knew about the gauge problem in Western countries. Afterwards there occurred several serious arguments about the revision of the railway gauge, especially from the military powers who wanted high speed and volume transport.

On the timing of the first imported locomotives there is a short exchange in the *Anglo-Japanese Gazette*. In November 1905, an article reported that 'we may here mention that Messrs Beyer, Peacock and Co. were the first British firm to supply locomotives for Japan'.[22] However, a correspondent in the next issue objected to the former article: 'We, however, can claim to have supplied locomotives to the Imperial Railway as far back as 1871, together with Messrs Sharp Stewart, the Yorkshire Engine Co., and the Vulcan Foundry: no. 1 locomotive was provided by Vulcan Foundry, nos. 2 and 4 by Sharp Stewart Co., no. 3 by Yorkshire Engine Co., and nos. 5 and 7 by Avonside Engine Co.' who were one of the original suppliers of locomotives to the Imperial Railway.[23] According to Japanese evidence, the Imperial Railway imported, in 1871, six tank engines (1-2 type) and two tender engines (2-1 type) from Sharp Stewart, one tank engine (1-2 type) from Vulcan Foundry and another from the Yorkshire Engine Works. The no. 1 locomotive was purchased from Vulcan Foundry Co., mainly for the construction of the lines and for the transport of the freight. At the same time no. 2 locomotive was imported from Sharp Stewart Co. for passenger and freight transport. Two locomotives were imported from the Avonside Engine Co. in 1871 as well. Japanese sources confirm the Avonside Engine Co.'s report in the *Anglo-Japanese Gazette*.[24]

Masaru Inoue led the early development of Japanese railways, and was eager to foster indigenous technologies and engineers. He was born in 1843 and violated the law of the Edo government, which prohibited Japanese from going abroad, by visiting Britain in 1864. After he returned to Japan, he became one of the advocates of the promotion of railways, and was appointed first head of the Railway Bureau in 1871. For more than 20 years he contributed to the Japanese railways' development and established the unique tradition of Japanese railway administration. He dared to construct the line from Kyoto to Otsu without any help of foreign engineers in 1880, though there was strong opposition to the idea. His original idea was that the government should own and control all the railway, but, owing to the scarcity of money, he had to make a concession and admit private railways.[25] The first grand project for a private railway was Nippon Railway from Tokyo to Aomori, the northernmost city of the main island, though it was constructed under the supervision of government officials and subsidized by the government which provided part of the dividends. The success of the Nippon Railway caused a boom in railway promotions among the businessmen and investors. Between 1885 and 1892, 50 schemes were proposed, though only 12 plans came into existence.

Under the pressure of establishing a modern transport system to serve industrial needs, the private railways extended rapidly: the total mileage of private railways increased to 853 in 1890, and then 1 706 in 1895, which exceeded by far that of the national railway – 553 miles in 1890 and 596 in 1895.[26]

THE BRITISH CONTEST AGAINST AMERICAN AND GERMAN LOCOMOTIVES IN JAPAN

As noted earlier, the first railway materials were almost all imported from Britain, but her share in the Japanese market gradually decreased because of the competition with the American and German manufacturers. Americans secured contracts in Hokkaido, the North of the Japanese islands, Germans in Kyushu, the South. After the Meiji Restoration, one of the policies adopted by the new government was to develop Hokkaido island, which needed American-style cultivation. The first magistrate of Hokkaido Development Agency, Kiyoteru Kuroda, invited Horace Capron from America to give advice to the Agency. Also he employed American civil engineers to construct railways for carrying coal from the pits. He ordered some of these American engineers to report on the possibility of constructing the railways in Hokkaido.

Benjamin S. Lyman, a geographer, investigated the possible routes from Ishikari colliery through Sapporo, capital of Hokkaido, to the port of Muroran. To realize the plan, Kuroda asked a Japanese minister in the USA to find an able railway engineer. J. U. Crawford was recommended by Thomas A. Scott, president of the Pennsylvania Railroad. Crawford had studied engineering at Pennsylvania University and was an experienced surveyor and superintendent who had worked on the Atlantic & Pacific and the Pennsylvania Railroads. In 1878 he arrived at Hokkaido as an adviser for the railways and civil engineering works under the Agency. Naturally Crawford called for other engineers (six in all) and materials for carriages and bridges from America.

The railway, called the Horonai Railway, opened with 22.27 miles between Temiya and Sapporo in 1880, being extended to 56.65 miles between Sapporo and Horonai colliery in 1882. Crawford recommended a 3 feet 6 inches (1 067 mm) gauge, because the Japanese government had already introduced this gauge at Shimbashi and Yokohama. He also considered the possibility of linking the line in Hokkaido with the lines in the main island, a farsighted idea.

In these circumstances, most of the railway materials in Hokkaido island were imported from America. Two locomotives, eight passenger carriages, 17 bolster wagons and nine wagons were imported from the USA. The first locomotives, tender type, were produced by H. K. Porter Co. in Pittsburgh and had air brakes made by Westinghouse Co. The total weight of locomotive was 26.1 tons with a cowcatcher at the front and big bell to warn people on the street.[27]

The Horonai Railway was not managed successfully and falling coal prices worsened its business. A private company organized in 1888 subcontracted with the Hokkaido Agency to manage the railway, but the problems of running the railway were solved by the Hokkaido Colliery Railway, which was newly organized in 1889 by major capitalists. One of their purposes was to purchase the Horonai Railway from the government and construct new lines from other collieries to the port of Muroran. The Hokkaido Colliery Railway purchased the Horonai immediately after the organization and extended other lines, to reach 207 miles by 1905.

The Hokkaido Colliery Railway also used mainly American railway materials and followed the systems of the Horonai Railway. Hokkaido Colliery inherited from the Horonai Railway nine tender locomotives, 13 passenger carriages and 277 wagons and vans, and increased their number to 79, 102 and 1 753 respectively by 1906, when the company was nationalized.[28]

The Kyushu Railway was another story of the introduction of foreign technologies besides British ones. Kyushu island, at the south of the main island, contrasted with Hokkaido island. Kyushu was one of the progressive regions where foreign news and goods were introduced earlier than other areas and played an important role in the creation of the Meiji government. A railway project was promoted by the local landowners and capitalists in 1886, four years after the opening of Horonai Railway in Hokkaido. The promoters of the Kyushu Railway asked the government for subsidies to support dividends to shareholders during construction. The government allowed a subsidy amounting to a dividend of 4 per cent.[29] It intervened in the Kyushu Railway in various ways. Responding to the request from promoters, S. Takahashi was recommended by the government as the president of the company. He was a director of the Agriculture and Trade Ministry, after experience as Japanese consul in New York. He once reported to the Foreign Minister in detail about the Denver & Rio Grande Railroad through the Rocky Mountains, and noted that the railway would be a good model for Japanese railways running through mountainous areas.[30] He was one of the bureaucrats of the Meiji government who had a strong interest in railways. Naturally his connection with the government influenced the development of the Kyushu Railway.

When a new railway company started it was important to decide what kinds of materials should be introduced and who would take charge of its engineering and mechanical department. The chief engineer of the Kyushu Railway company was nominated by the government. In this way, Hermann Rumschöttel, formerly a mechanical superintendent of the Prussian National Railway, came to Japan in November 1887 to be consulting engineer of this company. It is said that he ordered German railway materials through a German trading company, Illies & Co.,[31] but, according to the contemporary journals, the Japanese government had decided to introduce the German railway materials before he came to Japan.[32] The government was negotiating to revise the 'unequal' trade treaty which was concluded with European countries before the Meiji Restoration. Since then the government had been unable to secure autonomous tariff policy under the treaty. The German government was quite willing to admit the Japanese Government's wish, because they intended to use the treaty arrangements with Japan in order to sell her industrial goods. German government and business circles worked together to promote the sales of railway materials in Japan.

The British ambassador, Plunkett, reported to London on the German position in Japanese politics and economy:

> In a word, the Germans are pushing their popularity with Count Ito to an extent which may, I expect, defeat its end; but, in the meanwhile, I think it right to impress on your Lordship that, for the moment, Germany appears to be aiming at establishing a sort of Protectorate over Japan, which, if successful, would be most damaging to British interests.[33]

He also enclosed Vice-Consul Longford's report, in which German business activity in Japan was described vividly, especially concerning the introduction of German railway materials for the Kyushu Railway.

> The firm of Okura and co., immediately on the projection of the Company, subscribed for shares in it to the value of 300,000 yen, and they expected that ... they would be able to obtain the contract for supplying the necessary material, all of which they would, in keeping with their customs, have obtained form England. ... however, Mr. Ijuin, a Japanese partner of the German firm of Illies and Co., appeared on the scene, armed with letters of introduction from Count Inouye, Count Matsugata, and two other officials of the Japanese Government.[34]

The smallest estimate of the immediate cost of materials needed from Europe by the new Company exceeded one million dollars, and the main contract for supplying these materials looked as if it would be made with Okura & Co., the trading company which had close ties with British manufacturers. But in fact the orders were obtained from Germany instead of Britain. Through Illies & Co., the Kyushu Railway imported railway material produced by Dortmund Union & Co. and locomotives and carriages built by Krauss Co. in Munich. Three locomotives and 600 tons of rails were unloaded at Hakata in July 1889 from the first shipment. Altogether 48 locomotives were imported from Germany, three from Hohenzollern Co. and 45 from Krauss Co. by 1897.[35]

Rumschöttel invited a superintendent of mechanics and drivers from Germany, but one wonders how far Germans were responsible, practically, for directing the construction of the railway because Japanese civil engineers with experience of railway construction on other railways took the initiative in the works. H. Noheji, who graduated from Kobu Daigakko (one of the predecessors of the University of Tokyo) and had been in America to study the railway industry as a whole, became chief engineer of this company in March 1888 and worked there for two years. He supervised the construction of works which were subcontracted to civil engineering companies. These companies also employed young and able Japanese engineers who had studied up-to-date technologies at universities. For instance, T. Sugawara, chief engineer of the contractor of the third section of the works, had worked on the construction of the Nippon Railway after his graduation from Kobu Daigakko.[36] As far as the construction of the railway was concerned, Japanese engineering ability had already attained the level of 'autonomy' from foreign assistance when the Kyushu Railway was built in 1887–8. German influence in this respect was quite small. The company introduced British systems in working and running the railway, and English words were used for the rule book, signals and so on. Also, the bricklaying for bridges and platforms introduced a fashion for what is called English bond.

Germans were important on the mechanical side of the company, because their interest was closely related to sales of mechanical goods like rolling stock.

Figure 10.1   Total importation of rolling stock to Japan

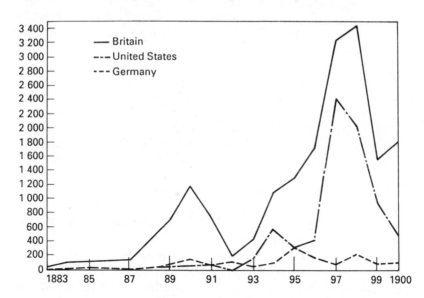

Source: Sawai, Minoru, 'The Development of the Japanese Rolling Stock Industry 1890s–1920s' *Shakaikagaku Kenkyu (The Journal of Social Science)* vol. XXXVII, no. 3 (1985) pp. 20–1.

However, after Rumschöttel left the company in 1892, orders for locomotives bought by the Kyushu Railway increasingly switched to American manufacturers, especially Schenectady Locomotive Co. Up to 1907, Schenectady locomotives numbered 133, more than half of the total 256 locomotives of the Kyushu Railway, with another 62 American locomotives, whereas the firm had only 48 German locomotives. According to the report of the investigation into the troubles caused by the company's deficit in 1899, business difficulties were partly due to the German locomotives, which were quite inefficient, and also to German goods purchased through Illies & Co., which were of poor quality and expensive. After the Kyushu Railway introduced a competitive tender when buying goods of more than 50 yen, Illies & Co. dropped out of competition.[37] As Figure 10.1 shows, German locomotive and carriage manufacturers missed the chance to invade Japanese markets before American makers established themselves there.

THE EMERGENCE OF LOCOMOTIVE MANUFACTURING INDUSTRY IN JAPAN

There were two stages in Japanese locomotive development. The first was the period of learning the skills of repairing and building locomotives under the guidance of British engineers. The second was the process of constructing locomotives at railway works wholly operated by Japanese, at first with major parts imported from foreign countries. As far as the imported locomotives from various countries and companies were concerned, Japanese users had problems in managing and controlling them consistently, and were anxious to establish their standardization and naturally to try to construct locomotives themselves.

There are several accounts of Japanese learning from British engineers. Japanese, who were working under foreign engineers, were called 'cadets' and they were keen to learn the new skills and know-how. According to recollections of 'the cadets', British chief engineers took charge of their training in preparation to become chief engineers. Eventually Japanese became independent of Europeans.[38] For example, around 1877, the construction of the railway from Kyoto to Otsu was organized under the control of Japanese engineers and in turn British engineers gradually retreated to the position of advisers. At the level of engine driver, most foreigners were dismissed by 1880, because Japanese had then mastered the skill of driving engines. One engine driver, who started his railway career as a worker in locomotive assembly and a fireman in 1871, was proud of his success in running the locomotives more efficiently than the foreign drivers, because his crew consumed 13.2 kg of coal per mile as compared with 15.6 kg consumed by foreign drivers. Furthermore labour costs were reduced when foreigners were replaced by Japanese: a foreign driver's wage was 150 yen per month, which contrasted sharply with the Japanese driver's wage of 20 yen.[39]

Under Richard F. Trevithick's guidance, the Kobe factory of the Government Railway was established in 1893 to construct the first locomotive in Japan.[40] A grandson of Richard Trevithick, the pioneer British railway engineer, R. F. Trevithick had entered the Crewe locomotive works of the London & North Western Railway in 1867. Following experience as chief mechanical engineer on railways in Argentina and Ceylon, he came to Japan as superintendent of locomotive works of the Government Railway at Kobe. He was not only a good engineer but also a good teacher. Many Japanese engineers were trained under him and later became leaders in Japanese railway engineering. In one case, he awarded a certificate to K. Ohta, who had no educational background but mastered drawings under him. It read as follows:

> During my tenure of office as Locomotive Superintendent of the Imperial Government Railways of Japan, Mr Kitimatsu *[sic]* Ohta was attached to my office as draughtsman for a period of about 12 years. He is a very skilful, accurate, and industrious draughtsman, capable of producing highly finished drawings, and during the 12 years above mentioned no work was ever spoilt from errors of draughtsmanship on his part.[41]

According to Ohta's recollection, Trevithick was rigorous in checking works and transferred British traditions of maintaining locomotives. Ohta moved to Kawasaki Shipyard in 1910 as manager of the locomotive and carriage drawing office when the works started to manufacture locomotives for the government. The Chief Engineer of the Railway Authority (Tetsudoin) regarded locomotives produced at Kawasaki Shipbuilding Works as not inferior to foreign ones, even rather superior to them.[42] Ohta was a good example of a Japanese who had trained under an English engineer and transferred his skill to a Japanese factory.

The immigrant chief engineer also contributed to the modification of the imported technology to suit Japanese conditions. Richard F. Trevithick manufactured at Kobe an English-style locomotive with a compound engine of two cylinders. It was said that its performance was good, and that it consumed 15 to 20 per cent less than the equivalent locomotives in Britain. Two years later, the Kobe factory manufactured tender engines as well.

Richard F. Trevithick reported on 'Locomotive Building in Japan' in the *Proceedings of the Institution of Mechanical Engineers* in April 1895. He analysed the mechanical characteristics of Japanese locomotives and their performance, comparing them with foreign ones. Though fundamental parts of the locomotives were imported from England, Japanese processed and finished them at the Kobe factory. Two frame-plates of mild Siemens–Martin steel, four steel plates forming the radial axle-box guides, four straight axles, eight steel tyres, a low-pressure piston of steel, copper tube-plates, boiler tubes, the bulk of the piping, india-rubber springs and so on were obtained from England. However the Kobe factory drilled or cut out all holes and gaps in the frame-plates, flanged and bent the steel plates to required radius, turned and fitted the tyres, and entirely flanged the tube-plates. On the other hand, the valve gear, sping gear, brake gear, draw-bar hooks and attachments were made in Kobe, almost entirely from scrap iron. The cylinders, axle-boxes, and all other fittings of cast-iron or brass were also cast and finished completely at the Kobe shops.[43]

Japanese technology at this stage was immature, especially in terms of locomotive buildings, but R. F. Trevithick's appreciation of the current level of the Japanese technology was as follows: 'The workmanship, both in detail and in the engine as a whole, leaves nothing to be desired, and compares favourably with that of the best engines imported'; and 'The significance of this result is emphasized when it is understood that it is entirely the product of Japanese labour led by Japanese foremen, no foreign foremen being employed in Kobe workshops'.[44] According to his table (Table 10.2), the Japanese compound engine was not at all inferior to foreign counterparts.

Table 10.2   Performance of Japanese and foreign locomotives, 1895

	Japan	England	America
Compound or non-compound	compound	non-compound	compound
Average weight of train (tons)	94.36	94.71	180.70
Coal consumption			
per engine-mile lb.	18.92	21.66	41.48
per ton-mile lb.	0.2005	0.2287	0.2296
Ton-miles per ton of total			
coal consumption (ton-miles)	11 172	9 794	9 756

Source: Proceedings of the Institution of Mechanical Engineers, April 1895.

He concluded: 'It will thus be seen that a locomotive has been built in Japan, which in first cost and efficiency will bear comparison with imported locomotives; and also that Japan, possessing cheap labour and coal, may at no distant date find it unnecessary to go to foreign makers for her locomotives.'[45]

Japanese factories completed 162 locomotives by July 1912, amounting to 6.7 per cent of the total locomotives available at that time. Between the wars, the ability to construct locomotives in Japan increased gradually and attained a high level of performance. Types 9600 and 8620 in c. 1914 and then type 18900 in 1919, showed very high levels of performance. For instance, type

9600 introduced high-pressure boilers using a wide boiler space over the wheels, and resulted in ending the use of Mallet-type locomotives with superheated steam which had quite complicated structures. Type 8620 embodied a frame designed in Japan and type 18900 succeeded in introducing wheels of 1750 mm in diameter, which were the largest in the world on a narrow gauge.[46]

The Private Railway Act of 1887 defined the organization and management of the private railway company, laid down regulations for common carriers, various facilities and equipment which should be provided by the company and other engineering details. This act also formally authorized the gauge of 3 feet 6 inches as a national standard. Afterwards the only exceptions to this gauge were special lines allowed by the government.

The Japanese government was eager to produce and use the indigenous locomotives, especially after the railway nationalization act of 1906. The consolidation of the railway system meant a big demand for standard locomotives and other carriages. The national railway, including the 17 newly nationalized companies, covered 91 per cent of the total railway mileage in Japan and it was a matter of urgency for the government to seek the standardization not only of locomotives but also of all railway systems. At the time of the nationalization, 1 147 locomotives of 147 different types came under government control, a mixture resulting from the different countries and different manufacturers which had earlier supplied the Japanese railway companies. Needless to say, each company had its own style, reflecting requirements in the home country. Generally speaking, British locomotives were heavy and consumed more coal than those of the USA and Germany because Britain was comparatively well endowed with coal. American locomotives were manufactured cheaply rather than aiming at long life and were designed to haul long distances with tenders on a poor railbed. German locomotives mixed the ideas of the British and American models and made a strong impact on the Japanese locomotive industry which sought engines with a lower coal consumption. Locomotives derived from different concepts naturally caused various inconveniences in running uniformly under a government system.[47] In particular, the standardization of coupling appliances and of wheel and axle sizes was urgently needed. Circumstances for the establishment of indigenous locomotive manufacture were favourable after the Russo-Japanese war (1904–5) because Japan could recover the autonomous right to decide the customs rate by herself and introduce protective tariffs to foster her infant industries, including locomotive manufacturers.

Educational and training facilities also made it possible for Japanese engineers to adopt foreign technologies smoothly. Edmund Morel in 1870 recommended that Count Ito establish a training school for able young students. He stressed that Japanese should prepare to be free from dependence on foreigners. Acting on his advice, the Kogakuryo (Engineering Bureau) was established in 1871 as one of the subordinate offices in the Kobusho (Ministry of Industry). It started to register students in 1873; 30 students were admitted in the first year and 50 students in the second. Students had to study for six years altogether: the first two years for general study, the next two for special subjects, and the last two for practical experience in the factories. However the Kogakuryo was reformed as the Kobu Daigakko in 1877 and the Railway Bureau was one of the most popular workplaces for the able graduates.

Meanwhile the Bureau itself started the education of the railway telegraph trainees in 1872, and launched an engineering training school in Osaka in 1877. Masaru Inoue had a strong interest in the education of employees and T. R. Shervinton, chief civil engineer, and E. G. Holtham, civil engineer, were invited to teach mainly civil engineering at that school. Shervinton, above all, worked out its curriculum. It is said that he was one of the individuals who rendered greatest assistance to Japanese railways in their efforts to be independent of foreign technologies. He stayed for seven years, returning to England in 1881. Holtham came to Japan in 1873 to work under R. V. Boyle and after teaching at the training school became a chief engineer. He not only supervised civil engineering works such as the line between Kyoto and Kobe and the construction of bridges over the Rokugo River on the border between the Tokyo and Kanagawa prefectures, but trained Japanese firemen to become drivers. Three Japanese became the first drivers in April 1878 and by November of the same year all the trains were driven by Japanese drivers. After Shervinton returned home, Holtham took over as chief engineer in the Kansai division, but went back to Britain in 1882.[48]

The engineering training school closed in 1882, because Kobu Daigakko began to send able engineers onto the railways. Though only 24 students graduated from the school, they played an important role in making the Japanese railway independent of foreign engineers. Meanwhile the Government Railway established a school for railway telegraph engineers in 1891 which simultaneously expanded education for railway employees in general. Students learnt for two to four months the technology of the telegraph, the rules of telegraphy, fitting telegraph machines, and the roman letters. The school lasted for about eight years. After that, the Railway Bureau tried several times to strengthen telegraph education and establish its own in-house system. Needless to say, nationalization required a comprehensive in-house training centre. Shinpei Goto, president of the National Railway, was keen to educate all employees and to establish systematic management and practice among the national railways. Numbers of employees increased rapidly, from 28 872 in 1905 to 59 647 in 1906. They were needed to master the complicated working methods, especially after nationalization. However that is another story.[49]

Generally speaking, Japanese railways were gradually becoming independent of foreign engineers around the end of the 1870s – about 10 years after the opening of the first railway. Japanese engineers relied on foreign engineers just for blue-prints of tunnels and direct advice on the construction of bridges, which needed technical knowledge in design and construction. Under the direction of a Japanese engineer, Y. Kunizawa, a tunnel of 664 metres was completed for the first time in 1878. Kunizawa was one of the graduate students of the engineering training school in Osaka.[50]

The government tried to produce rails in 1880 at one of the government factories, Kamaishi Iron Works, but, owing to the technical problems, they produced only 180 tons, about half the planned amount. After its establishment in 1901, the Yawata Iron Works supplied about half the national demand for rail. However it took a long time, to the end of the 1920s, for the Japanese-made rail to compete with foreign rail in terms of quality and price. On the other hand, passenger carriages and wagons, compared with locomotives, were easy to build, and they were mostly provided by Japanese factories, which attained nearly 100 per cent of self-supply at the beginning of the 1880s. They did, however, experience difficulty manufacturing bogie-type cars before the end of the nineteenth century.

CONCLUSION

The transfer of railway technologies into Japan occurred in three stages from the time British railway materials entered the Japanese market to the time when British suppliers were displaced. The first stage saw an overwhelming British influence on Japanese railway development in finance, technology and manufactured goods. The second stage came when British railway materials and technology gradually came to lose dominance in Japan by the end of the nineteenth century, as a result of competition from American and German rivals. The third was the process of independence of the Japanese railway industry from western countries' influence. In the course of the development of the indigenous railway industry, Japanese learned much from the British on the job and at training school.

In the course of the relative decline of the British presence in Japanese railways, American and German influences emerged in the North and South of Japan, respectively. Hokkaido was developed under American advice and consultation. The introduction of American engineers and railway materials was considered appropriate by the high officials of the Hokkaido Development Agency. Meanwhile, in Kyushu island in the South, German interests were strong and their railway engineers and materials were introduced as part of the diplomatic tactics of the Japanese government to revise the 'unequal' trade treaty. Indeed, by the end of the 1880s, German railway technology had reached the top level in this field and German supremacy in the Kyushu

Railway might be seen as the result of the trade competition with British and American counterparts. In fact German bureaucrats and diplomats were behind the contracts. However German locomotives were not efficient in terms of price and performance, as compared to American ones.

The third stage of technology transfer from the West to Japan could be explained by considering the reasons why Japan succeeded in supplying the railway materials by herself in such a short time. First the Japanese government encouraged the use of home products to save foreign currency and to foster infant industry. In March 1875 the government ordered an investigation into the possibility of switching railway materials, formerly imported from foreign countries, to ones made in Japan. They found that there were many items for the railway business available in Japan and at the same time cheaper, sometimes two or three times cheaper, than imported goods.[51] It was the policy of the government to use home products as much as possible, even when they were more expensive than foreign goods. William W. Cargill, an agent of the Oriental Bank and responsible for purchasing all railway material in Britain for the Japanese government, told the ministry of Kobusho (Industry), after he read the report, that he was very pleased to learn of the progress of Japanese goods and to note that their prices were lower than those of imported goods. Furthermore he encouraged the Minister in a policy of import substitution, even though some Japanese prices were more expensive at this time. In the long run the Kobusho would have the benefits from such a policy.[52]

The second reason lay in the teaching and learning process. British engineers were enthusiastic about training Japanese on the job and, on the other hand, Japanese workers were diligent students, keen to learn up-to-date skills from them. The British also taught Japanese students at a government training school and at the Kobu Daigakko, the most advanced study centre. Simultaneously Japanese students were dispatched by the government to British universities to absorb modern technology.

The third reason why Japan became self-sufficient in railway technology arose from the difficulties caused by the mixture of railway materials imported from various countries and firms which produced diverse kinds and standards of railway hardware. Especially after nationalization, the government urgently sought to consolidate standards and to use the same kinds of goods as much as possible. Of course developing countries in general always confronted the same problems of using various standards of imported goods, but they did not necessarily succeed in launching the railway industry in a short time, and therefore the third reason might be one of necessary conditions, not one of sufficient conditions.

NOTES

*I wish to thank Dr David Jeremy for his valuable comments.

1. H. G. Lewin, *Early British Railways, 1801–1844* (London & New York, 1925) ch. 5; G. R. Hawke, *Railways and Economic Growth in England and Wales 1840–1870* (Oxford, 1970) p. 203; H. Pollins, *Britain's Railways* (Newton Abbot, 1971) pp. 34–40.
2. Especially after the 1850s, investment in French railways and from 1860s in American railways. See L. H. Jenks, *The Migration of British Capital to 1875* (London & Edinburgh 1927) p. 165; D. R. Adler, *British Investment in American Railways, 1834–1898* (Charlottesville, 1970) pp. xii–xiii.
3. D. R. Headrick, *The Tools of Empire* (New York & Oxford, 1981), pp. 187–8.
4. W. W. Evans, *American v. English Locomotives* (Leeds, 1879).
5. Ibid., pp. 1–14.
6. Ibid., p. 23.
7. Ibid., p. 24.
8. For example, 'American v. English Locomotives', *The Engineer* (18 January 1878); 'English and American Locomotives', *The Railway Engineer* (March 1880); 'English and American locomotives', ibid., (December 1888); 'British V. American locomotives', ibid., (January 1891).
9. See *The Board of Trade Journal* (July 1897); November 1898.
10. Parliamentary Papers, 'Correspondence Respecting the Comparative Merits of British, Belgian, and American Locomotives in Egypt', 1902 (Cd. 1010) CIV. 105, p. 7.
11. Parliamentary Papers, 'Return of Correspondence with Certain British Firms as to the Competition between German and British Manufacturers of Railway Locomotives', 1902 (298) LXXI, 481, p. 3.
12. Ibid., p. 4.
13. Ibid., p. 12.
14. Order Book of Neilson & Co., vol. 2 (1863–1898) Mitchell Library, Glasgow.
15. Beyer, Peacock & Co., Names of Railways, BP/N/1-2, Manchester County Record Office.
16. Order Book of Sharp Stewart & Co., Mitchell Library, Glasgow.
17. Tetsudosho (Ministry of Railway), *Nippon Tetsudo-shi (Japan Railway History)* (Tokyo, 1921) vol. 1, pp. 20–6; Nippon Kokuyu Tetsudo (Japan National Railway), *Nippon Kokuyu Tetsudo Hyakunenshi (Centenary of Japan National Railway)*, vol. 1 (Tokyo, 1969) pp. 63–70.
18. Nippon Kotsu Kyokai (Japan Transport Association) (ed.), *Tetsudo Senjinroku (Dictionary of Railway Pioneers)* (Tokyo, 1972); Unesco Higashi Asia Bunka Centre (Unesco East Asia Culture Centre), *Shiryo Oyatoi Gaikokujin (Documents for Foreign Employees)* (Tokyo, 1975).
19. Naomasa Yamada, *Oyatoi Gaikokujin (Foreign Employees)* (Tokyo, 1968) pp. 36–56.
20. Fukuju Unno (ed.), *Gijutsu no Shakaishi (Social History of Technology)* (Tokyo, 1982) vol. 3, p. 117.
21. Tetsudosho, *Nippon Tetsudo-shi* pp. 43–6; Nippon Kokuyu Tetsudo, *Nippon Kokuyu...*, vol. 1, pp. 125–6; Kazuya Sawa, *Tetsudo-Meiji Sogyo Kaikodan (Recollections on Commencement of Railways in Meiji Period)* (1981).
22. 'British Locomotives in Japan', *Anglo-Japanese Gazette* (November 1905).
23. 'British Locomotives in Japan', ibid., (December 1905).
24. Watt Seitan Nihyakunen Kinenkai (Committee for Bicentenary of Birth of Watt) (ed.), *Nippon Jokikogyo Hattatsushi (Development of Japanese Steam Engine)* (Tokyo, 1938) pp. 185–95; Tsusho Sangyosho (MITI), *Shoko Seisaku-shi (History of the MITI's Policy)* (1976) vol. 18, p. 164; Naotaka Hirota, *Steam Locomotives of Japan* (Tokyo, 1972) p. 102.
25. Masaru Inoue, *Shishaku Inoue Masaru-kun Shoden (A Short Biography of Viscount Inoue Masaru)* (Tokyo, 1913) pp. 41–3.
26. Nippon Kokuyu Tetsudo, *Nippon Kokuyu* vol. 4, pp. 248–9.
27. Tetsudosho, *Nippon Tetsudo-shi*, pp. 300–22; Nippon Tetsudo Hokkaido Sokyoku

(Hokkaido Division of Japan National Railway), *Hokkaido Tetsudo Hyakunenshi (Centenary of Hokkaido Railway)* Sapporo, vol. 1, pp. 22–77.

28. Ibid., pp. 95–206.
29. Kyushu Ryokyaku Tetsudo Kabushiki-kaisha (Kyushu JR), *Tetsurin no Hibiki (Centenary of Kyusyu Railway)* Fukuoka, (1989) pp. 38–45; Tetsudosho, *Nippon Tetsudo-shi*, pp. 845–71; Takashi Deguchi, *Kyushu Tetsudo – Chayamachi Kyoryo (Kyushu Railway – Chayamachi Bridge)* (Kita-Kyushu, 1989) pp. 27–53.
30. Nippon Kokuyu Tetsudo, *Kobusho Kiroku (Documents of Ministry of Industry – Railway Division)*, Tokyo, vol.7 (1977) pp. 84–94.
31. For instance, see T. Deguchi, *Kyushu Tetsudo* p. 28; Nippon Kotsu Kyokai (ed.), *Tetsudo Senjinroku* pp. 406–7.
32. *Jiji Shimpo*, 21 May 1887, 26 May 1887; *Tokyo Nichi-nichi* 10 June 1887.
33. PRO, FO 46/365, 11 February 1887, p. 18.
34. Ibid., p. 19.
35. Kyushu Tetsudo Kabushiki-kaisha (Kyushu Railway Company), *Kyutetsu 20nen-shi (Twenty years of Kyushu Railway)* (Fukuoka, 1907) pp. 79–84.
36. Tetsudo Kensetsugyo Kyokai (Association of Railway Contractors), *Nippon Tetsudo Ukeoigyoshi Meiji-hen (History of Railway Contractors in Japan – Meiji period)* (Tokyo, 1944) pp. 134–48.
37. *Kyusyu Tetsudo Kabushiki-kaisha Chosahokokusho (Report of the Investigation in Kyusyu Railway)* (Fukuoka, 1899) p. 26.
38. K. Sawa, *Tetsudo-Meiji* pp. 190–3.
39. Ibid., pp. 193.
40. His younger brother, Francis Henry, who used to be chief locomotive engineer on the LNWR, came to Japan in 1876 and became superintendent of Kobe and Shimbashi factory of the Government Railway. He returned to England in 1897. Richard Francis Trevithick, the last foreign railway engineer employed by the government, left Japan in 1904.
41. Nippon Kokuyu Tetsudo, *Tetsudo Gijutsu Hattatsushi (Development of Railway Technology)* 4, (Tokyo, 1958) p. 12.
42. Kabushiki-kaisha Kawasaki Zosensho (Kawasaki Shipyard Co.), *40 nen-shi (40 years of Company History)* (Kobe, 1936) pp. 167–9.
43. *Proceedings of the Institution of Mechanical Engineers* (April 1895) pp. 298–302.
44. Ibid, pp. 302–3.
45. Ibid, pp. 303.
46. Watt Seitan Nihyakunen Kinenkai, *Nippon Jokikogyo Hattatsushi* pp. 177–81, Nippon Kokuyu Tetsudo, *Tetsudo Gijutsu Hattatsushi*, vol. 4, p. 270.
47. Tsusho Sangyosho, *Shoko Seisakushi*, vol. 18, pp. 164–5.
48. Nippon Kokuyu Tetsudo, *Tetsudo Gijutsu Hattatsushi*, vol.1, p. 256.
49. See Eisuke Daito, 'Railways and Scientific Management in Japan 1907–30' *Business History*, **31** (1989) pp. 1–28.
50. Especially in the case of civil engineering, Japanese traditional technology was available for such works as embankment, excavation and tunnelling. See Katsumasa Harada, *Tetsudoshi; Kenkyu Shiron (An Essay on Railway History)* (Tokyo, 1989) Chs 2 and 3, *passim*.
51. For instance, a large cart for use at a station cost 17.50 yen in Japan compared to 56.94 for an imported one; a printing machine for tickets, 400 yen against 1015.86 yen; a station lamp, 8.90 yen against 10.68 yen; a train head or rear lamp 10.00 yen against 13.58 yen; a station bell, 2.00 yen against 3.44 yen and so on.
52. N. Yamada, *Oyatoi Gaikokujin* pp. 146–7.

11. The Transfer of Electrical Technologies from the United States and Europe to Japan, 1869–1914

Hoshimi Uchida

INTRODUCTION

This chapter is concerned with the early phase of electrical technology in Japan beginning in 1869 with the first utilization of electricity, that is telegraphy, in the country, when it was wholly dependent on a British team and ending on the eve of the First World War when telecommunication and power-generating businesses were already established, and a number of domestic electrical manufacturers were trying to compete with the big firms of the USA and Germany. The 45 year period roughly coincides with the Meiji era in Japanese history, which is generally considered as the age of takeoff of the country. Since most of the technologies necessary were introduced from Europe or from the USA, transfer of electrical technology was representative for the industrialization of Japan of general trends.

Looking back from the present state of the Japanese electrical or electronic industry, the subject is of special interest. Japan, now occupies a superior position, in scale and in the sophistication of technology in the modern world, for the USA and European counterparts from whom it first learned. Transfer of electrical technology into Japan during the Meiji era was the overture for one of the greatest successes in modern industrial history, and may be regarded as an ideal of international technology transfer.

In the period under review, transfer of electrical technology assumed a peculiar character. Electricity was a *new* technology even in the Western nations. Its first practical use was telegraphy, invented in the USA and Britain during the 1840s, only a quarter-century before its introduction into Japan. And later development of electrical technology, the telephone and electric power, was attained in the USA and Germany after the 1880s. It almost coincides with the industrialization of Japan. In contrast, other technologies simultaneously introduced into Japan, such as the steam engine, mechanical spinning and iron

219

smelting with coke, were invented in eighteenth century Britain and had come to their maturity in the Western countries before their introduction into Japan.

Although the timing seemed to suggest that Japan could make almost the same start in the application of electricity as had Western nations, transfer of electrical technology was by no means easier than the transfer of older ones, for progress in the USA and Germany was too quick for the Japanese to follow, and the successive introduction of innovations was necessary.

Therefore the course of technology transfer in electricity to Japan involved a sequence of events in which various technologies were transferred from varied *donors* of technology to different *recipients* in Japan. Our account will inevitably follow these events. Happily we have a lot of evidence concerning the rise of electrical industries in Japan, including official reports of the Government, company records, contemporary articles in academic and commercial journals and personal recollections, which almost without exception refer to the introduction of technology from the Western countries. Based on these materials a number of books and essays were written from the viewpoints of economic, industrial, business and technical histories, although they were seldom translated into languages other than Japanese.[1] Moreover numerous studies on the development of electrical engineering or business on the donors' side, that is in the USA and Europe, have been published, especially in recent years. Most of them relate to the international diffusion of electrical technology, although they barely mention the contact with Japan.[2] The author of this chapter owes much to these Japanese and foreign works in finding facts on each event.

But we are not content with a mere enumeration of events extracted from those books and materials; we have to seek *characteristic* features of electrical technology and its introduction to Japan. Since the principal sources of electrical innovations had originated in two countries, the USA and Germany, other European countries were also recipients of the technology. But they more easily secured American and German technologies than did the Japanese, for people and business moved between Western countries carrying technologies with them, and they had established networks of information across the borders. This was never the case for relations between East and West. Such a handicap seemed common for all branches of technology. However there were additional difficulties inherent in electricity for non-European nations.

Electricity was an outgrowth of nineteenth-century physical science, in contrast to the mechanical and metallurgical technologies of the eighteenth century, which were developed by the empirical skill of traditional crafts. Since the European nations inherited a common tradition of natural science from the Renaissance, understanding the principles underlying the American or German innovations was easier for them than for the Japanese, who had to learn natural science and its applications at the same time.

A detailed examination of the principal events in the transfer of electrical technology to Japan reveals the way in which the recipients and the donors managed to overcome those difficulties. This, the object of the chapter, is pursued by the use of a method of *process analysis*, in the interpretation of events, referring to the following elements in the technology transfer:

1. Extent and character of technology gap between the donors and the recipient.
2. Motives of the donor and the recipient in seeking technology transfer.
3. Means of technology transfer: immigration, capital investment, turnkey contract, licensing agreement, or leak, such as via industrial espionage.
4. Media or vehicle of transfer: people , products, machinery or literature?
5. Objects of the transfer: scientific principle, patent right, system or product design, or manufacturing know-how, in limited or general electrical technology?
6. Effect of technology transfer upon the recipient.

The method will be applicable to the problems of technology transfer in any industry, in any country as well as in any age.[3] By integrating the elements for each event we can identify the actual meaning of technology transfer at a certain phase of the development of the Japanese electrical industries, and by comparing the events at different phases we can trace the progress in adaptability and capacity for new technologies in Japan, and at the same time trace the stages from dependence to self-reliance in technology.

TELEGRAPH: THE FIRST EXPERIENCE

The first encounter of the Japanese with electrical technology occurred in 1854, when Commodore Perry of the US fleet visited Japan to establish diplomatic relations. He demonstrated a set of telegraph apparatus and presented it to the Shogun. A US secretariat reported that the Japanese officials showed much interest in it.[4] Within a few years the Dutch, Prussian and Austrian ambassadors left similar gadgets as compliments before the fall of the Shogunate in 1868. Missions from the Shogun, to the USA in 1860, to the Netherlands in 1862 and to France in 1867, also reported the use of telegraphy in each country.[5] It is noteworthy that a Japanese military engineer named Sakuma Zozan conducted an experiment with the telegraph in 1858.[6] These facts suggest that the Japanese were anxious to learn about recent developments in electricity even before the political change – the Meiji Restoration – led to a deliberate governmental policy of industrialization by means of the introduction of Western technologies. The first practical telegraph line was laid in 1869, the year after the Restoration, by the new Government. George Gilbert, a British engineer, superintended the work between the Lighthouse and the Mayor's Office in Yokohama, the largest port opened to foreign traders. In 1871 the line was extended to the Tokyo Custom House and opened to the public. It was a year before the opening of the first railroad between the same two cities. It is said that the British Ambassador, Sir Harry Parkes, had strongly urged the Government to sponsor the telegraph before it promoted the railway.

The next year telegraphy was attached to the newly established 'Kobusho' (Ministry of Public Works) which controlled most of the government-owned enterprises applying Western technology such as railroads, mines and ship-yards. Kobusho hired a large number of foreigners, consisting of engineers and skilled workers, for related jobs. At the Telegraph Bureau as many as 59 foreigners were engaged, of whom 54 were British, led by Gilbert as Chief Engineer. In this manner the first electrical technology was transferred from Britain.[7]

In a few years a 1 200 km line to Nagasaki was completed; there it was connected with the submarine cables owned by the Great Northern Telegraph Co. to send messages directly to Europe via Siberia or the Indian Ocean. It meant the completion of transcontinental information networks formed over a period of ten years.[8] The diplomats, merchants and journalists from various countries benefited most from the international communication. Transferring telegraph technology served not only the Japanese people but also the British themselves, who were the donors; and during the late nineteenth century teams of British engineers and workmen used it while engaged in constructing infrastructure abroad.[9] These were the reasons on the donor's side for promoting the transfer of telegraph technology. In fact, the Telegraph Bureau transmitted messages in English as well as in Japanese.

The management of the telegraph business also looked like a British enterprise in Japan. Annual reports of the Bureau were printed in English and Japanese, and the First Report noted that the lines were worked 'cojointly by Europeans and Japanese. The latter acted under foreign superintendence as operators, clerks, engineers, inspectors and linemen.'[10]

The actual course of technology transfer was neither systematic nor smooth. Yoshida Masahide, who was regarded as the 'first electrical engineer in Japan', recalled:

> When in youth I was a student of English conversation in Yokohama, that was why I was recruited into the telegraphy. But the British foreman did not teach me the principle nor the working of the telegraph; I only imitated what he operated. In a few years I was moved to be a translator to a British engineer constructing long-distance lines to Nagasaki with the task of explaining to Japanese labourers how to install a pole and connect wires. It was very hard and difficult.[11]

Through these experiences, however, he acquired necessary telegraph practice; after 30 years he was promoted chief engineer of the telegraph.

The Bureau opened a school for operators in 1873, and within 12 years 1 282 boys graduated. But foreign instructors taught only Morse code and elementary English there. It was not until 1887 that the school opened a course in electrical engineering. The contribution of another branch of the Telegraph Bureau, the Machine shop, will be outlined later.

By 1881 British engineers and skilled workers had resigned from the Telegraph Bureau, leaving the day-to-day operations to Japanese staffs. The telegraph business continued to expand. This suggests that the Japanese had mastered practical telegraph engineering in a short time without systematic education. The success of the first transfer of electrical technology, telegraphy, was due partly to the transplantation of an established British system by using the necessary foreign manpower, and partly to the adaptability of the Japanese workers to the new technology.

But to catch up with the advances of electrical engineering in the West a different sort of manpower was necessary, although the experiences in wiring and insulation gained by the telegraph technicians were no doubt useful for the introduction of these new technologies: the telephone and electric power.

EDUCATION IN ENGINEERING SCIENCE AND THE RISE OF ELECTRIC POWER

In 1873 the Imperial College of Engineering was founded to train Japanese engineers in order to replace the foreigners in every undertaking of Kobusho. An outstanding fact about the College was that it had a Division of Electric Telegraphy along with other divisions; Civil and Mechanical Engineering, Architecture, Applied Chemistry, Mining and Metallurgy. In fact, it was the first independent division of higher electrical education in the world, for at the time electrical engineering was a part of physics at a few universities in Britain and in the USA, while it belonged to mechanical engineering at the German Technische Hochschulen. The first electrical engineering education in Britain began in 1878 at the City and Guilds of London Institute; Cornell and Columbia Universities in the USA opened courses in electrical engineering as late as 1883 and 1885, a decade after the Tokyo Imperial College.[12]

Henry Dyer, a Scottish-born mechanical engineer and the first Dean of the College, intended to form a school in which theory and practice were held in a reasonable balance, irrespective of the conservative system in his mother country. Students of the College spent the first two years learning English, mathematics and elementary science, the next two learning engineering science according to their divisions, and the last two years they worked on the job at the establishments of Kobusho and prepared essays for graduation.[13]

William Edward Ayrton, Professor of Telegraphy and Physics, had studied physics under Sir William Thomson, the most eminent figure in electricity at the time, at the University of Glasgow. After a short service working for Indian telegraphy, he was invited to Tokyo. No doubt he was one of a few academicians in electricity in the world, and in his lectures did not confine himself to telegraphy but taught the most up-to-date subjects in electricity. During his five years' stay in Tokyo he also conducted experimental research, assisted by his pupils. Therefore an education in electrical engineering at the Imperial College was regarded as one of the highest in the world at that time. Ayrton left Tokyo to take up a chair at the City and Guilds Institute. In 1892 he was elected President of the Institution of Electrical Engineers of Britain.[14]

The academic tradition of Ayrton was upheld by the Electrical Engineering Division of the Department of Technology, Tokyo Imperial University after the dissolution of the College of Engineering in 1886.[15] A new kind of technical manpower, the scientific engineer was born. After graduating, early students of the Imperial College and the University played a major role in the transfer of the new telephone and power technologies.

Ayrton had demonstrated the arc lamp to the Japanese public in 1878. After Thomas Edison succeeded in producing an incandescent lamp and then built a power station in New York, Fujioka Ichisuke, a former student of Ayrton, became the chief engineer of the newly-organized Tokyo Electric Light Co. It opened the first power station in Japan in 1888 using Edison's system. By 1890, seven electric power companies had been founded in major cities, where chief engineers were without exception graduates from the Division of Electricity of the Imperial College and Tokyo University (Table 11.1).

Thus two ways of generating and distributing electric power – direct current and alternating current – were transferred with the imported machinery only a few years after their first application in the USA and Europe. The essential difference in the technology transfer between electric power and telegraph lay in the changing role of the native engineers. A team of foreigners was not necessary anymore. The Edison Co. sent a single man, named Congton, to Tokyo Electric Light Co. to show how to assemble, install and operate the imported generators. Fujioka supervised the work with the junior graduate engineers, who soon learned how to establish a power station and later took charge of other power stations.[16]

Iwadare Kunihiko, Chief Engineer of the Osaka Electric Light Co., who had worked in the USA for Edison-General Co. after graduating from the Imperial College, chose the alternating system of Thomson Houston by himself, and the company also hired a single man, named Goddard, from Thomson.[17] The basic knowledge taught at school made it possible for Japanese engineers to choose

Table 11.1   *Earliest power companies in Japan*

Name of Company	Year of Foundation	System	Chief Engineer	Year of Graduation
Tokyo El Co.	1888	Edison DC	I. Fujioka	1881
Kobe El Co.	1889	Edison DC	J. Nakagawa	1889
Osaka El Co.	1889	TH AC	K. Iwadare	1882
Kyoto El Co.	1889	Edison DC	T. Ogi	1889
Nagoya El Co.	1889	Edison DC	M. Niwa	1887
Sinagawa El Co.	1890	MP AC	D. Ushioda	1891
Yokohama El Co.	1890	Edison DC	S. Kobori	1890

Notes: El: Electric Light; TH: Thomson Houston; MP: Mather Platt; DC: direct current; AC: alternating current.

an appropriate technology and to adopt the practice imported from a foreign manufacturer. Ayrton's teaching proved highly advantageous when Japan introduced electric power. He was worth more than 50 foreigners engaged in telegraphy.

Soon afterwards hydroelectric supply started in Kyoto, in 1891, and by the end of the century long-distance high-voltage power transmission began. Local stations increased in number year by year. The process was similar to that of earlier examples: native engineers planned and managed the undertakings with the aid of imported machines and the temporary service of foreign engineers.

Of course not all of the graduate electrical engineers worked for power companies. A number of them occupied seats at the Ministry of Communication, which took over the telegraph business from Kobusho. Their principal task was the introduction of a telephone system. They actually chose and assessed foreign technology and made long-term plans to build up a national communication system. When the telegraph was adopted only foreign engineers could execute these jobs; with the telephone indigenous engineers accomplished such tasks far better than they did.

Some of the graduates succeeded Ayrton as university professors as well as teachers at the technical colleges, mentioned later. They generally studied also at universities in the USA or Technische Hochschulen in Germany; here they absorbed recent developments in electrical engineering, which they taught to their students on their return. In fact, the university in the Meiji period was an organization for the transfer of engineering science from the most advanced countries. Graduate engineers developed and built larger-capacity power stations, higher-voltage, longer transmission lines and an effective telecommunication system with the most up-to-date technologies.

By 1914, only 30 years after the first installation of electric power, total power produced in the country reached some 1 555 *million* kilowatt hours. The number of power stations increased to 578, and the capacity of an individual station grew from 25 kilowatts in 1888 to 700 000 kilowatts in 1914.[18] At the same time, more than 3 000 telephone offices were relaying more than a billion messages a year, and the length of long-distance telephone lines totalled 2 000 kilometres.[19] The rapid expansion of electric utilities owes much to the increasing supply of electrical engineers. From 1879 to 1912, 386 students graduated from the Electrical Engineering Division of Tokyo University. But it was graduates of lower engineering schools who supported the growth of the electric utility industries in larger numbers.

The government established a workmen's school in 1885 and in 1897 upgraded it to a technical college to provide middle rank engineers. Electrical engineers first graduated from the Tokyo College in 1899, from the Sendai College in 1910, and from the Osaka College in 1911. By 1912, graduate electrical engineers from these three colleges totalled 437. In 1920, of a total of 923 university graduate electrical engineers, 116 worked in communication, 191 for power companies, 125 for electrical manufacturers, 57 for education and the rest were hired in the user industries; of 1 019 college graduate electrical engineers, 69 were engaged in communication, 250 in power companies and 259 in electrical manufacture.[20]

In addition to these engineers, private schools, including night classes, supplied a number of *electricians*. The first of these schools was Koshu Gakko (Technicians' School) founded in 1888. By 1920, 10 schools in Tokyo, Osaka and Nagoya produced more than 10 000 electricians.

University graduates taught at the technical colleges and college graduates in turn taught at the technicians' schools. Engineering science spread through the channels of education, resulting in the electrification of the country. The seed of electrical engineering which Ayrton had sown at the Imperial College of Engineering bore rich fruits within 30 years. Success in the transfer of engineering science seemed to be the most profitable event for the development of the Japanese electrical industries.

LIMITS OF COPIED PRODUCTION BY DOMESTIC MANUFACTURERS

In this manner electrical utility, including telecommunication and power supply, spread, but it still relied heavily upon imported machinery. Most of these machines were made in Britain, Germany or the USA, and in particular products of the big five manufacturers (Western Electric, General Electric and Westinghouse of the USA, and Siemens and AEG of Germany) accounted for the major shares (Table 11.2).

Table 11.2   *Value of imported electrical machines, 1893–1913* (¥000s)[21]

Year	Total	USA	Britain	Germany
1893	357	117	197	30
1894	226	146	49	18
1895	311	70	174	41
1896	681	280	248	152
1897	1 002	685	185	166
1898	606	407	134	64
1899	450	265	115	69
1900	726	502	144	76
1901	696	442	129	118
1902	810	682	60	64
1903	836	524	185	119
1904	1 266	812	228	222
1905	2 455	1 859	423	167
1906	1 405	862	326	185
1907	1 773	990	548	219
1908	2 050	1 381	369	293
1909	2 999	1 249	826	916
1910	2 196	902	611	634
1911	5 711	1 811	1 080	2 755
1912	4 140	1 605	1 312	1 119
1913	4 290	1 706	1 035	1 460

Note: Data relate to electric generators and motors.

These firms were not only the largest producers of electric machinery in the world, but also principal innovators in electrical technology, including telephone transmitters and exchanges, generators, alternating current, electric traction, electrochemistry and incandescent lamps. The machines imported into Japan embodied the most up-to-date advances in electrical engineering, so that the Japanese could make use of these innovations and the utility industries could emulate progress in power and communication technologies in the advanced countries.

Of course, making use of imported machines was the first step in technology transfer in the long run. Similar machines were produced within the adopting country, which at first copied the imported products and later designed others for themselves: in this way technology from advanced countries took a firm hold in Japan.

But at the start the growth of domestic electrical manufacture was slow as compared with electric utilization. The inconsistency involved the essential differences between electric utilization and the manufacture of equipment. The former industry supplies perishable goods such as electric current or information carried on it, which is consumed as soon as it is generated and cannot be stored over time. Therefore electric power supply or telecommunication businesses are located within the territory in which their products are consumed, and survive without competition from abroad. This feature gives a sort of natural monopoly to the domestic utilization industries.

In contrast, products of electrical manufacturers are hardware, which can be transported a long distance and preserved over time. This means that electrical machinery is an international good, and the domestic producers will always face competition from imported goods. Their consumers, utilization industries, can choose either domestic or imported machines. For the foreign electrical manufacturers the expanding telephone and power industries were promising markets, to which they were willing to transfer technology embodied in their products. These were the principal reasons for the rapid development of the utility industries and at the same time for the retarded growth of domestic equipment manufacture.

Manufacture of electrical equipment in Japan originated as early as the 1870s with the Seikisho (the Machine Shop) of the Telegraph Bureau, where a German mechanic named Louis Schaefer taught Japanese workers how to make telegraph apparatus. The Bureau also dispatched Tanaka Seisuke, a Japanese clockmaker, to Vienna to investigate the machines displayed at the International Exposition in 1873 and to learn machining technique there. By 1878, Seikisho had succeeded in copying 10 sets of Morse printing telegraph, and at the end of the 1880s all apparatus used in the Bureau was home-made.

The emergence of domestic manufacture was thus very rapid, even though the telegraph instruments copied by Japanese craftsmen were rough gadgets. In 1883 the Bureau tried to make a telephone set, but it seemed so complex and delicate, as compared to the telegraph, that they gave up home production. Nevertheless the influence of Seikisho in the rise of domestic electrical manufacture was important, for not a few skilled workers from the Bureau established their own shops, producing not only telecommunication apparatus but also machinery for the new power industry. Tanaka Daikichi founded in 1882, with his brother-in-law Seisuke, Tanaka Seisakusho, where they at first built telegraph apparatus for the Bureau and, then, after changing the name of the factory to Shibaura Works, enlarged their business to produce ammunition and steam engines. The firm was bought by Mitsui and became the largest manufacturer of electric machinery of every kind, growing into the Toshiba Corporation, one of the most diversified electrical manufacturers in the world today. Miyoshi Shoichi was the founder of Hakunetsusha, an enterprise set up to produce the first incandescent lamps in Japan with the technical assistance of Fujioka. Miyoshi had a machine shop, too, where he built the first electric motor and generator in the country. After he went bankrupt in 1889, two mechanics of the factory founded their own shops: Shigemune Hosui's Meidensha, which still exists as a maker of electric motors and Oda Sokichi's factory. Oki Kibataro maintained the closest connection with the Ministry of Communication after his departure in 1881, and Oki Denki Co. still exists as one of the largest manufacturers specializing in communication and information.[22]

Thus the techniques for the mechanical production of electrical apparatus were transferred from Schaefer, and an unknown Austrian who taught Tanaka Seisuke, to the first private manufacturers, forming the base for the technology of large Japanese electrical corporations today.

In the beginning there were favourable conditions for entry into the heavy electrical industry. The imported electrical machines of the 1880s were still in their infancy, with less power, lower voltage and simpler structures, so that domestic mechanics could easily copy them with poor tools and little skill. But as time went by, remarkable advances in the design and manufacture of electrical machinery were made in the West. The big American and German firms, applying the result of theoretical and experimental research accomplished by such talents as Ferranti, Stanley, Tesla, Dolivo-Dobrovolski and Steinmetz, made their products capable of larger power, higher voltage and greater long-distance transmission of electricity. US and German lamp makers were competing in the development of more brilliant and economical filament materials. Year by year imported products were improved in capacity as well as quality, embodying the most recent achievements in electrical technology, and it soon became clear that the domestic products, with scarcely any theoretical design and made from inadequate and impure materials, were uneconomical and unreliable.

However sympathetic the users had been to domestic production, they could not help choosing imported machinery. A three-phase alternator designed by Nakano Hatsune, a professor at Tokyo University, from an imported catalogue and built by Ishikawajima Shipyard and working at a station of Tokyo Electric Light Co., used to glow red-hot and was deformed so frequently that the operators were compelled to stop it many times a night. A generator made by the Miyoshi factory was rejected by Kobe Electric Light Co., and motors for the tramcars of Kyoto City provided by the same factory proved useless. The users changed to imported machinery.[23]

When in 1900 a student of electrical engineering named Shibusawa Motoji, who later became the Dean of the Nagoya University, designed a 100 kilowatt generator, he could not find an instrument to measure the magnetic property of tinplate, so he had to determine the necessary thickness from the data in a foreign text multiplied by a considerable safety factor. He said afterwards:

> Since the required strength of materials was small in the days of low voltage and small current, we were allowed to design machines without proper precision. After the installation of 10,000 volt cable, however, larger size and higher quality of machines required theoretical design which took a considerable time for us to learn.[24]

The technology gap between the imported and domestic machines became so great that mere copies from the appearance of imported goods were useless. Without any means of technology transfer from abroad the domestic producers could not have survived.

Otaguro Jugoro, the manager of Shibaura Works, thought at the end of the 1890s:

> Despite our recent progress in the manufacture of machines we are far behind the Western industries. In addition to the present gaps in technology, their rate of progress is much faster than ours, thanks to their larger scale of production, refined equipment and broader extent of research ... with all our engineers and mechanics we cannot make noticeable accomplishments in such an isolated state.[25]

WESTERN MANUFACTURERS' APPROACH TO THE JAPANESE MARKET

Since technology transfer could be never realized without the will of the donors to offer their patents or know-how to the recipients, we have to turn to the attitudes of the US and European electrical manufacturers to the world market.

At the turn of the century they were eager to export their products or to manufacture overseas at their subsidiary factories. AT&T, after winning the patent litigation over the telephone against Western Union and acquiring the latter's manufacturing facility, Western Electric Co., built a factory at Antwerp, Belgium, to supply telephone equipment to European governments. The first transmitter used by the Japanese government was also made in Belgium.

The Edison Co. and Thomson Houston set up their marketing and manufacturing facilities in Britain and France before they merged into General Electric in 1892. Westinghouse, too, began a world marketing operation after

1896. The German company Siemens had marketing and manufacturing branches as early as the 1850s in Russia and Britain.

It was Siemens who first identified the Japanese market, for they had been working with international telegraphy. As early as 1870, Werner Siemens wrote to his brother William in London asking about the feasibility of producing in Japan. In fact, most of the apparatus used at the Telegraph Bureau was made by Siemens. After meeting Ishii Tadasuke, Director of Telecommunication in the Japanese government, in Berlin in 1886, Werner made up his mind to send Herman Kessler to Japan. Kessler soon succeeded in selling electric transport and generating plants to Ashio Mine, owned by Furukawa Ichibei. Furukawa became the largest producer of copper in Japan and an exporter to the world. By 1896, Kessler had opened the Tokyo Office of Siemens, selling hydroelectric, electrochemical, electric traction and naval electric equipment. In 1907 the Office hired 16 service engineers, of whom nine were Japanese.[26]

Two of the native electrical engineers in Siemens became eminent entrepreneurs in the Japanese industrial history. One, Noguchi Shitagau, founded in 1906 Nippon Chisso Co. to introduce the calcium cyanamide process and plant from Siemens and its affiliate. The company soon grew to be the largest electrochemical manufacturer in Japan. The other ex-Siemens engineer, Kawakita Yoshio, established an engineering enterprise to build hydroelectric stations. These two examples illustrate how the application technology fostered within Siemens was transferred through the engineers to Japanese industries.[27]

Other big electrical concerns sold their products through agents in Tokyo or Yokohama. When Tokyo Electric Light Co. first imported a direct current system from Edison Co. in 1886, it was nominated an agent for the latter, selling and installing Edison generators in factories and other power stations. Similarly Osaka Electric Light Co. introduced in 1889 the first alternating current generator from Thomson Houston, who appointed them their Japanese agent. Tokyo Electric also changed to alternating current in 1894, importing generators from the German Allgemeine Elektrizität Co. (AEG).

The two routes for the transfer of alternating current left an irrational feature of regional inconsistency in the Japanese power supply system. The eastern half of Japan still uses 50Hz alternating current, which was the German standard, while the western part adopted 60Hz, the US standard. The difference in frequency resulted in much trouble and inconvenience in Japanese energy utilization. The example demonstrates how profoundly the first transfer of technology has repercussions within the adopted country. The agency contracts between American manufacturers and the Japanese power companies were liquidated soon after the merger of Edison and Thomson Houston into General Electric, and Japanese and American trading companies took the role of

importers. As Lockwood emphasized in his history of Japanese industrialization, trading companies were important channels of technology transfer.[28]

It seems that the most common imported electrical machinery during the
1890s was British generators for the cotton mills, which were being set up at
that time, made by Mather & Platt Co., attached to the spinning machines made
by Platt Brothers of Oldham, through the latter's sole agent, Mitsui & Co., the
largest trading company in Japan. Service engineers of Mitsui as well as those
employed in the cotton industry learned electrical engineering in the course of
installing and running these imported machines. In the 1900s the importation
of US and German large-capacity generating equipment for hydroelectric
stations increasingly came through the channels of trading companies (see
Table 11.2). General Electric appointed Bagnall & Hills in Yokohama their
sole agent in 1889. Westinghouse chose Takada & Co., the second largest
importer of machines, while Okura & Co. were made the agents for AEG and
other German electric lamp makers. Healing & Co., a British trading company,
was the agent for British electrical manufacturers such as Ferranti and Fowler.
Although the share of British electrical machinery decreased, Healing kept a
strong position in the provision of electric wires and cables.

By the end of the 1890s the big electrical manufacturers had almost
completed their channels of export to Japan, establishing a dominant position
in the growing market, while the small domestic manufacturers had to be
content with the sale of small-capacity machines and appliances. Then came a
critical time, both for the foreign exporters and for the domestic producers,
when the Japanese government set the time schedule for the revision of treaties
at the turn of the century. An expected outcome of the treaty revision was that
a free hand would be given to the Japanese government to raise protective
tariffs, which might injure foreign exporters. On the other hand, the revision
would establish the principle of equality between domestic and foreign
investors and patent applicants. In reality the revised Patent Law of 1889
ensured that foreigners could hold patent rights, and the Commercial Code
permitted direct investment by foreign firms into Japan.

In a rapidly advancing field like electricity exchange of patents tends to
benefit developed countries. In fact, before the revision only 32 electric patents
were filed by domestic inventors, but during the five years after the revision as
many as 190 were filed, of which 157 were applied by inventors abroad, most
of whom were linked with large electrical manufacturers.[29] The apparent result
was difficulty for domestic factories in copying imported machinery without
infringing the patent rights.

The crisis caused by the revision of the Patent Law was clearly recognized
by the top management of Mitsui, owner of Shibaura Works, which only held
a patent on a direct current generator. The minute of the Board of Mitsui dated
27 September 1897 reads:

While for the present we are able to copy the inventions of any nation, it would be impossible to produce goods patented by others after our country has joined the International Patent Convention. Therefore we are vulnerable.[30]

Mitsui had to reduce the business of Shibaura by firing a number of workers.

In contrast, foreign business found new opportunities. After the revision of the Commercial Code, Dr. Lönheln, a German lawyer and consultant to the Japanese government secretly informed Siemens:

The prospect for the capital investment in electric lamp, telegraph and traction business is hopeful in Japan ... There are problems of language and custom, indeed, but they are common in any country; we are able to overcome them by establishing a carefully managed subsidiary ... employing as many Japanese staffs as possible.[31]

Although Siemens did not take any action, its American rivals, Western Electric and General Electric, made a quick move to invest in manufacturing business in Japan. As stated earlier, it was the basic marketing strategy of these manufacturers to produce their patented goods abroad through jointly-owned subsidiaries. In so doing they could take royalties in addition to dividends, eliminating the risk of reduced exports caused by protective tariff and competition. American companies had been manufacturing solely in European countries where they could find the necessary engineers and mechanics. They gradually recognized that Japanese engineers and workmen were almost equally capable. This was a prerequisite for the transfer of technology into subsidiaries.

LICENSING AGREEMENTS AND THE PROCESS OF TECHNOLOGY TRANSFER

Three licensing agreements on electrical technology were signed between 1898 and 1909, accompanying capital investments from the USA. These were the first direct investments into the Japanese industry, and official technology transfer in consequence of the agreements opened a new era in the manufacturing of electrical machinery in Japan. There follows a description of the cause, process and effect of each agreement.[32]

Western Electric – Nippon Electric Co.

In 1889 it was decided that the telephone business in Japan should be a government monopoly. The Ministry of Communication imported necessary apparatus and then let the domestic manufacturers copy it. In spite of this nationalization policy, technological progress overseas was so fast that, in order to keep up with innovations abroad, the Ministry found it had to rely on imports for the most important parts of the system. Of ¥39 million spent for the purchase of apparatus and materials between 1889 and 1914, about one-third was for imported items.[33]

When the First Extension Plan started in 1896, the Ministry adopted the solid-back receiver and the standard switchboard utilized in the system of AT&T and manufactured by its subsidiary Western Electric Co. As early as 1888, Oi Saitaro, chief engineer of Telephony in the Ministry, had personal connections with the managers of AT&T and Western Electric: M. B. Thayer, J. J. Carty and F. R. Wells. Then, in 1895, Western Electric cancelled its agent contract with Takada & Co. and appointed a new sole agent, Iwadare Kunihiko, who had been the chief engineer of Osaka Electric Light Co. The next year, Thayer paid a visit to Japan to investigate the possibilities for business.[34]

There were many factors to take into consideration: increasing demand for the Western-type apparatus, maintenance work required for imports, the nationalization policy of the government, revision of the Commercial Code and Patent Law. To set up a manufacturing subsidiary would be the best solution. In 1898 Newcomb Carlton came to make a take-over offer to Oki Denki, who was to copy the Western-type receiver and switchboard for the Ministry of Communication. After three months' negotiation Oki rejected the proposal.[35]

Then Nippon Electric Ltd was formed by the partnership of Iwadare and Maeda Takehiko on the site of the bankrupt Miyoshi Shop, to import and repair the machinery of Western Electric. This company changed its name to Nippon Electric Co. (NEC) on 17 July 1899, the very day of the enforcement of the Commercial Code which authorized investment from foreign firms. NEC became the first joint venture in Japan under the law, Western Electric holding 54 per cent of the capital stock. Iwadare became managing director, while Carlton and E. W. Clement were elected directors.[36]

When NEC began production of telephone apparatus in addition to its earlier roles of import agent and maintenance centre a few years later, a rush of technology transfer took place. A new plant layout was designed and construction was supervised by the engineers of Western Electric; a complete set of production machinery was transported from the American factory. It was said that Western used to change its technical installations every five years and ship the older machines to overseas subsidiaries. They included automatic lathes seldom found in contemporary Japanese factories. Standardized material from the Supply Business Department of the parent company included such trivial goods as pencils and erasers, and standardized parts of transmitters and switchboards were assembled according to the specification of Western Electric.

In the workplace two American foremen kept watch over the Japanese workers, and letter forms within the company were written in English, exactly the same as in the USA. At first Japanese managers applied an internal contract system, in which each job was entrusted to a few skilled workers. This system was gradually abandoned after Iwadare's visit to the USA in 1905 and the return of two Japanese staff who had been studying the management of the parent company. In three years the following changes occurred; in addition to the skilled workers, clerks were assigned to pay wages directly to the apprentices; a young engineer traced production routes throughout the factory; a time and motion study was made for each job; a system of inspection was provided.[37]

Such enforced modernization implied transfer of production engineering into the Japanese factory. In the first decade of the twentieth century NEC was an exception, not only in electrical manufacturing, but in the whole industry, introducing the 'American System of Production'.

General Electric – Tokyo Electric Co.

Tokyo Electric Co. (TEC) was the successor of Hakunetsusha, the first producer of incandescent lamps. The company had been suffering from grave technological difficulties and from fierce competition with German lamps imported by Okura & Co. It was making losses every year, resulting in a frequent change of investors; electric power companies, who were at first sympathetic towards domestic production, turned to cheaper and superior imported lamps. In the early 1900s things looked hopeless for TEC when the chief manager of the company, Shinjo Yoshio, went to the USA to ask for technical assistance and capital investment. General Electric, the world's largest electric lamp producer, agreed to his proposal. In 1905, General Electric bought 51 per cent of the stock of TEC in exchange for exclusive rights over the patent and know-how in incandescent lamp production in Japan. Three Americans, Bagnall, Geary and McIvor, were elected directors of the company.

Imported machinery and materials, as well as the acquisition of manufacturing expertise partly embodied in the patent rights, played an important role in the transfer of lamp technology and in the reconstruction of TEC. Soon after the licensing agreement was signed, a set of machines, including headmaking, stemming, sealing and vacuum pumps, was sent from the USA. W. H. Chesney, an engineer, came to set up and run these machines and taught Japanese employees how to handle them. Critical parts such as carbon filaments and sockets were supplied from overseas, so that the same lamp as the 'Gem' lamp of General Electric could be assembled. General Electric allowed the trade marks 'Edison' and 'Mazda' to be used on the bulbs of TEC.

The imported machines and materials melted the ice in the technological bottleneck that existed in TEC, where previously almost all work had been done by hand, following methods based on foreign literature or on the brief impressions of an engineer in an American factory in 1896.[38] In the 10 years after the expiration of the Edison Patents in 1894 a remarkable mechanization was going ahead within the lamp factories of General Electric, with the introduction of Libby-Owens's semi-automatic glass blowing equipment, Howell's sealing machine, Howell and Burrow's stem machine and other devices for mechanizing the manufacture of lead wires, getters and filaments.[39] The introduction of these machines meant the first mechanization of the manufacturing process in TEC. The increased capital was invested in a glass factory and a larger lamp factory which were designed on a new site by A. H. Morse, an engineer from General Electric.

Soon after came the most important innovation: the tungsten filament. In 1905, General Electric acquired Just and Hannaman's pressed tungsten patent and planned to sell superior lamps incorporating the new material. Three years later Shinjo, President of TEC, was allowed to inspect and learn this new production method. By 1909 the same bulb was produced in TEC. An improvement, drawn tungsten wire, invented in the laboratory of General Electric, was also studied by three Japanese and brought into production in Japan.[40]

After the expiration of the basic patents on tungsten many small bulb makers appeared in Japan, as they did in the USA. Even so, TEC maintained a leading position in the business, thanks to the consumer's strong appreciation for quality. TEC was also the first producer of vacuum tubes in Japan under the agreement with General Electric, a fact which symbolized the beginning of the Japanese electronic age. The company later merged with Shibaura Works to form Toshiba Corporation.

General Electric – Shibaura Works

Shibaura Works, the largest domestic electrical manufacturer at the turn of the century, could only produce generators under 300 kilowatts and 3 500 volts, while imported machines reached 1 000 kilowatts and 10 000 volts. As stated earlier, its lack of competitive power against foreign manufacturers became a devil of a nuisance to its owner, the House of Mitsui. The management decided to ask for a licensing agreement to overcome the technology gap. In 1907, Masuda Takashi, manager of Mitsui & Co., met C. A. Coffin, president of General Electric, in New York and two years later a contract was drawn up by both companies, requiring Shibaura to offer 24 per cent of its capital stock and pay 1 per cent of its sales as royalty in return for patent licences, research information, training of Japanese engineers, blueprints of plant layout and instruction of managerial staff.[41]

This agreement did not tie the participants as closely as the two cases reported above, which made the Japanese factories subsidiaries of the American firms. The relationship was apparent in the minority holding of the stock of Shibaura by General Electric, while Mitsui kept a majority holding.

It is not certain whether Shibaura experienced a similar revolution in manufacturing methods to that of NEC and TEC. The benefit of the agreement for Shibaura lay principally in the use of the patents, which seemed to come into effect less immediately, for it was only as late as four years after the contract with General Electric that Shibaura succeeded in building the first 500 kilowatt generator for Oji Paper Mill. General Electric still exported to Japan its larger-capacity machines, and Toshiba remained an inferior competitor. Table 11.3 shows shares of imported and home-made machines in the Japanese electric power stations.[42]

Table 11.3   Number of generators in Japan, 1912

Maker	Over 500kw	Less than 500kw
Imported		
General Electric	19	72
Westinghouse	16	15
Siemens	12	8
AEG	6	4
Others	4	12
Subtotal	57	111
Home-made		
Shibaura	2	40
Others	0	6
Subtotal	2	46

American and German manufacturers were competing in the growing larger-capacity market, and General Electric retained the right to export in the agreement with Shibaura, to maintain its dominant position. Shibaura gained the status of leader among Japanese manufacturers, thanks to information flows from General Electric. These were the outcomes of the licensing agreement.

EXPERIENCES IN THE US FACTORIES AND INVISIBLE TRANSFER OF TECHNOLOGY

Transplanting designs and manufacturing practices on the basis of a licensing agreement was a direct method of effecting technology transfer. There were also indirect methods, either promoted by agreements or bypassing them in another way. By 1910 several non-licensed electrical manufacturers had developed in Japan, thanks to indirect or invisible technology transfer. For instance, a spill-over of licensed technology might occur from the licensee to a third person. Since the telephone apparatus of NEC was made the standard by the Ministry of Communication, another custom producer, Oki Denki, benefited from the specification given by the Ministry. This was a case of internal diffusion of technology through the customer. Movement of workers also helped the diffusion.

Chief engineers of Shibaura, as part-time lecturers, taught students at Tokyo University, and most of their students found jobs in other companies, including Hitachi and Mitsubishi. Thus technology diffusion based on a licensing agreement with a foreign company reached non-licensees through the school. In such ways the influence of licensing agreements was not confined to the licensees, but upgraded the general level of technology by means of invisible transfer.

The experience of engineers in factories in the USA was another effective source of technology transfer. As a result of agreements, NEC, TEC and Shibaura sent their engineers to the licenser in the USA every year. For the non-licensed manufacturers manpower with experience in a foreign factory was a more important source of technology than it was for the licensees. As shown in the examples in Table 11.4, over a dozen engineers worked in factories in the USA, sometimes voluntarily, sometimes ordered to do so by Japanese companies.

At the foreign factories they became acquainted with the design of products, manufacturing facilities, processing and assembly methods, rules of inspection, plant layout and so on. And they made use of the knowledge for the improvement of home factories.

These invisible means of technology transfer provided the basis for the non-licensees to establish themselves during the First World War, when the supply of imported machinery became short. After the war two licensing agreements were concluded, between Westinghouse and Mitsubishi, and between Siemens and Fuji Denki. Formal technology transfer again took place; the former case seemed similar to the General Electric–Shibaura agreement and the latter resembled the Western–NEC relationship, except that Siemens held no more than half of the capital of Fuji Denki. But we cannot enter into details of these events, for they occurred outside the period with which we are concerned.

Table 11.4   Engineers employed in foreign factories[43]

Name	Year of migration	Factory	Later employer
Iwadare Kunihiko	1886	Edison	Osaka Electric Light
Hasegawa Tei	1888	Thomson	Osaka Electric Light
Katogi Shigenori	1889	Western	Miyoshi
Iwai Kin'ichi	1897	G. E.	Hanshin Railway
Oda Sokichi	1897	Westinghouse	Oda Denki
Yamazaki Shisai	1902	G. E.	Keihin Railway
Fujimoto Goro	1903	Westinghouse	Meidensha
Tachihara Jin	1904	G. E.	Mitsubishi
Kasahara Kenjiro	1905	G. E.	Mitsubishi
Tachikawa Heiji	1905	G. E.	Mitsubishi
Yasukawa Daigoro	1913	Westinghouse	Yasukawa Denki
Yokota Chiaki	1915	Thomson (Britain)	Dainihon Lamp
Takeuchi Jutaro	1915	Westinghouse (Britain)	Meidensha

NOTES

Names in the text as well as in the notes appear as follows, according to nationality: Japanese, surname followed by forename; others, forename followed by surname. An asterisk denotes a Japanese publication.

1. *Katogi, Shigenori, *Honpo Denki Jigyoshi* (History of Electrical Business in Japan) (Tokyo, 1914); *Kogakukai (ed.), *Meiji Kogyoshi, Denkihen* (History of Industries in the Meiji Era, vol. 7, Electricity) (Tokyo, 1928); *Nihon Denki Kogyokai (ed.), *Nihon Denki Kogyoshi* (History of Electrical Manufacture in Japan) (Tokyo, 1956); *Nihon Tel.& Tel. Corp. (ed.), *Denshin-denwa Jigyoshi* (History of Telegraph and Telephone) (Tokyo, 1959); *Nihon Kagakushi Gakkai (ed.) *Nihon Kagaku-gijutsushi Taikei* (History of Science & Technology in Japan) vol. 19 (Tokyo, 1969).

2. G. Dettmar, *Die Entwicklung der Starkstromtechnik in Deutschland* (Berlin, 1940); A. A. Bright, *The Electric Lamp Industry* (New York, 1949); G. Siemens, *Geschichte des Hauses Siemens* (Munchen, 1947); H. C. Passer, *The Electrical Manufacturers, 1875–1900* (Cambridge, Mass., 1953); S. von Weiher and H. Goetzler, *The Siemens Company, its Role in the Progress of Electrical Engineering* (München, 1972); M. Fagen (ed.), *A History of Engineering and Science in the Bell System*, vol. 1, (New York, 1975); I. C. R. Byatt, *The British Electrical Industry* (Oxford, 1979); T. P. H. Hughes, *Networks of Power* (Baltimore, 1983); A. H. McMahon, *The Making of a Profession. A Century of Electrical Engineering in America* (New York, 1984), L. S. Reich, *The Making of American Industrial Research* (Cambridge, 1985); P. Cardot (ed.), *Un Siècle d'Electricité dans le Monde* (Paris, 1987).

3. *Uchida, H., 'Transfer and Development of Chemical Technology during the 1920s', *Japan Business History Review*, vol. 7. no. 2 (Tokyo, 1972).

4. F. L. Hawkes (ed.), *Narratives of the Expedition of an American Squadron to China and Japan* (Washington, 1856), Japanese translation, vol. 3. p. 200.

5. *Nihon Kagakushi Gakkai, op. cit. p. 32.

6. *Seki, A., 'Sakuma Zozan no Denshin Jikken', *Japan Industrial Archeology* no. 32, (Tokyo, 1984).
7. Takahashi, Y., 'The Beginning of the Telegraph System in Japan', paper presented at the Colloque *Télécommunication, Espaces et Innovations aux XIXe et XXe Siècles*, (Paris, 1989).
8. *History of the Cable & Wireless Ltd* (London, 1969), Japanese translation, pp. 1–10.
9. R. A. Buchanan, 'The Diaspora of British Engineering', *Technology and Culture*, vol. 27, no. 3, (July 1986) pp. 501–24; *Uchida, H., 'Denki Gijutsu no Donyu to Teichaku' (Transfer of Electrical Technology), Japan Science Foundation, *Reports on the Technology Transfer* (Tokyo, 1989) pp.154–5.
10. The Telegraph Bureau, *First Report of the Chief Commissioner for the Period from the First Projection of the Telegraph &c.* (Tokyo, 1875) p. 36.
11. *Yoshida, R., *Chichi o omou* (In memory of my father) (Kyoto, 1936) p. 7.
12. Takahashi, Y., 'Institutional Formation of Electricity in Japan', Cardot, *Un Siècle d'Électricité*, p. 301.
13. H. Dyer, *Valedictory Address to the Students of Imperial College of Engineering* (Tokyo, 1882); *Ministry of Finance (ed.), *Kobusho Enkaku Hokoku* (History of the Ministry of Public Works) (Tokyo, 1888) pp. 343–411; *Kita, M., *Kokusai Nihon o hiraita Hitobito* (Scottish Contribution to Japan) (Tokyo, 1984) pp. 93–121.
14. R. Appleyard, *History of the Institution of Electrical Engineers* (London, 1937) p. 291.
15. *The Association of Alumni, *Background of the Division of Electrical Engineering, Tokyo University* (Tokyo, 1959).
16. *Tokyo Electric Light Co., *Kaigyo 50 Nenshi* (Tokyo, 1936) pp. 22–34; *Kogaku Hakushi Fujioka Ichisuke Den* (Biography of Dr Eng. I. Fujioka) (Tokyo, 1933) pp. 17–18.
17. *Osaka Electric Light Co., *Enkakushi* (Osaka, 1925) p. 29; *Okamoto, S. (ed.), *Iwadare Kunihiko* (Kamakura, 1965) p. 28.
18. *Kurihara, T. (ed.), *Denryoku* (Electric Power). *Gendai Nihon Sangyo Hattatsushi*, vol. 3 (Tokyo, 1964) *Statistics*, pp. 18–19; Minami, R., *Power Revolution in the Industrialization of Japan*, vol. 2 (Tokyo, 1982) pp. 172–80.
19. *Amasawa, S. (ed.), *Tsushin* (Communication). *Gendai Nihon Sangyo Hattatsushi*, vol. 22 (Tokyo, 1965) *Statistics*, pp. 30–2.
20. Uchida, H., 'Japanese Technical Manpower in Industry, 1880–1930: a Quantitative Survey', in H. Gospel (ed), *Industrial Training and Technological Innovation: A Comparative and Historical Study* (London, 1988); *Uchida, H., 'Statistical Data for the Employment of Technical College Graduates, 1900–1920', *The Journal of the Tokyo College of Economics*, no. 108, (1978), pp. 139–82; *Uchida, H., 'Distribution of University Graduate Engineers, 1920, *ibid.*, no. 152, 1987, pp. 103–15.
21. *Ministry of Finance, *Foreign Trade Statistics* (Tokyo, 1894–1914).
22. Imazu, K., 'Modern Technology and Japanese Electrical Engineers', Okochi & Uchida (eds.), *Development and Diffusion of Technology* (Tokyo, 1980) p. 139.
23. Uchida, H., 'Western Big Business and the Adoption of New Technology', ibid., p. 149.
24. *Nihon Denki Kogyokai, *Nihon Denkin Kogyoshi*, p. 688.
25. *Jitsugyo no Nihon* 10 January 1910.
26. H. Kessler, 'Deutsche Mitarbeit in der Elektroindustrie Japans' (typescript), Siemens Archive, 1944; Momotani, R., 'Die Tätigkeit des Siemens in Japan' (typescript), Siemens Archive, 1954.
27. *Takanashi, K., *Noguchi S. Ou Tsuikairoku* (Osaka, 1952); *Chiba, S., *Kawakita Yoshio no Shogai* (Tokyo, 1963).
28. W. W. Lockwood, *The Economic Development of Japan* (London, 1954) p. 329.
29. *Kogakukai, *Meiji Kogyoshi*, p. 538.
30. *Mitsui Bunko, *Mitsui Jigyoshi Shiryo-hen*, vol. 4. no. 1 (Tokyo, 1971) p. 83.
31. L. Lönheln, 'Gutachten über die Einführung deutsches Kapitals in Japan' (manuscript), Siemens Archive, 1898.
32. Uchida, H., 'Western Big Business', pp. 155–8.
33. *Ministry of Communication, *Denwa Jigyo 25 Nenshi* (Tokyo, 1916) p. 86.
34. D. F. Elliott, 'Twenty-five Years of Successful Cooperation in Japan', *Electrical Communication*, vol. 12, no. 1, 1923, p. 95.

35. *Kuzumi, S., *Oki Kibataro* (Tokyo, 1932) p. 95.
36. *Nihon Electric Co., *70 Nenshi* (Tokyo, 1962) p. 45.
37. *Ibid., p. 56.
38. *Tokyo Electric Co., *50 Nenshi* (Tokyo, 1940) p. 73.
39. Bright, *The Electric Lamp Industry*, p. 204.
40. *Shijo, Y., 'Incandescent Lamp', *Denki Gakkai Zasshi*, no. 207, (1905), p. 727.
41. *Shibaura Works, *65 Nenshi* (Tokyo, 1940) p. 165.
42. Uchida, H., 'Western Big Business', p. 158.
43. *Uchida, H., 'Denki Gijutsu' Japan Science Foundation, p. 172.

Index

252   Index

Svedenstierna, Eric T. 14
Swan Hunter 77, 78
Swank, James 52, 54, 61
Sweden 14
Swedenborg, E. 14

Tadasuke, Ishii 231
Tagijev 163
'takabata' loom 186, 187
Takada & Co. 232, 234
Takamura, Professor Naosuke 192, 193
Takashi, Masuda 236
Takashi, S. 207
Takehiko, Maeda 234
Takosan Maru 78
Tanaka Seisakusho 228
tariffs 59, 66, 70, 89, 158, 171, 213
Taunton Manufacturing Co. 36
Tchistopol chemical works 163
Technische Hochschulen 223, 225
J.C. Teckleborg Aktien-Gesellschaft 82
Tei Hasegawa 239
telegraphy 95–114, 132, 136–8, 150, 151
    in France 104–7
    in Germany 102–4
    in Japan 219–35
    in UK 107–9
    in US 109–12
Telephon Apparat Fabrik 141
Telephone Co. of Brazil 133
telephone operators 127, 139
Tellier, C. 90
Tennou, Emperor 181
Tesla, Nikola 229
Tetsudoin 211
textile machines 35, 36, 37, 38, 39
textiles 3, 4, 12, 16, 17, 20, 21, 22, 24, 31–
    9, 44–5, 181–96
Thayer, M. B. 234
Thayer, Nathan 65
Thomas, David 54–6, 70
Thomas Iron Co. 56
Thomas, Sidney G. 51
    see also steel
Thomas Viaduct 44
Thomson, Edgar 65
    Steel Works 65, 66, 68
Thomson Houston 224, 225, 230, 231,
    239
Thomson, Sir William 224

throstle 181, 183
Tinsley, Mr 23
Tiquet, M. 25
TKK 77
Tokugawa shogun 181
Tokyo 194, 203, 204, 224, 229, 231
Tokyo College 226
Tokyo Electric Co. 235–6, 238
Tokyo Electric Light Co. 224, 225, 229,
    231
Tokyo Imperial College 223, 224
Tokyo University 224, 226, 238
Tolozan, J.-F. 27
Toshiba Corporation 229, 236
Trevithick, Richard F. 211, 212
Triewald, Martin 14
Trudaine, D.C. 27
Tsugaru 203
Tsuwano-han 192
Tula metal works 15
tungsten filament lamp 236
Turbinia 75

UK Telegraph Co. 107
Union Steamship Co. 76, 78
Union Telefonica 134
United Alkali Co. 164, 169, 171, 172
United River Plate Telephone Co. 134
United States Military Academy 41
United States Steel Corporation 67
United Telephone Co. 126, 135
University of
    Durham 81
    Glasgow 80, 81, 224
    Heidelberg 98
    Liverpool 81
    London 192

Vaderland 76
Vail, Alfred 99
Valley Forge, steel industry 58
Vickers 78, 79
Vienna International Exposition 228
Von Stephan 129
Vulcan Foundry Co. 205
Vulcan Iron Works 66, 68

Waern 17
Wallenburgs 87
Waltham system of manufacturing 38